National Parliaments and European Democracy

Europa Law Publishing, Groningen 2007

National Parliaments and European Democracy

A Bottom-up Approach to European Constitutionalism

Edited by Olaf Tans, Carla Zoethout and Jit Peters

Europa Law Publishing is a publishing company specializing in European Union law, international trade law, public international law, environmental law and comparative national law.
For further information please contact Europa Law Publishing via email: info@europalawpublishing.com or visit our website at: www.europalawpublishing.com.

Typeset in Scala and Scala Sans, Graphic design by G2K Designers, Groningen/Amsterdam

NUR 828; ISBN 978-90-76871-81-3

British Library Cataloguing-in-Publication Data
A catalogue record for this book is available from the British Library

Acknowledgments

In January 2004, three Dutch universities launched a research program entitled 'Political Control in a European and Constitutional Perspective'. The purpose of this research program is to examine how political control and accountability are to be organised in the future European Union, based on research and theory from legal studies and political science. It is financed by the Netherlands Organisation for Scientific Research (NWO). The team in charge consists of Luc Verhey (Professor of Constitutional Law, Maastricht University), Deirdre Curtin (Professor of International and European Governance, University of Utrecht), and Jit Peters (Professor of Constitutional Law, University of Amsterdam).

The program contains three sub-projects, the first of which has resulted in this book. It addresses the future role of national parliaments in the European democracy on the basis of a 'bottom-up' approach. This means that the political systems of the Member States are considered to be the prime source of inspiration to the process of establishing supranational norms. Therefore, distinguished scholars have been invited to analyse the constitutional order of a Member State with regard to parliamentary scrutiny of EU decision-making. By comparatively analysing these national studies, this book seeks to explore the binding factor – an element that could be fundamental to further integration and the development of European democracy.

The project could not have been realized without the help and support of others. We like to take this opportunity to thank, firstly, the other members of our research-group: Hansko Broeksteeg, Monica Claes, Deirdre Curtin, Ilse van den Driessche, Luc Verhey and Anchrit Wille. For a variety of other reasons, we also want to mention: Jacob de Boer, Geerten Boogaard, Tom Eijsbouts, Michael Frese, Taco Groenewegen, Ben Hoetjes, Ron Holzhacker, Philipp Kiiver, Javier Laso Perez, Albert Meijer, Jan Herman Reestman, Olivier Rozenberg, Tineke van Stralen-Mulders and Fieke Janse.

Olaf Tans, Carla Zoethout and Jit Peters

CHAPTER I

Introduction: National Parliaments and the European Union

In Search of Common Ground

Olaf Tans

1 Introduction

One of the main problems regarding the development of the European Union is the growing idea that Community decisions are insufficiently representative of, or accountable to, the nations and the people of Europe.[1] There seems to be general agreement on the fact that there is a democratic deficit affecting the legitimacy of the exercise of powers that have been transferred from the national to the Community level. As Curtin remarks, the classic argument is '...that the shift in the locus of decision-making (to the EU) has not been matched by a shift in the methods of holding the governors accountable to the people.'[2] In this respect Chryssochoou speaks of a '...growing dissonance between the essential requirements of modern democratic government and the actual conditions upon which the political management of the EU affairs is based.'[3] Van Ham puts it more briefly: 'Europe and democracy: please mind the gaps!'[4]

Although there is a European Parliament with the task to represent the people(s) of Europe and to take part in EU decision-making, and despite the fact that this European Parliament's legislative power has increased with successive treaty amendments, national parliaments are widely regarded to be crucial in redressing this democratic deficit. Two arguments mainly support this resort to the national level. According to the 'no instruments-argument', the European Parliament's influence is still too limited because of the necessity to exercise its legislative powers in concert with the Council of Ministers. This dependency is considered to weaken the European Parliament's control, which diminishes the democratic legitimacy of EU decision-making, which has to be compensated by national parliamentary control.[5] According to the 'no *demos*-argument', the functioning of the European parliament is more structurally hampered by the absence of what it is supposed to represent, namely, a European people.[6] Since there is no clear European *volonté générale* to be voiced and no European identity to be expressed by the European parliament, national parliaments are believed to be indispensable in connecting the EU to its social environment: a collection of political communities with divergent cultures, ethnicity and background.

It remains unclear, however, what should be the role of national parliaments in the European Union, and how this role is to be organised. In the past few decades, Member States have been developing their own distinct norms and practices with regard to national parliamentary control of EU decision-making, mostly by extrapolating their procedures with regard to domestic policymaking to the supranational level. At the same time, there have been attempts to arrive

1 Lord (1998) 165; Keohane & Hoffmann (1991) 162-171.

2 Curtin (1997) 45.

3 Chryssochoou (2003) 366.

4 Van Ham (2001) 160.

5 See: Van Gerven (2005) 16-17; Graig & De Búrca (2003) 167-175.

6 Weiler (1995).

at a Union-wide regime, which has resulted in the attachment of two protocols to the Treaty Establishing a Constitution for Europe, that turn national parliaments into guardians of the principles of subsidiarity and proportionality by introducing the so-called 'early warning system' and 'yellow card procedure'.[7] Apart from the fact that this Union-wide regime has an uncertain future, it is limited in that it only states general objectives with regard to the role of national parliaments. It does not specify any formal procedure.[8] Furthermore, the protocols only constitute a European role for national parliaments based on the principles of subsidiarity and proportionality, while leaving all the other ways in which national parliaments might affect the European decision-making process untouched. How are national parliaments to exert influence in the everyday practice of EU decision-making? How, in other words, are they to provide the extra democratic legitimacy that is called for? The famous Danish answer to this question is that ministers should only take part in EU decision-making on the basis of a binding parliamentary mandate. As will become clear in the following chapters, this mechanism has significant downsides from both the national and the supranational viewpoint. Another suggestion is that national parliaments should somehow become more directly involved in EU decision-making, for example by turning the European Parliament into a bicameral institution comprising a chamber in which the national parliaments are represented. This idea runs up to significant fundamental problems, let alone the practical complications inherent in it.

This book contributes to this debate by means of a comparative study of the organisation of national parliamentary control of EU decision-making in a number of Member States. More precisely, this book seeks to find *a common ground* in the way this control is organised: do Member States share certain legal institutions, practices, or ideas regarding national parliamentary control of decision-making in the EU? The thought behind this question is that the construction of a Union-wide regime for the role of national parliaments in the EU, and more generally, the construction of better mechanisms of control and accountability in this supranational political community, must involve the use of national building blocks. In this way, this book adopts a 'bottom-up' approach to European constitutionalism, which will be elaborated in the following paragraph.

2 A Bottom-up Approach to European Constitutionalism

Let us first relate this approach to the vivid debate about the European role of national parliaments in contemporary political and legal

7 In the early warning system, the European Commission would transmit legislative proposals directly to the national parliaments, and they would have the right to claim within six weeks that there has been a violation of the subsidiarity principle. If more than one third of the national parliaments were to give this 'yellow card', the European Commission would then be obliged to reconsider its proposal.

8 See: Cygan (2001) 9-11.

science. Political science, firstly, has produced a number of valuable insights. Philip Norton, for example, poses the question of how national parliaments have reacted to European integration.[9] In the conclusion of a comparative study he observes three stages of development. In the first stage, national parliaments were hardly involved in EU decision-making, due to the fact that 'Europe' was considered to be a matter for the executive. In the second stage (starting around 1973), national parliaments started to adapt to changes taking place in the Community: they became more active, more specialised and better organised in dealing with European affairs. A major influence was the publication of the White Paper on the Completion of the Single Market and the enactment of the Single European Act, which extended the EC's competence to policy areas that were previously exclusively the domain of national governments. Thirdly and finally, Norton observes that national parliaments are increasingly viewed as a means to redress the democratic deficit, but he adds that a number of circumstances complicate this view. In fact the author concludes: 'If national parliaments are going to contribute to remedying this deficit – and, for reasons already discussed, that remains a very big and much contested if – then it is far from clear what they can do in order to achieve that.'[10]

In their much cited comparative study of scrutiny systems, Wolfgang Maurer and Andreas Wessels significantly contribute to the debate by analysing the role of national parliaments in the EU in a number of perspectives.[11] The overall picture they sketch shows that many national parliaments have adapted slowly to European integration, that they are reluctantly trying to become national players in a supranational game and are generally weak performers in this respect. Interestingly, these authors conclude that this negative balance sheet may be caused by the fact that national parliaments are trapped in their national role: 'Our assessment that many parliaments are slow adapters or weak performers is thus a depending variable on the role which national parliaments implicitly attribute to their parliaments.'[12] Other research has brought more detail to this picture, for example by arguing that the 'executive-legislative relationship' in the national political setting is the key variable in explaining the strength of parliamentary scrutiny, which is further analysed on the basis of factors such as political culture, federalism/unitarism and frequency of minority government.[13] Tapio Raunio and Matti Wiberg, finally, defend that the variation in the level of European scrutiny is primarily explained by two factors: the role of the parliament in the domestic political system, and the EU related public and party opinion.[14]

---

9 Norton (1996).

10 Norton (1996) 192.

11 Maurer & Wessels (2001).

12 Maurer & Wessels (2001) 464.

13 See for example: Bergman (1997).

14 Raunio (2005); Raunio & Wiberg (2000). And Raunio's contribution to this book.

These are valuable insights, but they leave the normative side of the story relatively untouched. More precisely, the political science perspective tends to focus on national parliamentary control of EU decision-making as an empirical phenomenon, answering questions such as: How have national parliaments reacted to European integration? How can the strength of parliamentary control be measured? In contradistinction, this volume focuses on national parliamentary control of EU decision-making as a subject of the primarily normatively oriented movement of European constitutionalism. Our starting point is the observation that the EU is engaged in a long-term process of designing its constitutional framework, a process in which the democratic deficit remains a stumbling stone, and that national parliaments are expected to come to rescue. Given those facts, this volume seeks to contribute to the perspective of institutional design, that is, to look over the shoulder of the European legislator and pose the question: how to find constitutional norms to improve the 'postnational' European democracy?[15]

One may argue that such an approach has become outdated in light of the negative outcomes of the French and Dutch referenda on the Draft Treaty Establishing a Constitution for Europe. Admittedly, these outcomes are a setback to the constitution-building process, but this does not mean that the search for foundational norms has come to an end. On the contrary. The French and the Dutch 'no' are indicative of the fact that not all nations were convinced by the content of the norms laid down in the constitutional treaty. One may say that these referenda reveal a lack of 'social legitimacy' of this step in the integration process. In our view, this means that the search for foundational norms is all but over. Rather, European constitutionalism has to regroup and reorient itself. In order for future versions of a European constitution to be ratified by all Member States, it shall have to find ways to establish foundational norms that are more convincing to the peoples of Europe. This asks for new research into the proper ways of European constitution-building, in order to arrive at an institutional design that fits better to its social environment.

As opposed to the top-down approach that seems to have dominated European constitutional ambitions over the last decades, this book is based on a bottom-up approach. This means that the national political systems and cultures of the Member States are considered to be the prime source of inspiration, the main input, to the process of establishing supranational norms. One could also speak of an 'inductive' method. Rather than deducing European constitutional norms for the role of national parliaments from abstract democratic theories and principles, thus trying to submit the EU to an even higher normative framework, it is our intention to depart from the Member States' constitutions, as they exist today. From this actual state of affairs, we want to extract an essence, a binding factor, and then discuss to what extent this can serve as a basis for national parliamentary control in the future EU.

---

15 Curtin (1997). See also: Verhey (2005).

This bottom-up approach draws from a number of traditions in legal and political thought. Historically, it is related to the Medieval attempt to as establish a *ius commune*: a supranational legal system that was learned and produced by European universities by observing and analysing Roman and all sorts of local customary laws.[16] Furthermore, it can be related to what Elkin and Soltan have introduced under the heading 'new constitutionalism': an approach that seeks to arrive at a more fruitful application of the perspective of institutional design.[17] More precisely these authors reject the narrow perspective of institutional design that focuses on the simple application of prescriptive standards, and plea for a more *constructive* attitude: 'In designing institutions we are not only concerned with the choice of the best means to some established end; we are also concerned with something more, though it is not so easily agreed what that is, and what follows for institutional design.'[18]

Other authors have inspired us to look for this 'something more' in the currently existing political and constitutional reality. Baun, for example, stresses the importance of combining constitutional ambitions with an eye for the political culture. More precisely he adheres to a 'conventional' understanding of the relationship between political culture and constitutionalism, in which culture is considered to be logically prior: 'In other words, unless a constitution reflects the predominant values of a society, its prospects for stable and successful operation – and the prospects for constitutionalism – are poor.'[19] With regard to the EU, Van Gerven appears to adopt a similar bottom-up approach, by stating that he aims to show '...how the distinctive features of a democratic polity that characterise the Member States can be gradually transplanted to the European Union'.[20]

Our research also draws from recent publications that, albeit not in a bottom-up approach, address the role of national parliaments in the EU in a more or less normative perspective. Adam Cygan provides a thorough comparative analysis of the German and British scrutiny systems that shows how the legislatures of these two Member States have responded to the increased competence of the European Union.[21] Klará Szalay does something similar with regard to the new Member States.[22] Philipp Kiiver, furthermore, provides a more general analysis of the role of national parliaments in the EU.[23] One of his main conclusions is that the debate directed at enhancing the role of national parliaments in the EU has a number of inherent flaws, among which the fact that European national parliaments are treated as a group of similar, easily comparable institutions,

---

16 Van Caenegem (2001) 1-21.

17 Elkin & Soltan (1993).

18 Soltan (1993) 13.

19 Baun (1995) 79.

20 Van Gerven (2005).

21 Cygan (2001).

22 Szalay (2005).

23 Kiiver (2006).

whereas in reality they show significant differences. Another misconception lies in the fact that national parliaments are often seen as unitary institutions that oppose and control their governments, whereas in fact they are divided, for example because parliamentary majorities tend to support the government and leave the critical role to the opposing minority. Harlow, finally, analyses the role of national parliaments in light of the more general subject 'accountability in the European Union' and concludes that: '...if national parliaments are to retain their central place in European democracy, it is essential that they should find innovative ways to collaborate with each other.'[24]

These and other studies have significantly contributed to the design of our research project and to its conclusions.[25] What is still lacking, however, is a thorough analysis of the constitutional and social background of the various scrutiny systems, an analysis that brings us closer to driving forces behind the actual organisation of national parliamentary control. By tracing these driving forces, and by posing the question whether they have something in common, this book intends to contribute to our knowledge of what could guide future European constitutionalism.

3 Research-design

In order to trace these driving forces, and their common ground, the following chapters present a comparative study of the organisation of national parliamentary control of EU decision-making. Distinguished specialists have been invited to analyse the constitutional regime of a Member State on the basis of the questionnaire that can be found in the appendix at the end of this chapter. Before elaborating on the way these constitutional regimes are analysed, a number of preliminary conceptual issues will be addressed in the following paragraph.

3.1 Conceptualising 'National Parliamentary Control of EU Decision-making'

The concept of 'national parliamentary control of EU decision-making' refers to three phenomena, namely 'national parliaments', 'control' and 'EU decision-making'. The following figure gives a first impression of how these phenomena, and their relation, are perceived in this study:[26]

24 Harlow (2002) 107.

25 See also: Smith (1996); Besselink (2006); Hautala (2005); De Búrca (2005); Laursen & Papas (1995); Rizzuto (2003); Katz & Wessels (1999).

26 This is a simplified version of a model in a publication of The European Centre for Parliamentary Research and Documentation (2002) 20. See also: Raunio (1999); Pelle & Van Schendelen (1993).

Figure 1. Model of national parliamentary control of EU decision-making

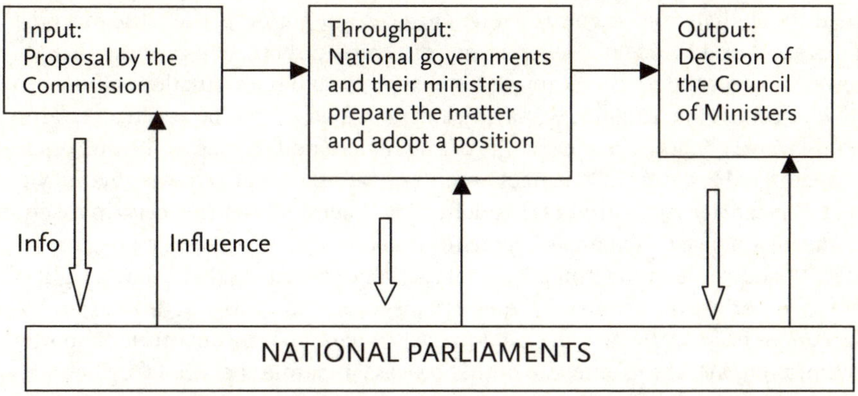

Let us discuss the various components of this scheme. As for the concept 'national parliament', it seems sufficient to state that in the context of this research 'national parliament' refers to the uni- or bicameral institutions that exist in all Member States of the EU, and that represent their peoples in the exercise of legislative power and/or political control. As far as they have a role in European scrutiny, attention shall also be paid to regional parliaments.

As for the concept 'EU decision-making' it is assumed that, as far as national parliaments can have any control over it, EU decision-making can be understood as the input-throughput-output system forming the upper part of the figure. It all starts when the Commission uses its right to initiate legislation by making a proposal, thus providing the input of the decision-making process. In the throughput-phase, this proposal becomes the object of the national political process directed at influencing the government's position. In the last phase, the Council of Ministers will take a decision and thus determine the output of the process. National parliaments may try to control this decision-making process in all three phases.

It must be stressed that this focus on decision-making implies that a number of other possible objects of national parliamentary control fall outside the scope of this book. Most significantly, it means that this volume does not pay attention to national parliamentary control of the *implementation* of EU decision-making. Although this type of control is definitely important, we take it that in light of our ambition to improve the EU's democratic legitimacy, decision-making should be our prime concern. By taking decisions, namely, the popular will that is supposed to guide rulers is most clearly expressed. This is another way of saying that European democracy can be perceived as a political system in the sense that, for instance, Schumpeter describes as follows: 'Democracy is a political method, that is to say, a certain type of institutional arrangement for arriving at political – legislative and administrative – decisions…'[27]

[27] Schumpeter (1981) 242.

As for the concept of 'control', one needs to go in more detail. In general, one may say that 'to have control' refers to a certain power to affect the outcome of a process or a course of events. In general, furthermore, one may say that 'power to affect the outcome' refers to a state of actual manipulation, of having a real effect. If, for instance, we say that someone has much power in a certain assembly, we generally mean that he or she makes a difference in the outcome of meetings. However, in this book we refer to another type of power, namely a state of authority. According to this definition, having power in a certain assembly means that we can identify a (constitutional) norm attributing a power to affect the outcome of meetings, for instance a norm stating that X has a right of veto. In other words, 'control' is conceptualised as a normative state of affairs. A parliament has control over decision-making when it has a constitutional power (authority) to affect the outcome of this process, regardless of the fact whether this power is put to effect.

More specifically, this study is premised on the idea that a national parliament's constitutional power to control EU decision-making has two basic elements that can be characterised as (1) having the power to know about it, and (2) having the power to do something about it.[28] Starting with the latter: if a national parliament is to have some sort of constitutional controlling power, there must be constitutional norms enabling it to influence the object of control. This (potential) influence is indicated by the arrows pointing upwards. As for the former: a national parliament cannot really have any influence if it has no information about the decision-making process. This flow of information, indicated by the arrows pointing downwards, may not be very relevant in everyday-situations of control, but it is quite crucial in the case of controlling a complex process such as EU decision-making. In fact, this is one of the main issues in the debate on the EU's democratic deficit and the focus of attention of the most significant attempts to redress it.

3.2 A Threefold Analysis of National Constitutional Regimes

As mentioned, our bottom-up approach to European constitutionalism implies that we seek to build on the Member States' constitutional regimes, as they exist today. This raises the question of what is meant by a 'constitutional regime' and how this phenomenon is perceived in the following chapters. This paragraph explains and defends a threefold approach.[29]

First and foremost, the contributions to this volume describe and analyse constitutional norms that purport to regulate parliamentary control of EU decision-making, and that are recognized in a national legal order. In this way, this book seeks to map out how parliamentary control of EU decision-making

[28] This means that we use two of the three key factors determining national parliamentary influence (availability of information, availability of time, parliamentary ability to bind their governments), as described in: Maurer & Wessels (2001).

[29] See also the questionnaire in the appendix.

is constitutionally regulated in various Member States. Secondly, the contributions describe (parliamentary) practices that are not prescribed by an explicit constitutional norm, but that nevertheless significantly affect national parliamentary control of EU decision-making. In this way, this book seeks to touch upon the so-called 'invisible constitution' of Member States: the norms that have grown from custom, from the way things are done. Thirdly, the contributions analyse how the constitutional norms of Member States regarding national parliamentary control of EU decision-making fit in their surrounding political systems. In this way, this book aims to gain understanding of the logic of the Member States' general organization of political control. What are the underlying reasons, the driving forces, for Member States to have their specific regulations? These three aspects of Member States' constitutional regimes with regard to national parliamentary control of EU decision-making will now be explored in more detail.

I Constitutional Norms Regarding National Parliamentary Control of EU Decision-making

This concept of 'constitutional norm' has two constituent parts, namely 'constitution' and 'norm'. Starting with the first, we define *constitution* as the set of norms that prescribe the basic system of government of a political community. This definition unites the various legal traditions that are under scrutiny in this book, by stating that a constitution is not to be understood as a single document, or as the Supreme Law of the land, but simply as all the norms having a constitutional status within the political community of a Member State.[30] Generally speaking, this means that constitutional norms are elements of a system of rules that can be found in sources such as:[31]

a) the written constitution, if there is one;

[30] This definition is quite close to the British understanding of a constitution, as described, for instance, by Bolingbroke: 'By constitution we mean...that assemblage of laws, institutions and customs, derived from certain fixed principles of reason, directed to certain fixed objects of public good, that compose the general system, according to which the community hath agreed to be governed.' Quoted in: Griffin (1996) 11. See also: Lane (1996) 7; Peczenik (1989).

[31] We leave in the middle whether constitutional norms are always part of the law. As far as we can see, this is the dominant view. Kay remarks, for example, that (American) constitutionalism relies on the thought of a 'proper use of state authority' by means of 'the promulgation and enforcement of positive law'. This basically means that constitutions are expected to yield rules that are legally applicable in concrete situations. Griffin expresses the same idea when stating that constitutionalism is based on 'an analogy between a constitution and ordinary law'. It is however also possible to conceive of some constitutional norms as non-legal phenomena. Hood Philips and Jackson, for example, describe conventions as: '...rules of political practice which are regarded as binding by those to whom they apply, but which are not laws as they are not enforced by the courts or by the Houses of Parliament'. This book considers both options to be equally valid. As long as a certain norm counts as constitutional in a certain political community, and as long as this norm purports to regulate national parliamentary control of EU-deci-

b) ordinary statute laws with constitutional implications;
c) constitutional customs;
d) judicial decisions in which the courts interpret the constitution;
e) preparatory material to constitutional legislation.

More concretely, the contributors to this volume have been asked to focus on two sets of constitutional norms that correspond to the two elements of parliamentary control identified above: (1) constitutional norms governing the flow of information about EU decision-making to a national parliament;[32] (2) constitutional norms governing a national parliament's ability to influence the EU decision-making process. As the following chapters show, these norms vary from general prescriptions of the relationship between the government and the parliament to rather detailed information and scrutiny-procedures. Furthermore, the controlling-powers that are established by these constitutional norms can have a variable degree of force. Article 23 of the *Grundgesetz*, for example, gives the Bundesrat a power of 'consent' with regard to transfer of sovereign powers, which indicates a relatively large power to influence the decision-making process.[33] The rule of ministerial responsibility confers a power to 'hold accountable', which indicates a smaller or at least different impact on the decision-making process. Other degrees and types of constitutional powers to affect the outcome of EU decision-making are expressed by the right to co-decide, the right to give advice, the right to veto, etc.

Using the input-output model of EU decision-making adopted above, there is another way to analyse the impact of parliamentary controlling powers over EU decision-making. The location of these powers in (one of the three phases of) the decision-making process, namely, can make quite a difference. Some

sion-making, it counts as a relevant element of a constitutional regime in the context of this research. See: Kay (1998) 19; Griffin (1996) 13; Tushnet (1998) 193-202.

32 Constitutional norms about the information-aspect can prescribe, for example, *who* has to provide *whom* with information about EU decision-making. Is this a task of a minister, or a cabinet, or a third party? And, is the parliament informed as a whole, or only part of it? There can also be norms about the *content* and *form* of the information that has to be provided, for example, when a measure of detail, or quantity, or style is prescribed. Also important are norms about the *timing, frequency* and the *initiative* of the information-process. When is information provided, how often, and does this happen actively or reactively? Finally, it is relevant to know if, according to these norms, a parliament is to be informed about the input-, the throughput- or the output-phase of the decision-making process. As will be discussed below, namely, a parliament's controlling power does not only depend on the quality of the information and the type of controlling power it is provided with, but also on the phase of the decision-making process that is thus affected.

33 Art. 23, paragraph 1, of the German *Grundgesetz*: 'With a view to establishing a united Europe the Federal Republic of Germany shall participate in the development of the European Union, which is committed to democratic, rule of law, social and federal principles as well as the principle of subsidiarity, and ensure protection of basic rights comparable in substance to that afforded by the Basic Law. To this end the Federation may transfer sovereign powers by law with the consent of the Bundesrat....'

authors defend that the more a parliamentary control-mechanism is located at the input-side, the more significant its impact on the decision-making process will be.[34] If, namely, a parliament can control the content of the proposals that enter the system at the input side, it has the power to set conditions under which decision-making will take place. One can also say that the parliament thus has control in the common English sense of the word, namely, being able to steer, to actively move a certain process in a certain direction. This is clearly the case when parliaments have a certain control over the machinery that produces the Commission's proposals, or when they control ministers having a certain influence on that machinery.[35]

As far as we can see, however, the majority of national parliamentary control mechanisms affect either the throughput- (*ex dumque*) or the output-phase (*ex post*) of the EU decision-making process. In the former case, a parliament cannot set conditions of decision-making, but it can invoke a certain compliance by negotiating, applying pressure, dealing and wheeling, for instance when it is entitled to adopt motions or to engage in public debate. One can also say that this type of control is 'reciprocal', in the sense that the parliament can only affect the outcome of the decision-making process by reacting on a given input, such as a legislative proposal or a European policy. A typical example of such ex dumque control is the public debate in which parliaments try to influence the conduct of ministers in the Council with regard to existing proposals. This is most likely to occur in the co-operation and co-decision procedures (art. 251 and 252 EC), in which proposals are re-examined and amended under the influence the European Parliament's opinion, a process that takes time and may be influenced by national parliaments.

If a control-mechanism is located at the output-side of the decision-making process (*ex post*), a parliament generally only has the power to check. This reading is closest to the origin of the word 'control', namely the Latin *contra rotulus*, which referred to a second register (a counter-roll) containing data that could confirm the correctness of the first register, for instance in bookkeeping. Originally, the act of control was thus a matter of verifying whether something met a certain standard. This may often be the case when a parliament has a power to check, for instance on the basis of its right to ask questions, conduct investigations or review the conduct of ministers, but we do not want to presuppose that this necessarily involves the application of a standard. The essence is that a parliament is entitled to scrutinize what has already happened. This type of control is relatively 'passive', and often considered to have the smallest impact.

---

34 Pelle & Van Schendelen (1993).

35 The content of Commission proposals is a result of the interaction between the Commission, interest groups, national experts and civil servants. National parliaments may have certain means to directly influence this interaction. More indirectly, they may hold ministers accountable for their behavior in the Council with regard to, for example, its 'common position' concerning proposals. Craig & De Búrca (2003) 163.

II The Relevance of Practices and Habits

Although this research is primarily focused on describing and comparing the constitutional foundations of national parliamentary control of EU decision-making, it cannot close its eyes to the social environment in which parliamentary control takes place. The constitutions of some Member States, namely, are relatively silent about the way EU decision-making is to be controlled by the parliament. The controlling power of the Dutch parliament, for instance, is of course regulated by provisions attributing general competences, such as to ask questions, adopt motions, hold ministers accountable, conduct investigations, but parliamentary control of EU decision-making has hardly been specifically regulated in statutes or other sources of constitutional norms.[36] Rather, the issue is dealt with in a purely habitual manner, for example by installing a special European affairs-committee, or by developing a routine in the way ministers inform the parliament, or simply by repeatedly expressing a belief about the role to be played by the parliament.[37] In other words: Dutch parliamentary control of EU decision-making seems to be organised mostly informally, that is, in parliamentary practices that have no constitutional foundation. As far as we can see, the same holds true for the constitutional systems of many other Member States.

The question is how to deal with these habits and practices. In a purely normative perspective, we could simply disregard them. We would state that we are interested in constitutional norms, and that behavioural patterns are the concern of a totally different discipline, namely sociology. This approach is unsatisfying for several reasons. Scientifically speaking, it would lead to a fairly limited comparative analysis, as there appears to be little constitutional material to be compared. More importantly, it would be unsatisfying to disregard a phenomenon that may not be relevant from a purely normative perspective, but that has (a) huge practical importance and is (b) frequently described and analysed in constitutional literature. This indicates that in one way or the other, practices and habits are considered to be constitutionally relevant.

Moreover, there is a theoretical reason to take them into account. Although it runs counter to the purpose of modern constitutionalism, many theorists have expressed the idea that constitutions are more than simply a set of foundational norms. Schindler, for instance, holds that positive constitutional law has an 'ambiance', a social environment, to which it is adapted, and in which it is eventually realised.[38] Making the same distinction, others have stressed the fact that

---

[36] In the Netherlands, some progress has been made in the approval acts of the treaties of Amsterdam and Nice. These acts contain provisions giving the Dutch parliament a right to be instantly informed about intended decision-making in the Counsil of Ministers concerning the titles IV and IIIA EC, and a right to give its consent to the cooperation of Dutch representatives to such decision-making (Acts of 24-12-1998 and 19-12-2001, *Staatsblad* 1998, 737 en 2001, 667).

[37] Del Grosso (2000) 165-200.

[38] Schindler (1970).

there tends to be a 'mismatch' between constitutional norms and their social environment, due to the '...limited capacity of words to limit public power...'.[39] This is another way of saying that political communities also have a 'living' constitution, a thought that Dworkin has put to words in yet another way.[40] According to this author, the political and legal practice of a political community expresses a so-called 'political morality': a story about the way the community is organised.[41]

On the basis of these considerations, the contributors to this volume have been asked to take into account practices and habits that are not prescribed by a constitutional norm but nevertheless affect national parliamentary control of EU decision-making. It primarily concerns parliamentary practices and habits, for example regarding the way the parliament is informed about EU-matters, or the way parliamentary debate is organised, or the way special committees are appointed to exercise political control, and if so, regarding the way these committees fulfil their task. We do not want to go as far as saying that these practices and habits reflect a political morality à la Dworkin, but we do defend that a comparative analysis of constitutional norms regarding parliamentary control of EU decision-making would be unsatisfying if these habits and practices were disregarded. One may say that these habits and practices are potential constitutional customs: regularities in the behaviour of constitutional actors that foreshadow the normative status they might acquire in the future.

III Widening the Scope to the Political System and Culture at Large

Finally, the constitutional norms, habits and practices affecting parliamentary control of EU decision-making are related to their constitutional context. How do these particular regimes fit in the general political system and culture of the corresponding Member States? The reason for this wider scope is that in order to find a common ground between various Member States, it would be insufficient to focus only on their specific constitutional norms and behaviours regarding political control of EU decision-making. These norms do not stand alone, but have meaning in relation to the political environment from which they sprang and in which they are likely to have some sort of support. In

39 Lane (1996) 11; Kay (1998) 29.

40 Dworkin (1996); Dworkin (1986). See also: Pino (1999).

41 According to Dworkin, this can be deduced from the way legal arguments develop in practice. When discussing constitutional problems, lawyers use arguments related to the domain of 'political morality'. This means that they look for an essence, an overall rationale, in the political and legal practice of their political communities, and apply it to concrete cases. The same thought is echoed by many other authors. Phillipp Bobbitt, for instance, argues that constitutional decision-making is often a matter of interpreting the constitutional *ethos* of a political community, which refers to its character, its identity, or – if you like – its immanent morality. Dworkin (1996) 131-149; Dworkin (1986) 355-399; Bobbitt (1982).

other words, we believe that this wider scope can bring us closer to the underlying reasons, the driving forces, for Member States to have their specific regimes. Moreover, this approach could be fruitful to the eventual purpose of constructing a common concept of political control for the EU. Such a concept might need a justification on the level of political philosophy, to which our comparative analysis can contribute.

More specifically, the contributors have been asked to focus on two aspects. Firstly, we found it interesting to know how a certain regime regarding parliamentary control of EU decision-making can be explained (or not) in the light of the general system of political control of that Member State. On the one hand, it is possible that such a regime somehow fits in a more encompassing picture of the political system at large. The German regime, for example, seems to fit in the larger picture of a state in which the *Länder* are to some extent independent from the federal government, as the *Grundgesetz* provides a basis for the involvement of both the *Bundestag* (the national parliament) and the *Bundesrat* (in which the governments of the *Länder* are represented) in European affairs.[42] The Danish mandate procedure, furthermore, could be partly explained in the context of a political system that is dominated by minority-governments. This, namely, implies that the viewpoints of Danish ministers taking part in EU decision-making are by no means guaranteed to be supported by a parliamentary majority.[43] On the other hand, it is possible that a particular regime regarding parliamentary control of EU decision-making does not fit the political system at large. A Member State may have organised this in a way that does not make sense in the light of its general constitutional framework, for example due to incompetence or nonchalance. Considering the purpose of this book and the eventual purpose of the research-programme, it would be quite important to know about such a mismatch. We might, for instance, choose to consider this regime to be an omission and look for common ground in the political system at large.

Secondly, we found it interesting to know whether Member States have underlying reasons to have their specific regimes or political systems. These underlying reasons may have to do with history, political theory, basic principles, sheer pragmatism, etc., as long as they are a justification of the actual system and its regime regarding political control of EU decision-making. The majority of the EU Member States, for example, seem to adhere to the theory that 'democracy' is a political community in which the people (*demos*) rules (*kratein*). This theory, one may say, is the general underlying reason why these Member States have constitutional norms establishing suffrage, ministerial accountability, or political representation. Member States may also have more reasons to have their specific regime or political systems. It is quite relevant, for instance, to know that the Danish tradition of minority government and the tendency to provide the *Folketing* (the Danish parliament) with strong controlling powers, are the

[42] Art. 23 GG.

[43] Jensen (1996).

result of a historical development that made the Danes especially sensitive to loss of parliamentary influence, and that made them adhere to the principle of negative parliamentarism.[44]

This is not to say that all constitutional norms, habits and practices regarding parliamentary control of EU decision-making can be traced back to clear-cut underlying reasons. In many cases, these regimes may exist for no specific reason at all and be simply the result of a gradual, historical, legal or political development. Furthermore, they may be based on a compromise, that is, be the outcome of the interaction of conflicting considerations. Again, we like to stress that this type of observation is equally valuable, as it indicates that a certain Member State has not developed a clear or dominant philosophy about the way parliamentary control of EU decision-making is to be organised. As long as such philosophies can be identified, however, they could contribute to a better understanding of constitutional regimes as they exist today, and provide material for the common ground we are looking for.

4 Conclusion

The rest of this book comprises basically two parts. The following nine chapters contain in depth analyses of the constitutional regimes of a Member State on the basis of the questionnaire that can be found in the appendix. The result is an illuminating picture of various scrutiny systems, offering insight in legal, empirical and political-cultural aspects, and revealing both the differences and the commonalities. The final chapter offers a comparative analysis of these national regimes. It explores the common ground in the organisation of national parliamentary control of EU decision-making as it exists today, and goes on to discuss to what extent this common ground can serve as a basis for the future development of (the role of national parliaments) in the European democracy.

---

[44] For decades (1870-1920), the *Folketing* fought for parliamentary sovereignty whereas the King kept appointing minority governments. This struggle strengthened parliamentarism and made the Danes observe the principle according to which a government cannot be formed or continue to sit if a majority in the parliament passes a vote of no confidence. Jensen (1996) 39/40.

Appendix: Questionnaire

The contributors to this book have been asked to construct their texts around the following research questions:

1. What are the constitutional norms regulating the flow of information about EU decision-making to the national parliament, in the Member State you are discussing? One could think of:
   a) Constitutional norms about who has to inform what part of the parliament, and about what phase of the EU decision-making process (input, throughput, output) is thus clarified;
   b) Constitutional norms about the content and form of the information;
   c) Constitutional norms about the timing, frequency and initiative of the information-process.
2. What are the constitutional norms regulating national parliamentary control of EU decision-making? More precisely, could you describe:
   a) The controlling-powers that are established by these norms;
   b) The relative force of these powers: do they give the right to give advice, to co-decide, to veto, etc;
   c) The phase of the EU decision-making process that can be controlled by these powers: the input-phase, the throughput-phase or the output-phase? Are we, in other words talking about *ex ante, ex dumque*, or *ex post* scrutiny mechanisms?
3. Apart from these constitutional norms, what habits and practices structurally affect the flow of information to the parliament and its control over EU decision-making? One could think of:
   a) Ministerial habits and practices.
   b) Parliamentary habits and practices, such as the functioning of a European Affairs Committee, or certain modes of communication between the executive and the legislature, lobbying-mechanisms etc.
4. How does this regime fit in the political system at large?
   a) Can it, for instance, be explained as a logical consequence of the way political control is generally organised, or is it rather disharmonious?
   b) Or is there, for instance, a dominant democratic philosophy or principle, and if so, could you say that it is reflected, or rather infringed by the way parliamentary control of EU decision-making is organised?
   c) Are there other generally accepted underlying reasons for the member-state to have its specific regime, for instance related to the Member States' history, political culture or social structure?
5. How would you describe the problems, if there are any, related to this constitutional regime regarding national parliamentary control of EU decision-making?
6. Do you have any ideas about a future and better organisation of national parliamentary control of EU decision-making?

References

M.J. Baun, "The Federal Republic of Germany", in: D.P. Franklin & M.J. Baun, *Political Culture and Constitutionalism. A Comparative Approach* (London/New York: M.E. Sharpe, 1995) 79-97.

T. Bergman, "National Parliaments and EU Affairs Committees: notes on empirical variation and competing explanations", *Journal of European Public Policy* 4:3 (1997) 373-387.

T. Bergman, W.C. Müller, K. Ström, "Parliamentary democracy and the chain of delegation", *European Journal of Political Research* 37 (2000) 255-260.

L.F.M. Besselink, "National Parliaments in the EU's Composite Constitution. A Plea for a Shift in Paradigm", in: Ph. Kiiver (ed.), *National and Regional Parliaments in the European Constitutional Order* (Groningen: Europa Law Publishing, 2006) 117-132.

P. Bobbitt, *Constitutional Fate, Theory of the Constitution* (Oxford: Oxford UP, 1982).

G. De Búrca, *The EU Constitution: in Search of Europe's International Identity* (Groningen: Europa Law Publishing, 2005).

R.C. van Caenegem, *European Law in the Past and the Future, Unity and Diversity over two Millenia* (Cambridge: Cambridge UP, 2001).

D.N. Chryssochoou, "EU democracy and the democratic deficit," in: M. Cini (ed.), *European Union Politics* (Oxford: Oxford UP, 2003) 365-382.

P. Craig, G. de Búrca, *EU Law, Text, Cases, and Materials* (Oxford/New York: Oxford UP, 2003).

D.M. Curtin, *Postnational democracy, The European Union in search of a political philosophy* (The Hague: Kluwer, 1997).

A.J. Cygan, *National Parliaments in an Integrated Europe, an Anglo-German perspective* (The Hague/London/New York: Kluwer Law International, 2001).

N.Y. Del Grosso, *Parlement en Europese Integratie* (Deventer: Kluwer, 2000).

R. Dworkin, *Taking Rights Seriously* (Londen: Duckworth, 1996).

R. Dworkin, *Law's Empire* (Cambridge Mass.: Harvard UP, 1986).

S.L. Elkin & K.E. Soltan (eds.), *A New Constitutionalism. Designing Political Institutions for a Good Society* (Chicago: Chicago UP, 1993).

E.O. Eriksen & J.E. Fossum (eds.), *Democracy in the European Union, Integration through deliberation?* (London: Routledge, 2000).

European Centre for Parliamentary Research and Documentation: *European Affairs Committees, The Influence of National Parliaments on European Policies* (Dick Toornstra: Brussels, 2002).

W. van Gerven, *The European Union, A Polity of States and Peoples* (Oxford/Portland Oregon: Hart, 2005).

S.M. Griffin, *American constitutionalism, from theory to politics* (Princeton: Princeton UP, 1996).

P. van Ham, *European Integration and the Postmodern Condition* (London: Routledge, 2001).

C. Harlow, *Accountability in the European Union* (Oxford: Oxford UP, 2002).

H. Hautala, "The Role of National Parliaments in the EU: A Partnership or Rivalry?", in: D. Curtin, A.E. Kellerman, S. Blockmans (eds.), *The EU Constitution: The Best Way Forward?* (The Hague: T.M.C. Asser Press, 2005) 223-231.

O. Hood Philips & P. Jackson, *Constitutional and Administrative Law* (London: Sweet & Maxwell, 1987).

J.A. Jensen, "Prior Parliamentary Consent to Danish EU Policies", in: E. Smith (ed.), *National Parliaments as Cornerstones of European Integration* (London: Kluwer, 1996) 39-48.

R.S. Katz & B. Wessels (eds.), *The European Parliament, the National Parliaments, and European Integration* (Oxford: Oxford UP, 1999).

R.S. Kay, "American Constitutionalism", in: L. Alexander, *Constitutionalism, Philosophical Foundations* (Cambridge: Cambridge University Press, 1998) 16-63.

R.O. Keohane & S. Hoffmann (eds.), *The New European Community, Decision-making and Institutional Change* (Boulder/Oxford: Westview Press, 1991).

Ph. Kiiver, *The National Parliaments in the European Union: A Critical View on EU Constitution Building* (The Hague/London/New York: Kluwer Law International, 2006).

J.E. Lane, *Constitutions and Political Theory* (Manchester: Manchester University Press, 1996).

F. Laursen & S.A. Pappas (eds.), *The Changing Role of Parliaments in the European Union* (Maastricht: European Institute of Public Administration, 1995).

J. Lodge, "The European Parliament", in: S.S. Andersen, K.A. Eliassen, *The European Union: How Democratic is it?* (London: Sage Publications, 1996) 187-214.

C. Lord, *Democracy in the European Union* (Sheffield: Sheffield Academic Press, 1998).

A. Maurer & W. Wessels (eds.), *National Parliaments on their Ways to Europe: Losers or Latecomers?* (Baden-Baden: Nomos, 2001)(Bonn, Schriften des Zentrums fur Europaische Integrationsforschung der rheinischen Friedrich-WilhelmsUniversitat, 2001).

Ph. Norton (ed.), *National Parliaments and the European Union* (London/New York: Routledge, 1996).

A. Peczenik, *On Law and Reason* (Dordrecht: Kluwer Academic Publishers, 1989).

J.J. Pelle, M.P.C.M. van Schendelen, "Dutch Parliamentary Control in Theory and Practice," in: C.M. Zoethout, G. van der Tang, P. Akkermans (eds.), *Control in Constitutional Law* (Dordrecht: Martinus Nijhoff Publishers, 1993) 129-141.

G. Pino, "The Place of Legal Positivism in Contemporary Constitutional States", *Law And Philosophy* 5:18 (1999) 513-536.

T. Raunio, "Holding governments accountable in European affairs: Explaining cross-national variation", *Journal of Legislative Studies* 11:3-4 (2005) 319-342.

T. Raunio & M. Wiberg, "Does Consensus lead to Ignorance? National Parliaments and the Legitimacy of EU Governance", *Acta Politica* 35:2 (2000) 146-168.

T. Raunio, "Always one step behind? National Legislatures and the European Union", *Government and Opposition* 34:2 (1999) 180-202.

F. Rizzuto, "National parliaments and the European Union: part of the problem or part of the solution to the democratic deficit in the European constitutional settlement?", *Journal of Legislative Studies* 9:3 (2003) 87-109.

K.E. Soltan, "What Is the New Constitutionalism ?", in: Elkin & Soltan (1993) 3-19.

D. Schindler, *Verfassungsrecht und soziale Struktur* (Zürich: Schultess Polygraphischer Verlag AG, 1970).

J.A. Schumpeter, *Capitalism, Socialism and Democracy* (third impression)(London: Unwin University Books, 1981).

R. Scully, "The European Parliament", in M. Cini (ed.), *European Union Politics* (Oxford: Oxford UP, 2003) 166-178.

E. Smith (ed.), *National Parliaments as Cornerstones of European Integration* (London/Boston: Kluwer Law International, 1996).

K. Ström, "Delegation and accountability in parliamentary democracies", *European Journal of Political Research* 37 (2000) 261-289.

K. Szalay, *Scrutiny of EU Affairs in the National Parliaments of the New Member States – comparative analysis* – (Budapest: Hungarian National Assembly, 2005).

M. Tushnet, "Understanding the non-legalized constitution", in: *Law and Philosophy* 17 (1998) 193-202.

L.F.M. Verhey, "Good Governance: Lessons from Constitutional Law", in: D.M. Curtin & R.A. Wessel (eds.), *Good Governance and the European Union* (Antwerpen-Oxford: Intersentia, 2005) 49-67.

J. Weiler, "Does Europe need a Constitution? Demos, Telos and the German Maastricht Decision", *European Law Journal* 1:3 (1995) 219-258.

S. Williams, "Sovereignty and Accountability in the EC," in: R.O. Keohane, S. Hoffmann (eds.), *The New European Community, Decisionmaking and Institutional Change* (Boulder/ Oxford: Westview Press, 1991) 155-176.

CHAPTER 2

The Finnish Eduskunta: Effective Scrutiny, Partisan Consensus

Tapio Raunio

1 Introduction

Finland's integration policy can be characterised as flexible and constructive and one of its objectives is to consolidate Finland's position in the inner core of the European Union (EU). The government has constantly underlined the importance of being present where decisions concerning Finland are taken. According to the political elite, national interests can be best pursued through active and constructive participation in decision-making. Underlying this stance is a strong conviction that a strong and efficient Union can best protect the rights and interests of smaller member states, as intergovernmental processes tend to favour larger member states. Hence, Finland has consistently supported the further extension of qualified majority voting in the Council, and the strengthening or at least safeguarding of the roles of the Commission and the European Parliament (EP).[1]

The improvement in the role of national parliaments in the EU has been another important element in the Finnish strategy for increasing democracy in the Union. Indeed, the Finnish political elite, including the government, the Eduskunta and the main parties, have continued to balance their broad pro-integrationist statements and policies with a relatively conservative approach to institutional reform. The Finnish government has repeatedly argued that national parliaments are the primary channel for providing democratic legitimacy to EU decision-making, with the EP complementing the role of national legislatures. The importance attached to the role of national legislatures reflects the recent parliamentarization of the Finnish political system. These priorities and political preferences have been clearly evident in the three Intergovernmental Conferences (IGC) held since Finland joined the Union.

Comparative research has indicated that the variation in the level of parliamentary scrutiny on EU affairs by domestic legislatures is primarily explained by two factors: the role of the parliament in the domestic political system and public and party opinion on European integration. The key variable has been argued to be the executive-legislature relationship, with the parliament controlling the government to the same extent in European matters as it does in the context of domestic legislation. Similarly, the contentiousness of the European dimension is important, with divisions over integration leading to tighter scrutiny mechanisms.[2] Both preconditions for tight control of government are therefore in place in Finland – political parties and especially voters are divided over integration, and recent constitutional changes have significantly altered the Finnish political system, bringing Finland closer to standard parliamentary democracy and strengthening the powers of the Eduskunta, the unicameral national parliament.

---

1 Raunio & Tiilikainen (2003).

2 For research on explaining cross-national variation in the level of parliamentary scrutiny in EU affairs, see: Raunio (2005a).

This chapter analyses the role of the Eduskunta in controlling the government in EU matters and in influencing national integration policy. The next section examines the period before Finland joined the Union in 1995, showing that the parliamentary preparations for EU membership went hand in hand with the constitutional reforms that strengthened parliamentarism. Section three explores the constitutional powers of Eduskunta and its actual possibilities for shaping the direction of national EU policy and of government behaviour in the Council. The fourth section briefly explores the Eduskunta's views on the new Protocols dealing with national parliaments included in the new Constitutional Treaty. The concluding summary highlights the main benefits and problems of the Finnish system. The data consists of interviews with MPs and parliamentary civil servants, official documents including the national constitution and the Eduskunta's rules of procedure, and statistics of parliamentary activities. The main findings are that constitutionally the Eduskunta has considerable powers to control the government, and that the decentralized model established for monitoring the government in EU matters works rather well, with the mandatory committee deliberations giving all deputies an opportunity to develop knowledge on European matters. Reflecting the domestic political culture, the overall approach of the Eduskunta to EU matters has been pragmatic and consensual, focusing on committee-based scrutiny of EU legislation instead of plenary debates on the future of integration.

2 Background: Constitutional Reform and Preparing for EU-Membership

The Finnish political system has normally been categorized as semi-presidential, with the executive functions divided between an elected president and a government that is accountable to the parliament. However, recent constitutional reforms have quite radically altered the Finnish political system, with the government and the prime minister emerging from the shadow of the president as the leaders of the political process.[3] The new constitution, which entered into force in 2000, completed a period of far-reaching constitutional change that curtailed presidential powers and brought the Finnish political system closer to a standard version of parliamentary democracy. While the executive branch still dominates national politics, at least now that executive is accountable to the Eduskunta. The Finnish political system was therefore experiencing major changes even independent of integration. Hence, membership in the EU presented a challenge for the parliament, concerned about not seeing its position weaken as a result of the political dynamics of the EU policy process.

Many of the constitutional amendments and procedural innovations inside the Eduskunta were already introduced when preparing for European Economic Area (EEA) membership. Finland's participation in the EEA would have implied,

3 Nousiainen (2001); Paloheimo (2001); and Raunio (2004).

in accordance with a strict interpretation of the constitution, the inclusion of the entire EEA policy in the competence of the president. The constitution had therefore to be amended in order to enable the participation of the parliament and the government in EEA matters. The result was first an addition to Section 33 of the Form of Government Act[4], and finally, the whole Section was modified in the new unified constitution. This amendment (Section 33a) purported to balance the division of powers between the president and the government in EEA matters and to prevent the powers that by definition belonged to the sphere of domestic policy from being transferred to the president.[5] Section 33a was historical as it brought the government into the sphere of foreign policy for the first time in Finland's history.

The importance of the amendment increased when Finland joined the Union. Section 33 of the Form of Government Act was applied to Finland's EU membership in the sense that as a part of his general foreign policy leadership, the Common Foreign and Security Policy (CFSP) as well as amendments to the EU treaties were interpreted to belong to the president's jurisdiction while other EU matters belonged to the government.[6] Under the new constitution, the government is the key actor in EU policy and also – jointly with the president – in foreign policy. The text of the new Section 93 reads:

> The foreign policy of Finland is directed by the President of the Republic in co-operation with the Government. However, the Parliament accepts Finland's

4 Finland used to have four different laws which together constituted the constitution: the Form of Government Act (1919), the Parliament Act (1928), the Act Concerning Ministerial Responsibility (1922) and the High Court of Impeachment Act (1922).

5 'The Parliament shall participate in the approval of those decisions taken by international organs which according to the Constitution require the consent of the Parliament in the manner stipulated by the Parliament Act. The Council of State shall decide on the approval and implementation of the decisions covered by the subsection 1 if the decision does not require the Parliament's approval and does not because of its substance necessitate that an order is issued.' The Form of Government Act, Section 33a.

6 A disagreement emerged between the parliament and the president about the correct interpretation of the constitutional passage. The Committee for Constitutional Law of the Eduskunta adopted a position according to which the government – and not the president – was the key actor representing Finland in the European Council. National preparation of the European Council meetings takes place under the auspices of the government and the prime minister informs the parliament about these meetings. The Committee for Constitutional Law, therefore, saw that the decision on Finland's participation in the European Council belonged to the government on the basis of Section 33a of the Form of Government Act. When president Martti Ahtisaari (1994-2000) confirmed the laws enforcing the amendments caused by Finland's EU membership, he adopted an interpretation deviating from the position of the committee. According to Ahtisaari, in order not to undermine the division of powers in foreign policy, the president should have the right to decide on his participation in the European Council meetings. This was confirmed between prime minister Paavo Lipponen and president Ahtisaari in 1995 and forms the current praxis. The dispute is important from the point of view of the Eduskunta, as the president is not accountable to the parliament.

> international obligations and their denouncement and decides on the bringing into force of Finland's international obligations in so far as provided in this Constitution. The President decides on matters of war and peace, with the consent of the Parliament.
>
> The Government is responsible for the national preparation of the decisions to be made in the European Union, and decides on the concomitant Finnish measures, unless the decision requires the approval of the Parliament. The Parliament participates in the national preparation of decisions to be made in the European Union, as provided in this Constitution.
>
> The communication of important foreign policy positions to foreign States and international organizations is the responsibility of the Minister with competence in foreign affairs.[7]

In parallel with these amendments caused in part by adaptation to integration, a comprehensive revision of the Finnish constitution took place during the 1990s, aiming to consolidate the four separate constitutional acts into one constitution and to further parlamentarize the political system. The constitutional reforms of the 1990s were in part a response to the excesses of the presidency of Urho Kekkonen (1956-1981), who had made full use of his powers and even overstepped the constitutional prerogatives of the presidency. President Mauno Koivisto (1982-1994) and the political elite in general favoured the strengthening of parliamentarism and curtailing the powers of the president. There was thus widespread consensus – at least among the political elite – about the need to parliamentarize the political system. A further impetus to change came from the end of the Cold War. Relations with the Soviet Union were at the top level primarily based on negotiations between the Finnish president and the leaders in Kremlin, and the dissolution of the Soviet empire reduced the importance of such personalized foreign policy leadership. The gradual consolidation of parliamentary democracy was also facilitated by government stability. Since 1983, all governments except one have stayed in office for the whole electoral term of four years, and have done so without serious internal problems or even without real effective opposition.[8]

The constitutional and political changes have drastically changed the nature of the Finnish polity, with the government and particularly the prime minister emerging as the dominant actors. Now the government is the supreme execu-

---

7 The Constitution of Finland, 11 June 1999 (731/1999), Section 93.

8 The only exception was the short-lived coalition between the Centre, Social Democrats and the Swedish People's Party that took office after the elections held in March 2003. The prime minister Anneli Jäätteenmäki was forced to resign in June of that year after allegations concerning her use of secret foreign ministry documents during the election campaign. The same three parties formed a new cabinet immediately after Jäätteenmäki had resigned. In addition, three small parties have left the governments: the Rural Party in 1990 over budgetary disagreements, the Christian Democrats in 1994 owing to the government's pro-EU stance, and the Green League in 2002 because of the decision to build a fifth nuclear reactor. These defections have not threatened the overall stability of the cabinets.

tive authority, not the president, and the powers of the latter are more clearly restricted. EU membership has contributed to this development in two ways. First, according to the constitution, the government formulates and decides national EU policy, with the president's powers mainly limited to second pillar matters. Secondly, the process of European integration effectively blurs the distinction between foreign and domestic policy, with trade and increasingly also traditional foreign policies decided collectively by member states or together with the EU institutions at the European level. Therefore, the share of matters falling under the jurisdiction of the Finnish president is gradually declining. Nevertheless, the president is not (at least not yet) a mere ceremonial figurehead.[9] As a result, the new Finnish political system sits rather uneasily in the semi-presidential category.

Adaptation to European integration within the Eduskunta started already in 1990, when the Foreign Affairs Committee demanded that the parliament and particularly its committees have access to information and the ability to influence national policy in EEA decision-making. There was broad agreement among the main parties, including those in the opposition, about the need to safeguard the participation rights of the Eduskunta. The goal was to guarantee the Eduskunta as powerful a position in EU decision-making as is possible for any national legislature. Here the Eduskunta, notably its civil servants, studied closely the work of the existing EU committees in the national legislatures, particularly in the Danish Folketinget. At the same time, the constitutional amendments aimed at respecting the separation between executive and legislative branches: the parliament was given the right to participate in national policy formulation in EU matters while the government was assigned the right to decide on such matters and to represent Finland at the European level.[10]

3 Controlling the Government in EU Matters

3.1 Accountability and Control Instruments

Recent constitutional reforms have significantly altered the balance of power among Finnish political institutions, empowering the Eduskunta and the government at the expense of the president. Hence, the parliament has overall better opportunities for controlling the government.

The government is accountable to the Eduskunta, and, hence, the latter can force the cabinet to resign. But more important are the various ways in which the Eduskunta can influence government behaviour. Firstly, the new constitution (Section 61) parliamentarised government formation, with the Eduskunta electing the prime minister, who is thereafter formally appointed

9 Raunio & Tiilikainen (2003) 96-112.

10 Jääskinen (2000).

by the president. The president appoints the other cabinet members in accordance with a proposal made by the prime minister.[11] Prior to the enactment of the 1991 constitutional amendment, the cabinet was not obliged to present its programme in the Eduskunta. The new vote of investiture was first used in 1995, when the rainbow coalition headed by Paavo Lipponen took office. Under the new constitution, the government shall without delay submit its programme to the parliament in the form of a statement, which is then followed by a debate and a mandatory confidence vote. The decision rule is simple majority.[12] It must be emphasized here that these government programmes – which cover all policy areas and have become much longer since the early 1990s – are politically binding documents that define the subsequent behaviour and priorities of the government.

For controlling the cabinet while the latter is in office, the bluntest tool is the vote of no confidence, of which there are three types. The decision rule is simple majority. First, there are votes of no confidence that always follow an interpellation. Although an individual MP can initiate interpellations, they are usually put forward by party groups of the opposition parties. A minimum of 20 signatures (10% of MPs) is needed for an interpellation to be presented to the cabinet or an individual minister. While the last cabinet resignation owing to a vote of no confidence following an interpellation occurred in 1958, MPs make more use of this instrument than before. Second, the cabinet can in practice initiate confidence votes, understanding that a defeat will lead to its downfall. Third, the opposition can, without prior warning and in connection with any policy issue, request a confidence vote during the plenary. So far, such votes of no confidence have not led to a resignation.

The role of parliamentary questions has become more important over time. Originally MPs could table only written questions (introduced in 1906), with oral questions introduced in 1966 and questions to the Council of State (*i.e.*, the government) introduced in 1989. Whereas the first two options were available to individual MPs, questions to the Council of State had to be signed by at least four representatives, and they had to be on matters that were both 'current' and 'of consequence'. The monthly questions to the Council of State were introduced in order to enable the parliament and the government to engage in a more open dialogue on topical issues. In 1993, the procedure for oral questions was redesigned so that any MP could put forward questions to the cabinet ministers present in the chamber. In 1999, the oral questions and written questions to the Council of State were merged into a question time, during which MPs can spontaneously put questions to the ministers on topics of their own choice. These question times are held on Thursdays and shown live on the main state-owned TV channel. While the impact of questions is hard to measure, their steady increase shows that members find them worthwhile.[13]

---

11 The Constitution of Finland, 11 June 1999 (731/1999), Section 61.

12 The Constitution of Finland, 11 June 1999 (731/1999), Section 62.

13 See the chapters in Wiberg (1994); and Raunio & Wiberg (2003).

Like the other Nordic legislatures, the Eduskunta can be categorized as a 'working parliament'; with emphasis on work carried out in parliamentary committees.[14] A strong committee system facilitates efficient control over government. Literature on committees has emphasized that committees provide MPs with the opportunity to specialize, and that such specialization can benefit the whole parliament. Moreover, committees that have stable memberships and whose jurisdictions mirror the division of labour among ministries should be better equipped to control the government.[15] In the Eduskunta, committee deliberation is compulsory and committees must report to the plenary on all matters under consideration except private members' bills and motions. Committees meet behind closed doors and ministers do not hold seats on committees. Committees can invite ministers to hearings, but cabinet representatives are not legally obligated to appear in person. The major reform of the committee system carried out in 1991, involving the abolition of two committees, establishment of three committees, and reshuffling of the committees' jurisdictions, produced a situation where the competencies of the individual committees mirror (by and large) the jurisdiction of the respective ministries. It also appears that the frequency of committee meetings has risen over time.[16]

A crucial element in holding the government accountable is access to information, and, in this sense, the Eduskunta's powers have traditionally been very strong. The right of the parliament to receive information from the government is regulated in Section 47 of the Constitution:

> The Parliament has the right to receive from the Government the information it needs in the consideration of matters. The appropriate minister shall ensure that Committees and other parliamentary organs receive without delay the necessary documents and other information in the possession of the authorities. A Committee has the right to receive information from the Government or the appropriate ministry on a matter within its competence. The Committee may issue a statement to the Government or the ministry on the basis of the information. A representative has the right to information which is in the possession of authorities and which is necessary for the performance of the duties of the Representative, in so far as the information is not secret or it does not pertain to a State budget proposal under preparation. In addition, the right of the Parliament to information on international affairs is governed by the provisions included elsewhere in this Constitution.[17]

These strong information rights are complemented by the right to receive information on matters relating to the EU (Section 96); reports from the government

[14] Arter (1999) 211-217.

[15] Mattson & Strøm (1995).

[16] For a detailed analysis of the committee structure in the Eduskunta, with particular focus on committee assignments, see: Forsten (2005).

[17] The Constitution of Finland, 11 June 1999 (731/1999), Section 47.

(Section 44); the government's annual reports on its activities; measures undertaken in response to parliamentary decisions; state finances and adherence to the budget (Section 46); and international affairs (Section 97). The rights to receive information on EU matters and on international affairs, both introduced in connection with Finland joining the EU, have improved the Eduskunta's capacity to control the government.

This brief overview of the accountability and control mechanisms shows that overall the Eduskunta is now better equipped to control the government than was the case under the old constitution or when Finland joined the EU. Hence, it was not surprising that the parliament wanted to safeguard its prerogatives when designing its system for controlling the government in EU matters.

3.2 Scrutiny of EU Matters[18]

There is no doubt that the institutional rules established for parliamentary scrutiny of EU matters work rather well. Politicians in Finland and civil servants from the legislatures of other EU member states have considered the Finnish model a success, and the most comprehensive study of the role of national parliaments in European integration identified the Eduskunta as having the strongest scrutiny mechanism after the Danish parliament.[19] The scrutiny model of the Eduskunta has four main strengths: the position of the parliament is regulated in the constitution; the Eduskunta gets relatively early involved in the processing of EU legislation; the parliament enjoys unlimited access to information from the government; and the responsibility of preparing and monitoring European matters is delegated downwards to specialized committees.[20]

The scrutiny system is primarily designed for controlling the government on individual pieces of EU legislation and other decisions. The Grand Committee (*Suuri valiokunta*) and the Foreign Affairs Committee are the main committees responsible for European questions. The former handles first and third pillar issues, the latter second pillar matters and decisions relating to Treaty amendments. The Grand Committee has 25 members and 13 substitutes. In addition, the MP representing the Åland Islands is always entitled to participate in Grand Committee meetings. The Grand Committee convenes normally on Wednesdays and Fridays, on both days from 1.30pm to 3.30pm. The Grand Committee has enjoyed high status in the parliament since Finland joined the EU, and among its members are chairpersons of standing committees and representatives from the leaderships of the party groups.

---

18 This and the next subsection draw on previous work by the author. See: Raunio & Wiberg (1997); Raunio & Wiberg (2000); and Raunio (2001). See also Jääskinen & Kivisaari (1997); and especially Jääskinen (2000).

19 See Maurer & Wessels (2001); and Raunio (2005a).

20 Jääskinen (2000).

The documents considered by the Grand Committee, together with the minutes of the meeting, usually become public when the minutes are signed as a correct record. Additionally, a press release is published after each meeting and is also available in the Internet. At the request of the government, however, the Grand Committee may decide that its members will maintain the confidentiality of certain questions. This usually occurs when the government cannot reveal its margin of manoeuvre in the negotiations. It is also customary not to publish the negotiating positions of other member states. When the Grand Committee decides to maintain the confidentiality of the question, the relevant documents and the views of the Committee are not appended to public documents.

The involvement of the Grand Committee in EU matters is three-fold. It participates in national policy formulation on issues decided at the European level, gives instructions to cabinet ministers attending the meetings of the Council, and scrutinizes the behaviour of Finnish representatives in the European Council.[21] The Constitution (Section 96) defines the parliament's role in European matters as follows:

> The Parliament considers those proposals for acts, agreements and other measures which are to be decided in the European Union and which otherwise, according to the Constitution, would fall within the competence of the Parliament.
>
> The Government shall, for the determination of the position of the Parliament, communicate a proposal referred to in paragraph (1) to the Parliament by a communication of the Government, without delay, after receiving notice of the proposal. The proposal is considered in the Grand Committee and ordinarily in one or more of the other Committees that issue statements to the Grand Committee. However, the Foreign Affairs Committee considers a proposal pertaining to foreign and security policy. Where necessary, the Grand Committee or the Foreign Affairs Committee may issue to the Government a statement on the proposal. In addition, the Speaker's Council may decide that the matter may be taken up for debate in plenary session, during which, however, no decision is made by the Parliament.
>
> The Government shall provide the appropriate Committees with information on the consideration of the matter in the European Union. The Grand Committee or the Foreign Affairs Committee shall also be informed of the position of the Government on the matter.[22]

The government must inform the parliament without delay of any proposal for a Council decision. These so-called 'U-matters' are usually Commission's legisla-

[21] The technical details of the procedures were initially formulated in Suuren valiokunnan lausunto 3/1995 vp, Euroopan unionin asioiden käsittelystä suuressa valiokunnassa ja sille lausunnon antavissa erikoisvaliokunnissa, 22.11.1995 (SuVL 3/1995 vp). Information on the processing of EU matters, together with statistics, is also found in English and in French at the Eduskunta's web site (http://www.eduskunta.fi).

[22] The Constitution of Finland, 11 June 1999 (731/1999), Section 96.

tive proposals that fall within the competence of the parliament. The government must also send the Grand Committee information on the preparation of any issue relating to the EU that might belong to the competence of the parliament. Also, according to Section 97 of the Constitution, the Grand Committee "shall receive reports on the preparation of other matters in the European Union."[23] These other matters are 'E-matters', with the difference between E-matters and U-matters being that the former do not belong to the remit of the parliament. The government delivers to the Grand Committee a report on an E-matter, either upon request from the Committee or on its own initiative. Typical E-matters are the Commission's legislative initiatives that fall outside the jurisdiction of the Eduskunta and non-legislative documents published by the Commission (*i.e.*, green and white papers and Commission's opinions). Other E-matters include reports on Finland's integration policy or on court cases concerning Finland in the European Court of Justice.[24]

The process begins with the government sending a formal letter to the Speaker. The letter includes a summary and normally the full text of the proposal, its relevance and consequences for Finland, and the (tentative) position of the government. The government has also the duty to provide, on its own initiative, the Grand Committee and the competent standing committees all relevant documents relating to the decisions handled by the parliament. Occasionally the Eduskunta has complained that the information provided by the government is too extensive, making it difficult for MPs to identify the key points of the proposals. The Speaker forwards the matter to the Grand Committee and requests the competent specialised committee or committees to give their opinion to the Grand Committee.

The majority of U-matters are processed by more than one specialized committee. Committee involvement in European matters depends on their policy jurisdiction. The specialized committees issued in 1995-2003 on average 159 written opinions per year on U- and E-matters. The Finance Committee was most burdened with EU legislation, with also the Agriculture and Forestry Committee, the Economic Affairs Committee, the Environment Committee, Administration Committee and the Transport and Communications Committee producing actively opinions on EU matters. The Defence Committee (1 opinion) and the Committee for the Future (2 opinions) processed least EU issues. The number of domestic legislative initiatives was approximately 250 per year during the same period.

The specialized committees prepare their opinions in light of information about the government's tentative position and after having heard expert testimony. It has been estimated that in approximately 90% of the cases the Grand

[23] The Constitution of Finland, 11 June 1999 (731/1999), Section 97.

[24] This division to U-matters and E-matters does not reflect the importance of the issues. As the Eduskunta itself has remarked, some E-matters are very far-reaching and important questions, while many legislative U-matters can be fairly minor technical matters. See: Eduskunta (2005) 11.

Committee agrees with the opinion of the specialised committee.[25] When more than one specialised committee delivers an opinion, the Grand Committee summarises and mediates. After debating the issue, the Grand Committee formulates a position – which is a parliamentary recommendation, not a formal decision – in the form of a summary from the chairperson. The government representatives are notified of the decision. In order to enhance the ability of the Eduskunta to monitor and guide government behaviour in the Council, an effort is made to formulate the view of the Grand Committee before the consideration of the matter begins in the preparatory organs of the Council. The Grand Committee and the specialised committees monitor the progress of the initiative. The government has occasionally failed to inform the Eduskunta of legislative amendments enacted by the Council and the EP, forcing the committees to take steps to acquire the relevant information.

The Grand Committee convenes, usually on Fridays, to hear ministers about Council meetings scheduled for the following week. Committee members receive the agendas of the meetings, as approved by COREPER, in advance. They also receive, for each agenda item, a standardised memo with appropriate document references, a historical background summary, a summary of outstanding questions and the government's proposed course of action. The ministers must give the Committee the chance to express its opinion on all matters before final decisions are taken in the Council. The Grand Committee has insisted on this, and the government representatives have occasionally used this parliamentary scrutiny reserve in negotiations at the European level, for example during the 1996-1997 IGC. After Council meetings, the Committee always receives a report on the Council meeting. Ministers must be also prepared to appear before the Committee and to explain in detail any deviations from the given policy guidelines.

Advance scrutiny of Council agenda items means, in most cases, discussing the relevant issues and their implications, usually from the Finnish perspective. Actual voting instructions are only given at the final stage of the process and constitute a small percent, albeit an important one, of all instructions. These voting instructions by the Grand Committee are not constitutionally binding. Politically, however, they are important because the government must enjoy the support of the legislature. The Grand Committee usually does not impose very strict mandates, thus leaving ministers a certain amount of freedom of manoeuvre. This is reflected in the behaviour of the Finnish government in the Council, which has mainly been characterized by flexibility and the desire to build compromises. Moreover, the Grand Committee focuses its scrutiny on selected issues, often those of special interest to the MPs. The overwhelming majority of European matters do not cause any controversy.

According to Section 97 of the Constitution "the Prime Minister shall provide the Parliament or a Committee with information on matters to be dealt with in a European Council beforehand and without delay after a meeting of

[25] Lampinen & Räsänen (1998).

the Council. The same applies when amendments are being prepared to the treaties establishing the European Union."[26] The prime minister must inform the Grand Committee in advance of questions to be addressed by the European Council. After European Council meetings, she/he must provide the plenary session or the Committee with information on what took place. The prime minister informs the Foreign Affairs Committee about CFSP matters discussed in the European Council.

As indicated above, the informational rights of the Eduskunta in EU matters are very strong. Section 47 of the constitution is particularly important in terms of the specialized committees' access to EU information. The right of the Grand Committee and the Foreign Affairs Committee to receive information on EU matters is instead based on Sections 96 (U-matters) and 97 (E-matters) of the Constitution. The constitutionally regulated, basically unlimited, access to information from the government is an essential prerequisite for effective parliamentary scrutiny. The Grand Committee may request information on the preparation of any matter within the European Union. The government is also under an obligation to provide information of this kind to the Grand Committee on its own initiative when necessary. This access to information is especially relevant regarding two procedures related to EU decision-making: written reports from the government to the Grand Committee ('E-matters') and hearings with ministers in the Grand Committee prior to Council meetings. In decision-making related to the foreign and security policy of the EU, the Foreign Affairs Committee enjoys the same rights to receive information and to express the view of parliament as the Grand Committee enjoys in relation to other EU matters.

The functional capacity of the Grand Committee has been enhanced by its secretariat. In 2004, the Grand Committee employed three committee counsellors and four secretaries. When additional staff is required, the Grand Committee primarily relies on the staff of the specialized committees. Committee counsellors with personal experience of EU matters have been especially important, suggesting that it would facilitate parliamentary scrutiny if each committee had one functionary specializing in European issues. The Eduskunta has its own EU information service. The Secretariat for EU Affairs of the Parliament consists of the counsel to the Grand Committee and the Foreign Affairs Committee, the Brussels-based Eduskunta's representative at the EU, and a research officer and an information officer at the Public Information Unit. All members and staff of the Eduskunta have unrestricted online access to the sources of the government, including its central and non-public database of EU documents, and to the public services of the EU institutions.

The plenary can become involved both before and after decisions are taken at the European level. The plenary session may, after a proposal by the Speaker's Council, request the Grand Committee to submit the Commission's proposals to the whole parliament, along with all information provided to the Committee by the government. The plenary may debate the proposals, but does not make

[26] The Constitution of Finland, 11 June 1999 (731/1999), Section 97.

formal decisions in such cases. A formal Act of Parliament, that is, a decision made after plenary debate, is necessary when the implementation of directives requires legislation. Treaty amendments also require the consent of national parliaments. While routine EU legislation is rarely debated on the floor, far-reaching political decisions such as the Economic and Monetary Union (EMU), Agenda 2000, IGCs, and notably the development of CFSP have inspired long plenary debates. MPs who do not sit on the Grand Committee have expressed their concern about the difficulty of following European matters, arguing that more EU issues should be debated on the floor.

3.3 Partisan Consensus

The low involvement of the plenary means that while the Eduskunta deserves credit for establishing an effective committee-based system of parliamentary scrutiny, the debating function of the parliament has so far remained marginalised in European matters. Two main factors explain this brevity of integration debates. First, the Eduskunta is a committee-based institution, with the plenary in a secondary role also in the context of domestic legislation. Secondly, despite the overall consensus in the Grand Committee, European matters continue to produce disagreement within and among parties, and public debates on the floor might damage the parties by highlighting these internal cleavages.

Overall, the processing of EU matters in the parliament has been characterised by consensus and pragmatism, with little if any (public) conflicts between or within the parties. Several factors contribute to this low level of conflict between the Eduskunta and the government. The Finnish political system is often characterised as both consensual and elitist.[27] This applies particularly to foreign policy in which maintaining an amicable relation with the Soviet Union was of overriding importance during the Cold War. Even though the range of actors involved in making foreign and security policy has broadened, largely the same logic continues to guide decision-making in foreign policy and EU issues, with emphasis on achieving national unity and avoiding public cleavages. Decision-making in other policy domains is likewise broadly inclusive and based on extensive consultation with key interest groups.

The shape of the Finnish party system, with no party as a rule winning more than around 25% of votes in parliamentary elections, also facilitates consensual governance and ideological convergence between all parties aspiring to enter the government. Table 1 shows the distribution of votes between parties in national parliamentary and European elections held since the early 1990s. The fragmented nature of the party system forces parties to make concessions. Parties and their leaders are engaged in an almost constant process of negotiation and the art of building compromises and package deals is an essential feature of party politics. Until 1992, one-third of MPs (67/200) could postpone the final

---

[27] Ruostetsaari (2003a).

adoption of an ordinary law over the elections, with the proposal adopted if a majority in the new parliament supported it. This deferment rule explained partially the propensity to form oversized coalitions and contributed to the practice of inclusive, consensual decision-making that reduced the gap between the government and opposition.[28] The dividing line between government and opposition has increased in significance as a result of a series of constitutional reforms that have brought Finland closer to a standard parliamentary democracy, but the pragmatic and consensual style of politics still prevails, particularly so in European and foreign policy matters.

The early involvement of the Eduskunta in processing the Commission's initiatives also reduces conflicts. It enables the parliament to monitor the preferences of the other member states and the Commission and the EP, and to frame its own position accordingly. Also hearings with civil servants enable the Eduskunta to identify key issues and to learn about issues under preparation at the European level and in national ministries. For example, the Environment Committee has regular meetings with civil servants from the Environment Ministry. Such direct contacts with civil servants are important, for middle-level civil servants have a central role in the preparation and processing of European legislation in Finland. Ministers or even high-level bureaucrats seldom have a significant impact on the substance of the issues. Civil servants appreciate these meetings, particularly in politically controversial matters, for they enable the civil servants to hear the MPs' views and to acquire the backing of the relevant Eduskunta committee for their preparatory work. Meetings also serve as occasions for conflict management, where possible differences between the ministries and the parliament are ironed out, and thereby reduce conflicts between the cabinet and the Parliament.

Finally, committee scrutiny of European matters differs in one important respect from domestic legislation: the government-opposition dimension does not play the only significant role in either the Grand Committee or in specialized committees. The Grand Committee has insisted that all relevant information is to be made available to both the government and opposition representatives on equal terms. The main goal is understood to be to achieve parliamentary, and thus national, unanimity or at least broad consensus, which can arguably be translated into additional influence in the Council.[29] This consensus-oriented behaviour does reduce conflicts between parties and hence also public debates on EU matters, but it does provide consistency and long-term

---

[28] Mattila (1997).

[29] Tuomioja (1998). However, it is very difficult to examine whether such national unity does indeed lead to more bargaining power at the EU level. While there are anecdotal suggestions (see for example "Finland's premier gives voice to the fears of EU's small states", *Financial Times*, 9 September 2003) that Finland has performed rather well in negotiations in Brussels, and while Finland has, under the right circumstances, been able to introduce her own items to the EU agenda (*e.g.*, the Swedish-Finnish initiative on crisis management included in the Amsterdam Treaty, the Northern Dimension Initiative), this does not necessarily imply overall effectiveness in negotiations.

legitimacy for the policy choices. After all, with no single party forming the cabinet or even controlling anywhere near the majority of Eduskunta seats, the opposition has hardly any realistic chances of radically altering national European policy without the support of the other parties.[30]

3.4 Attitudes towards Interparliamentary Cooperation

With parliamentary activity geared towards scrutinizing the government on individual EU decisions, it is not very surprising that the approach of Finnish MPs towards interparliamentary cooperation has so far been fairly passive. Finnish parliamentarians and civil servants do take part in the various interparliamentary activities, but it would be wrong to say that there is much enthusiasm in the Eduskunta towards such cooperation. This is illustrated in relations between the parliament and Finnish Members of the European Parliament (MEPs) and in the interest shown towards the Conference of Community and European Affairs Committees of Parliaments of the European Union (COSAC).

The Eduskunta has made very limited use of the MEPs' expertise, primarily due to the fact that the Eduskunta has not seen Finnish MEPs as useful channels of information or influence. Finnish MEPs are not allowed to attend the meetings of the Grand Committee, and so far the Committee has not invited MEPs to give testimony. The EU Secretariat of the Eduskunta does, however, forward all agendas and press releases, and, upon request, the minutes of the meetings, of the Grand Committee to the Finnish MEPs. The Eduskunta's representative in the EU acts also as a link between the MEPs and the MPs. The Grand Committee and the Finnish MEPs hold a joint seminar twice a year, once in Strasbourg/Brussels, and once in Helsinki. The autumn seminar focuses on the EU budget while the spring meeting focuses on topical issues. Lasting only a couple of hours, the seminar is more a social occasion than a forum for exchanging detailed policy information. Moreover, only the minority of Grand Committee MPs and MEPs has attended the seminars. Also the specialized committees have made little use of the MEPs' policy expertise.

However, most of the Finnish MEPs are closely involved in the work of their national parties, and thus they can provide the party leadership with information on European matters (in most parties at least one MEP belongs to the executive party organs). Nevertheless, it is still obvious that much depends on the status of individual MEPs within the party. In addition, while there is less institutionalised co-operation between the MEPs and the Eduskunta, the former are in regular contact with their parties' Grand Committee members. In general, it appears that there is little genuine interest in the Eduskunta to develop contacts with MEPs, the main reason being that the MPs do not see

---

30 See: Raunio (2005b).

MEPs as useful sources of information or as an effective channel to influence EU decision-making.[31]

The six-member COSAC delegation has usually one representative per party group, with rotation among the smaller party groups. Occasionally it has been difficult to find volunteers for travelling to COSAC meetings, and, hence, it has not been uncommon for the Finnish delegation to have less than six MPs. After COSAC meetings, a parliamentary civil servant produces a summary of the meeting which is distributed to the MPs. Since Finland joined the EU, COSAC's meetings or resolutions have not resulted in any debates or questions in the parliament – neither before COSAC convenes, nor after the meetings.

4 The Eduskunta and the Constitutional Treaty

The Finnish government and the parliament were by and large satisfied with the outcome of the Convention and the 2003-2004 IGC.[32] Basically, all political parties agreed that while the Constitutional Treaty left room for improvement, it was probably the best deal that could realistically be achieved in difficult circumstances. Concerning the role of national parliaments, the Grand Committee repeated its earlier statements concerning openness in the Council: "the legislative body should function publicly and on the basis of binding rules of procedure that ensure the participation of national parliaments and scrutiny by civil society."[33] The government and the parliament were also against the idea of The Congress of Peoples that was discussed during the Convention.[34]

The Eduskunta has adopted a lukewarm approach – to say the least – to the Protocol on the Role of National Parliaments in the European Union attached to the Constitutional Treaty. The Eduskunta welcomed the fact that the new Protocol will give national parliaments better and more direct access to documents, but at the same time it emphasized – along the lines of the Protocol – that the involvement of national parliaments in the EU's policy process is a matter that should not be regulated at the European level. Hence, the parliament supported the Protocol without any notable enthusiasm as it did not consider the Protocol to be that relevant or important (at least not from the point of view of the Eduskunta that already enjoys strong access to information). It is worth quoting at length the position of the Grand Committee on the Protocol, as it effectively illustrates the approach of Finnish politicians on this question:

---

31 See: Linnapuomi (1999); and Ruostetsaari (2003b).

32 See for example: Valtioneuvoston selonteko eduskunnalle Euroopan unionin perustuslakisopimuksesta (VNS 6/2005 vp).

33 Statement of the Grand Committee, The Government Report on Finland's positions concerning questions arising at the Convention on the future of Europe (SuVL 1/2003 vp – E 139/2002 vp).

34 See Statement of the Grand Committee, Report of the Council of State on Finland's positions concerning the future of Europe and issues arisen during the Convention (SuVL 6/2002 vp – E 139/2002 vp).

The Grand Committee has had and continues to have reservations about any proposals aimed at regulating in detail the role of national parliaments by Union legislation. The Committee considers that such arrangements are neither necessary nor sufficient to ensure the position of national parliaments. They may, in certain circumstances, undermine the Finnish Eduskunta's constitutional role by creating a default value for parliamentary participation that is less than the current Finnish situation. National parliaments influence national policies through their governments. The relationship between a national parliament and government are among those core issues of national sovereignty that should not be regulated at the European level. The Grand Committee assumes that national parliaments in every member state can participate in and supervise their country's European policies – if these parliaments choose to exercise their powers.

> 'The Grand Committee recognises that, for reasons related to the political culture in most member states, many national parliaments view the protocol arrangement as necessary ... The Committee is therefore prepared to accept the arrangement in the protocol on the following conditions:
> - the protocol must under no circumstances impair the Eduskunta's constitutional powers or its right to receive information;
> - the Government, acting subject to the confidence of the Eduskunta, shall continue to be Finland's only representative in the Union's institutions;
> - the protocol's provisions concerning the institutions' duty to provide information and documents to national parliaments shall not impair the Government's duties or the Eduskunta's rights under sections 96 and 97 of the Constitution;
> - the Government shall at the intergovernmental conference in appropriate form indicate the primacy of the Finnish Constitution in regulating relations between the Government and the Eduskunta.
>
> If the protocol is to have any real effect on the position of national parliaments, it should state, more clearly than now, that national parliaments are one pillar of the Union's democratic legitimacy, the European Parliament being the other, and that national parliaments are, in the constitutions of all member states, the supreme holders of all public power. Without intruding on national constitutional arrangements, the protocol could note the current consensus on minimal requirements arising from the role of national parliaments. Such minimum standards were approved by the national parliaments' European committees and representatives of the European Parliament at COSAC in December 2002 (the so-called Copenhagen Parliamentary Guidelines).'[35]

The same attitude characterised the parliament's approach to the 'early warning system' included in the Protocol on the Application of the Principles of Subsidiarity and Proportionality. The whole issue was considered to be of little importance, particularly as the Eduskunta had not, during the almost decade of Finnish EU membership, noticed a single case where the Commission's legislative initiative would have violated the principle of subsidiarity.

---

[35] SuVL 1/2003 vp.

> 'The Grand Committee has serious reservations about the notion that national parliaments should appear as independent actors in relation to the Union's institutions. In the Finnish constitutional context, this would be both strange and pointless. If it were to observe a breach of the principle of subsidiarity or proportionality, the Eduskunta would naturally instruct the Government to take appropriate action in the Council, just as it directs the Government on any substantive issue.'[36]

The Protocol on the role of national parliaments or the 'early warning system', if implemented, will hence not result in any major organisational changes within the Parliament.[37]

5 Conclusion

There is no doubt that the system established for parliamentary scrutiny of European matters works rather well. Particularly the decentralization of scrutiny and policy formulation to specialized committees increases the ability of the whole parliament to influence the position of the government. The active scrutiny of European legislation has arguably improved the overall dialogue between the government and the Eduskunta, thus strengthening parliamentary accountability also in domestic issues. The regular appearance of ministers before the Grand Committee has had a positive impact on the internal work of the government, leading to improved policy coordination within the cabinet and among the ministries and forcing the ministers to study the issues more thoroughly than might otherwise be the case. In sum, the system established for scrutinising the government in European affairs works efficiently, and there are no plans for reforming the procedures.

To conclude, it is worth highlighting the features of the Finnish model that could be exported to other national parliaments.[38] Most significantly, it is important that all MPs – regardless of their views on integration, status within the parliament, or partisan affiliation – are involved in the handling of European affairs. The most effective way of achieving this objective is through delegating authority to specialized committees so that they must process EU issues, preferably before the matter is debated and decided by the plenary or the EU Committee. This way all representatives become familiar with European integration and simultaneously the whole parliament and its EU committee benefit from the policy expertise of the deputies. Secondly, the government needs to be made legally bound to provide the parliament on its own account information about

---

[36] SuVL 1/2003 vp.

[37] See: Eduskunta (2005).

[38] Indeed, this is what the Finnish parliament tried to do during the Convention. The chair of the Working Group (WG IV) on the role of national parliaments visited the Eduskunta upon invitation of the chair of the Grand Committee. The Working Group also heard a presentation on the Finnish scrutiny system. See: Kiljunen (2002).

(preferably all) matters that are processed in the EU institutions. This includes matters that are still under preparation, particularly if they are considered as nationally important. While this implies that the parliament is then potentially faced with huge amounts of information, most of which may not be that relevant, it is at least then the parliament – and not the executive – that decides which matters deserve consideration and which do not.

Table 1. *Party positions on membership and distribution of votes in Finnish national and European parliamentary elections (EP) since the early 1990s (Sources: Statistics Finland; and Paloheimo (2000) 58.)*

Party	Party line in the 1994 Referendum[3]	1991 %	1995 %	1996 EP %	1999 %	1999 EP %	2003 %	2004 EP %
Centre Party	Yes	24.8	19.8	24.4	22.4	21.3	24.7	23.4
Social Democratic Party	Yes	22.1	28.3	21.5	22.9	17.8	24.5	21.2
National Coalition	Yes	19.3	17.9	20.2	21.0	25.3	18.6	23.7
Left Alliance	No decision	10.1	11.2	10.5	10.9	9.1	9.9	9.1
Green League	No decision	6.8	6.5	7.6	7.3	13.4	8.0	10.4
Swedish People's Party	Yes	5.5	5.1	5.8	5.1	6.8	4.6	5.7
Christian Democrats	No	3.1	3.0	2.8	4.2	2.4	5.3	4.3
Rural Party[1]	No	4.8	1.3					
Young Finns[2]	Yes		2.8	3.0	1.0			
True Finns				0.7	1.0	0.8	1.6	0.5
Others		3.5	4.1	3.5	4.2	3.1	2.8	1.7
TOTAL		100	100	100	100	100	100	100

1 The Rural Party was disbanded after the 1995 elections. The True Finns, established that same year, can be considered as its successor.

2 The right-wing Young Finns was established in 1994. The party failed to gain seats in the 1999 elections and was subsequently disbanded.

3 The Left Alliance and the Green League did not adopt official positions prior to the referendum. The Centre Party adopted a pro-membership line in its party congress, but only after the party chairman and the prime minister Esko Aho had threatened to resign were the party to oppose membership. The share of party supporters voting in favour of membership were: National Coalition 89%, Swedish People's Party 85%, Social Democratic Party 75%, Green League 55%, the Centre 36%, Left Alliance 24%, Rural Party/True Finns 20%, and Christian Democrats 10%.

References

David Arter, *Scandinavian Politics Today* (Manchester: Manchester University Press, 1999).

Eduskunta, *EU-menettelyjen kehittäminen. EU-menettelyjen tarkistustoimikunnan mietintö* (Helsinki: Eduskunnan kanslian julkaisu 2, 2005).

Timo Forsten, *Valiokuntapeli eduskunnassa. Valiokuntajäsenyydet 1945-2002* (Turku: Turun yliopiston julkaisuja C:223, 2005).

Niilo Jääskinen, "Eduskunta: Aktiivinen sopeutuja", in: Tapio Raunio and Matti Wiberg (eds), *EU ja Suomi: Unionijäsenyyden vaikutukset suomalaiseen yhteiskuntaan* (Helsinki: Edita, 2000) 114-134.

Niilo Jääskinen and Tiina Kivisaari, "Parliamentary Scrutiny of European Union Affairs in Finland", in: Matti Wiberg (ed.), *Trying to Make Democracy Work: The Nordic Parliaments and the European Union* (Stockholm: Gidlunds, 1997) 29-47.

Kimmo Kiljunen, "Principles of the European Affairs scrutiny system of the Finnish Parliament", Working Group IV, Working document 20 (WG IV – WD 20), The European Convention, The Secretariat, 9 September 2002.

Risto Lampinen and Ilkka Räsänen, "Eduskunnan asema EU-asioiden valmistelussa", in: Risto Lampinen, Olli Rehn, and Petri Uusikylä (eds.), *EU-asioiden valmistelu Suomessa* (Helsinki: Eduskunnan kanslian julkaisu 7, 1998) 121-132.

Mari Linnapuomi, "Täällä Strasbourg, kuuleeko Helsinki? Suomalaiset europarlamentaarikot eurooppalaisen ja kansallisen tason yhteensovittajina", in: Tuomo Martikainen and Kyösti Pekonen (eds.), *Eurovaalit Suomessa 1996: Vaalihumusta päätöksenteon arkeen* (Helsinki: Acta Politica, No. 10, Yleisen valtio-opin laitos, Helsingin yliopisto, 1999) 228-280.

Mikko Mattila, "From Qualified Majority to Simple Majority: The effects of the 1992 Change in the Finnish Constitution", *Scandinavian Political Studies* 20:4 (1997) 331-345.

Ingvar Mattson and Kaare Strøm, "Parliamentary Committees", in: Herbert Döring (ed.), *Parliaments and Majority Rule in Western Europe* (Frankfurt, New York: Campus and St. Martin's Press, 1995) 249-307.

Andreas Maurer and Wolfgang Wessels (eds), *National Parliaments on their Ways to Europe: Losers or Latecomers?* (Baden-Baden: Nomos, 2001).

Jaakko Nousiainen, "From Semi-presidentialism to Parliamentary Government: Political and Constitutional Developments in Finland", *Scandinavian Political Studies* 24:2 (2001) 95-109.

Heikki Paloheimo, "Divided Government in Finland: From a Semi-Presidential to a Parliamentary Democracy", in: Robert Elgie (ed.), *Divided Government in Comparative Perspective* (Oxford: Oxford University Press, 2001) 86-105.

Heikki Paloheimo, "Vaaliohjelmat ja ehdokkaiden mielipiteet", in: Pertti Pesonen (ed.), *Suomen europarlamenttivaalit* (Tampere: Tampere University Press, 2000).

Tapio Raunio, "Holding Governments Accountable in European Affairs: Explaining Cross-National Variation", *Journal of Legislative Studies*, 11: 3-4 (2005a) 319-342.

Tapio Raunio, "Hesitant Voters, Committed Elite: Explaining the Lack of Eurosceptic Parties in Finland", *Journal of European Integration* 27:4 (2005b) 381-395.

Tapio Raunio, "The Changing Finnish Democracy: Stronger Parliamentary Accountability, Coalescing Political Parties and Weaker External Constraints", *Scandinavian Political Studies* 27:2 (2004) 133-152.

Tapio Raunio and Teija Tiilikainen, *Finland in the European Union* (London: Frank Cass, 2003).

Tapio Raunio and Matti Wiberg, "Finland: Polarized Pluralism in the Shadow of a Strong President", in: Kaare Strøm, Wolfgang C. Müller and Torbjörn Bergman (eds.), *Delegation and Accountability in Parliamentary Democracies* (Oxford: Oxford University Press, 2003) 301-324.

Tapio Raunio, "The Parliament of Finland: A Model Case for Effective Scrutiny?", in: Maurer & Wessels (2001) 173-198.

Tapio Raunio and Matti Wiberg, "Building Elite Consensus: Parliamentary Accountability in Finland", *Journal of Legislative Studies* 6:1 (2000) 59-80.

Tapio Raunio and Matti Wiberg, "Efficiency Through Decentralisation, The Finnish Eduskunta and the European Union", in: Matti Wiberg (ed.), *Trying to Make Democracy Work: The Nordic Parliaments and the European Union* (Stockholm: Gidlunds, 1997) 48-69.

Ilkka Ruostetsaari, *Valta muutoksessa* (Helsinki: WSOY, 2003a).

Ilkka Ruostetsaari, "Euroeliitissä vai politiikan sivuraiteella? Europarlamentaarikoiden asema suomalaisessa valtarakenteessa", *Politiikka* 45:3 (2003b) 194-211.

Erkki Tuomioja, "Konsensus tärkeää pienelle maalle", *Hallinto* 4 (1998) 3-7.

Matti Wiberg (ed.), *Parliamentary Control in the Nordic Countries: Forms of Questioning and Behavioural Trends* (Jyväskylä: Finnish Political Science Association, 1994).

CHAPTER 3

Parliamentary Control of EU Decision-making in Germany

Supportive Federal Scrutiny and Restrictive Regional Action

Daniel Thym

1 Introduction

Germany's constitutional norms on parliamentary control of EU decision-making are complex and cumbersome, often mirroring the specific design of German constitutionalism. Its analysis must therefore be construed against the background of the two defining features of the German parliamentary system. First is the parliamentary system at the federal level with its close working relations between the federal government and the parliamentary majority in the first chamber, the *Bundestag*, with effective parliamentary control of the executive being exercised by the parliamentary opposition. Second is the federal structure of the German state with the specific function of the second chamber, the *Bundesrat*, which is not primarily a body of democratic control, but of regional representation aiming at the preservation of the federal balance. These defining features of the German parliamentary system help us to better understand the contents of the existing rules and to evaluate the extent to which they pass the reality check of parliamentary control of EU decision-making in practice.

The analysis starts with a brief introduction to the constitutional framework underlying the constitutional norms on parliamentary control of EU affairs (section 2), whose regulatory framework is described in a second step (section 3). Against this background, it will be possible to enter the constitutional substance and analyse the rules governing the flow of information (section 4). We shall see in the final sections on substantive parliamentary control powers during the decision-making process that the existing rules were largely designed at the academic drawing table, stemming either from new and untested constitutional hypotheses or mirroring domestic federal arrangements. Both might explain why they have largely failed the reality check, both in the case of the *Bundestag* (section 5) and regarding the *Bundesrat* (section 6). It might therefore not be surprising that the *Bundestag* in particular is returning to the roots and focusing its scrutiny on decisions which require its original involvement in EU affairs, such as Treaty change or the implementation of directives and framework decisions.

2 Constitutional Framework

In deliberate contrast to the hierarchical subordination of the whole state to the Nazi dictatorship, the German constitution established multiple inter-woven layers of checks and balances at federal and regional levels, complemented by the explicit desire to embed Germany firmly into future *fora* of international co-operation. The latter principle of 'open statehood'[1] is enshrined

[1] Many thanks to Philipp Dann for his constructive comments on an earlier version of this article, the usual disclaimer applies. See the classic analysis by Klaus Vogel (1964), at 33 et seq.: 'offene Staatlichkeit.'

in various constitutional provisions favourable of international co-operation. For Germany, there was therefore no inherent contradiction between its internal constitutional identity and the increased flow of powers to the supranational level. On the contrary: the incorporation of the Federal Republic into the supranational European Communities realised the European vocation of its constitution, the *Grundgesetz* (hereafter: GG), which explicitly foresaw the transfer of sovereign powers and called upon Germany 'to promote world peace as an equal partner in a united Europe'.[2]

In the course of time, the German *Länder* felt the pressure of a centripetal tendency with more and more powers being exercised on the federal level. Constitutional lawyers characterized this tendency as 'unitary federalism'[3] with the *Länder* compensating their loss of legislative powers through reinforced participation in decision-making at the federal level. As a result of this compensation, most federal laws have until very recently required the consent of the second chamber, the *Bundesrat*. Fritz Scharpf famously described the resulting complex system as the 'joint-decision trap' (*Politikverflechtungsfalle*), where overlapping and inter-woven competencies and decision-making powers considerably reduce the actual problem-solving capacity of the overall entity.[4] A first attempt to disentangle the 'joint-decision trap' was undertaken with the constitutional reform package after reunification.[5] More recently, the Committee on Modernising German Federalism laid the ground for a comprehensive constitutional reform, which was eventually agreed upon by the 'grand coalition' of Christian and Social Democrats after the 2005 elections and entered into force in autumn 2006. It constitutes the most far-reaching reform of German federalism since 1949 and aims at disentangling the respective powers of the federal and the regional levels by handing certain regulatory powers, *e.g.* in the field of education, back to the *Länder* in return for a considerable reduction of co-decision powers of the *Bundesrat*, which effectively broadens the freedom of manoeuvre of the parliamentary majority in the *Bundestag*.[6]

The aforementioned developments are crucial for the understanding of Germany's constitutional regime of parliamentary control of EU decision-making. The increased legislative activities of the European Communities during the single market programme caused frustration on the side of the *Länder*. Not only did they witness a creeping loss of regulatory freedom as a result of European harmonisation; they moreover perceived a tendency of the federation to compensate its respective loss of competence to the European

---

2 The citation is taken from the preamble of the Grundgesetz, while Art. 24 (1) has foreseen the transfer of sovereign powers since 1949.

3 Hesse (1962).

4 See originally Scharpf (1985), and in English Scharpf (1988).

5 Whose reinforcement of the principle of subsidiarity in Art. 72(2) GG has been applied more rigorously by the federal constitutional court since the *Nursing Act* case annotated by Markus Rau (2003). <www.germanlawjournal.com>.

6 Constitutional Amendment of 2006 (Federal Law Gazette 2006 I).

level with a further extension of its powers to the detriment of the *Länder*. While the federal government participated actively in the shaping of European laws through the Council, the regional governments were excluded from the decision-making in Brussels. Mirroring the original domestic experience of compensating the loss of regional powers through regional co-decision in the *Bundesrat*, they called for the latter's involvement in EU affairs. A constitutional amendment in this respect was first initiated in December 1989 and eventually agreed upon in the post-reunification constitutional reform commission during 2002. The new Article 23 GG was inserted in the German constitution on the occasion of the ratification of the Maastricht Treaty in December 1992.[7] Its provisions remain the backbone of Germany's constitutional norms for parliamentary control of EU affairs until today.

In 2004, the Committee on Modernising German Federalism took up an occasionally heated debate on EU affairs, but did eventually not foresee wide-ranging changes.[8] The minor adaptations to Article 23 GG agreed upon as part of the comprehensive constitutional reform package of 2006 will be referred to in the relevant section.[9] Moreover, some more technical changes were realized on the occasion of the ratification of the Treaty establishing a Constitution for Europe in May 2005.[10] The entry into force of the domestic reform package currently depends on the fate of the European Constitution, but, in its 2005 election manifesto, the conservative party promised to bring forward its application regardless of the fate of the Constitutional Treaty.[11] For the time being, the government has however not taken any initiative to anticipate domestic changes to the parliamentary control powers and/or the corresponding early warning mechanism on the role of national parliaments at European level in order to avoid any step which might be interpreted as a political departure from German support for the Constitutional Treaty, of which the government wants to save as many aspects as possible, preferably the integral text.

It is important to keep in mind that the repeated impetus of the *Länder* for demanding and enforcing an empowerment of the second parliamentary chamber at the federal level are not primarily the democratic scrutiny and legitimacy of EU action – although they would of course argue that any enhancement of their rights increases democratic legitimacy, since they are as smaller entities closer to the hearts and minds of the citizens. Instead, their primary concerns are regional powers. Tellingly, the original *Bundesrat* draft constitutional amend-

---

7 Constitutional Amendment of 21 December 1992 (Federal Law Gazette 1992 I, 2086).

8 An overview of the debate is provided by Hrbek (2005); and Bartelt (2005).

9 Cf. in particular section 6.3.

10 Act on the Extension and Reinforcement of the Rights of the *Bundestag* and the *Bundesrat* in EU affairs of 17 November 2005 (Federal Law Gazette 2005 I, 3178).

11 See the conservative party manifesto for the 2005 elections CDU/CSU, Deutschlands Chancen nutzen – Regierungsprogramm 2005-2009, 11 July 2005 <www.cdu.de>, section 6.1, which – besides explicit support for the Constitutional Treaty – calls for the application of its rules relating to the role of national parliaments 'prior to its entry into force.'

ment for the present Article 23 GG did not contain any reference to the need for reinforced democratic scrutiny. Its official motivation only refers to the need to 'give the *Länder* a role in the shaping of EU affairs in order to preserve the federal balance.'[12]

The *Bundestag* on the contrary has never sought a considerable extension of its powers vis-à-vis the federal government in EU affairs and seems largely happy with the powers it obtained as a result of the insertion of Article 23 GG. There are various reasons for this restraint, which will be discussed later. One may however observe a renewed focus on the importance of the *Bundestag* for the democratic legitimacy of EU action. The best testimony in this respect is the Maastricht judgement of the *Bundesverfassungsgericht*, which the German constitutional court rendered after the insertion of Article 23 in the *Grundgesetz*. Much of its sometimes strong language may be attributed to the personal convictions of the reporting justice, Paul Kirchhof.[13] However, it nonetheless reflects an increased awareness of the important democratic role and function of the *Bundestag* also in EU affairs:

'If the Union carries out sovereign tasks and exercises sovereign powers for those purposes, it is first and foremost the national peoples of the member-States who, through their national parliaments, have to provide the democratic legitimation for its so doing... Democracy, if it is not to remain a merely formal principle of accountability, is dependent on the presence of certain pre-legal conditions, such as a continuous free debate between opposing social forces, interests and ideas... (T)herefore, democratic legitimation necessarily comes about through the feed-back of the actions of the European institutions into the parliaments of the Member States.'[14]

3 Normative Framework

Article 23 GG remains the backbone of Germany's constitutional rules on parliamentary involvement in EU decision-making, which has been changed recently for the first time with a minor modification being agreed upon in the framework comprehensive constitutional reform package of 2006.[15] The constitution's Article 23 is complemented and specified by the Act on the Co-operation between the Federal Government and the *Bundestag* in matters concerning the European Union of 12 March 1993 (hereafter: Bundestag-EU-Act) and the corresponding Act on the co-operation with the *Bundesrat* of the

---

12 Draft constitutional amendment of 16 May 1991, Bundestag-Drucksache 12/549.

13 He has repeatedly spoken out in favour of curbing European integration and preserving the powers of the nation state; see for instance Kirchhof (1999).

14 See *Bundesverfassungsgericht*, Judgement of 12 October 2003, Cases 2 BvR 2134/92 & 2159/92 – *Maastricht*, BVerfGE 89, 155-213 at 184-5; reported in English as *Manfred Brunner and Others v. European Union Treaty, Common Market Law Review*, 1994, 57-108 at 86-7.

15 See *supra* note 7.

same day (hereafter: Bundesrat-EU-Act).[16] Changes to these rules with a view to the European Constitutional Treaty were laid down in a separate Act of Parliament whose entry into force currently depend on the entry into force of the Constitutional Treaty, but whose implementation might be brought forward regardless of the fate of the Constitutional Treaty.[17]

As simple laws, any amendment to the aforementioned laws may be agreed upon in the ordinary legislative procedure, while any change to Article 23 GG would require a majority of two thirds in both houses of Parliament. The 1992 constitutional amendment also provided for the establishment of an EU Committee within the *Bundestag* with certain privileges under Article 45 GG, specified in the Parliament's Rules of Procedure.[18] Aware of its importance in the age of Europeanization, the German *Bundesrat* is particularly active in providing the necessary information on its EU-related activities online in English.[19] The contents of the constitutional norms enlisted above will be presented, analyzed and evaluated in more detail in the following sections.

Of course, the *Bundestag* in particular may also rely on its general control powers vis-à-vis the government in EU affairs with the ultimate right to censure the government and elect a new chancellor being its ultimate weapon to change the future political orientation of the executive or sanction it for past behaviour.[20] From a strict legal point of view, the *Bundestag* may only censure the Chancellor, not individual ministers. But in political practice, the public debate does of course tend to focus on the wrongdoing of the individual concerned, thereby effectively holding individual ministers to account.[21] Other regular instruments of parliamentary control, such as Committees of Inquiries, which were not designed specifically for matters of EU policy, but have been applied and fine-tuned in domestic policies for more than fifty years, are also being activated in European affairs.[22]

---

16 Federal Law Gazette 1993 I, 311. An English translation of the relevant legal bases concerning the *Bundestag* may be downloaded at <www.bundestag.de/htdocs_e/committees/a21/legalbasis/index.html>.

17 *Supra* notes 10 and 11.

18 See, again, the English translation *supra* note 16.

19 Online at <www.bundesrat.de/Site/Inhalt/EN>.

20 For the 'constructive vote of confidence' resulting in the institution of a new government see Art. 67 GG and on the 'simple vote of confidence' whose negative outcome might trigger new elections see Art. 68 GG.

21 On the nomination and dismissal of individual ministers by the President upon the proposal of the Chancellor, see Art. 64 GG; the aforementioned parliamentary powers formally target the position of the Chancellor upon which the government as a college depends.

22 See *infra*.

4 Information: Irrelevance through Overload?

As active members of the information society, most academics tend to forget the importance which the timely and comprehensive flow of information had until very recently. Only ten years ago, it was difficult to get hold of developments in Brussels and Luxembourg without delays caused by the publication process and the scarcity of directly accessible sources. The German parliamentary chambers faced similar problems when it came to the flow of information on EU decision-making. To prevent a lack of information from rendering the substantive control powers ineffective, the 1992 constitutional reform package laid down wide-ranging normative obligations of the government, which have recently undergone institutional and procedural adaptation to take account of parliamentary complaints about an avalanche of documentation preventing effective oversight.

4.1 Normative Concept

In theory, the *Bundestag* is an omniscient European actor with complete and timely information on all matters of potential interest. Under section 3 of the Bundestag-EU-Act, the government shall inform the legislators 'comprehensibly and as quickly as possible of all initiatives within the framework of the European Union which could be of interest to the Federal Republic of Germany.' There are no hidden caveats limiting the *Bundestag*'s right to obtain the relevant information. In particular, neither European Council documents nor documents relating to police and justice co-operation in criminal matters under the 'third pillar' or soft law instruments such as Commission communications are excluded from the scope of the provision.[23] Even matters concerning the Common Foreign and Security Policy (CFSP) are forwarded to the *Bundestag*, which is arguably of particular importance due to the limited role of the European Parliament in this policy field.[24]

In contrast to the general provision of *all* EU documents under the general rule, more detailed information on the course of the inter-institutional and intra-Council debate is constitutionally provided only with regard to the 'legislative process' (Article 23(3) GG), while the implementing act only refers to 'draft directives and draft regulations' (Section 4 Bundestag-EU-Act). A strict interpretation of the latter wording would exclude police and judicial co-operation in criminal matters. Since 'framework decisions' and 'decisions' under the reformed third pillar must however be qualified as legally binding secondary Union law, they are covered by the constitutional obligation on detailed infor-

[23] On the normative shortcomings of the Amsterdam Protocol on the Role of National Parliaments in this respect, see Maurer (2001) 62-4.

[24] See my analysis of normative concepts and political practice in Thym (2006). Only the *Bundesrat* is not necessarily informed fully in this respect, reflecting the wide-ranging prerogatives of the federal level in foreign policy issues.

mation flow, in whose light the statutory instruments have to be interpreted. In practice, such documents have always been forwarded to the *Bundestag* in accordance with the Interministerial Agreement of 10 November 1995 on the notification of the Bundestag.[25]

The government does not simply forward legislative documents to the *Bundestag*, but is under an obligation to add a summary of the main contents and objectives, the procedure applicable and the foreseeable date of debate in the Council. Moreover, it shall 'inform the Bundestag of the decisions that it intends to take, the course of the deliberations, the opinions of the (European institutions and the other Member States) and of the decision taken.'[26] The rationale underlying these manifold information requirements during the legislative process are clear: the *Bundestag* shall not only be informed about the contents of EU proposals and other official EU documents relating to it (such as the various intermediate steps of the co-decision procedure under Article 251 EC). It shall instead get the 'inside story' of the course of negotiations and ideally grasp the situation at the negotiation table as a 'virtual reality.'[27] However, the statutory rules only foresee information on the debate at Council level, while in practice most compromises are already reached or substantially prepared at working group level.[28] The eventual obligation to provide information on the decision taken gives the *Bundestag* the opportunity to scrutinize *ex post* to what extend the government followed its possible recommendations.[29] The *Bundesrat* is generally excluded from the detailed information flow, which is however more than compensated for by his participation in the decision-making process as such (see section 6.1).

4.2 Practice and Problems

Based on these detailed rules, the flow of information to Parliament has always proceeded smoothly. The geographical proximity between Brussels and Bonn, seat of the *Bundestag* until 1999, and the almost proverbial

[25] See sections I.1. and II of the agreement, whose adoption is foreseen in Section 3 Bundestag-EU-Act and which is also published on the *Bundestag*'s EU Committee website, *supra* note 16.

[26] Section 4, sentence 2 of the Bundestag-EU-Act.

[27] The lack of detailed information, or the understanding for its meaning and context, is often identified as a major structural deficiency preventing the effective involvement of national parliaments in EU affairs; see for example the smart analysis by Dann (2002) 16, which also provides an English summary of Dann (2004).

[28] Interestingly, the existing rules do not explicitly provide the Bundestag with a right to request specific information on selected issues in more detail, *e.g.* the debate in a specific working group on a particularly important piece of legislation. The Bundestag as such (Art. 43(1) GG) or its committees (Section 68 Rules of Procedure) may however rely on their general control rights in this respect and ask written and oral questions or request the presence of specific persons to provide the information desired.

[29] See section 4 Bundestag-EU-Act and the more detailed rules in section II.2 of the Interministerial Agreement, *supra* note 25.

efficiency of German bureaucracy certainly facilitated the timely and comprehensive provision of information before the information age. In more practical terms, most documents are forwarded by the government to the secretariat of the *Bundestag*'s EU Committee, whose staff level has been repeatedly reinforced in recent years and which distributes the documents to the parliamentary substructures responsible.[30] The smooth information flow is certainly the expression of the good intention to give the *Bundestag* full oversight over developments in Brussels. Members of the *Bundestag*'s EU Committee however point out that the sheer volume of legislative proposals and related documents does not only consume unnecessary resources. They moreover warn that the intensity of information threatens to 'paralyse the parliamentary control functions.'[31] Most proposals are only taken note of without any discussion at all; the wide range of activities and developments makes it very difficult to separate 'standard' business from potentially sensitive and politically 'significant' issues.[32] In short, the practical efficiency of the information flow entails the danger of irrelevance through intensity.

4.3 The Way Ahead

Parliament is not willing to resign in the face of the information flood. On the occasion of the ratification of the Constitutional Treaty, a new clause was inserted in the Bundestag-EU-Act that parliament may 'decide to forgo being sent or notified of individual or groups or proposals, initiatives or motions for legislative acts.'[33] This pre-selection by Parliament itself of certain policy areas on which no documents shall be forwarded evades the difficulties in identifying (un)important material by the government itself, which certainly has the inside knowledge to do so, but might be suspected of trying to circumvent Parliament by classifying important business as routine.[34] Moreover, a special safeguard clause for parliamentary minorities prevents the parliamentary majority from abusing the pre-selection procedure to shield the government its support from parliamentary scrutiny.[35] Of course, the *Bundesrat* may at any time decide to change the pre-selection or rely on its general control rights vis-à-vis

---

30 See section I of the Interministerial Agreement, *supra* note 25, and the description by the academic associate of the EU Committee Secretariat Sven Hölscheidt (2005) 95-6.

31 See the plain and highly recommended account of the challenges facing the work of the Committee by its former members Christian Sterzing and Stefan Tidow (2001) 282.

32 Sterzing & Tidow (2001) 281-3, and similarly the former President of the Committee Friedbert Pflüger, in Pflüger (2002a) at 20.

33 New Section 4, Sentence 2 Bundestag-EU-Act, *supra* note 10.

34 For the rejection of governmental pre-selection, see Sterzing & Tidow (2001) 282.

35 A new sentence 3 gives each parliamentary group with at least 5% of the seats a veto.

the government to obtain information on events on which it was originally not informed due to negative pre-selection.[36]

Interestingly, only the Bundestag-EU-Act was amended with a view to pre-selection, while the second chamber did not demand a similar amendment of the Bundesrat-EU-Act on the same occasion. This disparity may be explained by the structural differences between the institutions: while the *Bundestag* is a 'regular' parliamentary chamber with directly elected politicians exercising democratic control over the government, the *Bundesrat* represents the regional governments and is in itself an executive body, whose working methods are – like the work of the Council in Brussels – dominated by civil servants, who are well positioned and used to deal with a considerable load of documents and information. In one respect the *Bundestag* is however preparing to emulate the model of the *Bundesrat*. The German MPs had already agreed to open a parliamentary liaison office in Brussels staffed with 5 or 6 members of its EU Committee Secretariat before the surprise snap election in autumn 2005 provisionally halted the plans.[37] It shall serve as an early warning outpost which draws the attention of the national parliamentarians in Berlin to emerging political battle fields and may moreover facilitate direct contact with political actors in the European institutions.[38] The *Länder* have long been represented in Brussels with regional 'embassies'. These fulfil various functions ranging from lobby activities in support of regional businesses, *e.g.* in competition law cases, to the backing of regional applicants for EU money; but regional representations do also serve as facilitators of parliamentary scrutiny through the *Bundesrat*.[39]

5 *Bundestag*: Supportive Scrutiny

The 1992 constitutional reform package, supplemented by the implementing acts mentioned at the outset, was primarily motivated by the desire to give the *Länder* a say in EU matters through the involvement of the second chamber, the *Bundesrat*. The corresponding procedures and rules shall be described below (section 6). This section focuses on the constitutional control

36 The amendment or revocation of the pre-selection is not explicitly foreseen, but systematically possible by means of adoption of a new pre-selection decision. On the *Bundestag*'s general information rights to which it might also have recourse in EU affairs *supra* note 28.

37 See Kafsack (2005). The liaison office shall be located in the European Parliament joining similar representations of other national parliaments.

38 Similar plans had been supported with the said intention by the former chairman of the EU Committee for some time; see Pflüger (2002a) 20.

39 For more information on the regional representations, see Pahl (2004) 266-72. The regional representations of Bavaria and North-Rhine Westphalia are among the most impressive, see <www.bayern.de/Europa/Bruessel> and <www.europa.nrw.de>. Of course, it should be kept in mind that these two regions in particular are 'bigger' than many small EU Member States in terms of population and economic clout.

powers of the first parliamentary chamber, the *Bundestag*, whose directly elected MPs are the primary object of interest of any comparative survey of parliamentary control of EU decision-making. We shall see that the sophisticated procedures and normative rules were largely designed in the abstract, which might explain why they have failed the reality check in the eyes of many observers.

5.1 Normative Concept

According to Article 23(3) GG, the government 'shall give the Bundestag the opportunity to state its opinion before participating in the legislative process of the European Union.' Whenever the *Bundestag* decides to voice its opinion, the government has the constitutional obligation to 'take the opinion of the Bundestag into account in the negotiations.' Again, there are no caveats in the legal small print limiting the *Bundestag*'s involvement at the abstract level of constitutional rules. Section 5 of the Bundestag-EU-Act rather specifies that the 'period within which the opinion is to be stated shall be such that the Bundestag has sufficient opportunity to consider the item concerned' and that the obligation to take the *Bundestag*'s opinion into account requires the government to 'use the opinion as a basis for its negotiations.' A first look at these rules does already indicate that the EU decision-making process as a whole is covered by the parliamentary control rights, reflecting the similarly comprehensive reach of the information rights discussed above. The *Bundestag* may influence the EU decision-making at any stage.

During the input-phase of legislative drafting, the *Bundestag* may not only scrutinize new Commission proposals with a view to influence the government's position from the very beginning of the negotiations in Brussels, but may also examine 'soft' documents such as the Commission's Green and White Papers which often lay the ground for later legislative proposals in the strict sense and are usually considered to be much easier to influence than formal proposals.[40] Once the negotiations in the Council, its working groups and between the EU institutions start, the *Bundestag* has the constitutional right to discuss the issue throughout the negotiations on the basis of the information it obtains on their course, including the positions taken by the other actors which ideally give the German MPs a realistic idea of the situation at the negotiation table.[41] The constitutional norms cited above are in particular not limited to the formal decision at ministerial level, but explicitly oblige the government to 'take the opinion of the Bundestag into account *in the negotiations*.'[42] The absence of any rule on the timing of the *Bundestag*'s intervention at an early or late stage in

---

40 On the corresponding information right, see text accompanying note 23 *supra* in section 4.1. The term 'legislative process' in Art. 23(3) GG must be understood to encompass not only the formal EU decision-making procedure, but any other practice which eventually leads to the adoption of a legislative instrument; see Pernice (1998) at para. 98.

41 See in this respect the text accompanying note 27 *supra* in section 4.

42 Art. 23(3) GG, emphasis added.

the legislative process effectively lays it in the hands of the *Bundestag* to decide when it deems necessary to discuss a topic and voice its opinion.

At all stages of the legislative process, the view of the *Bundestag* has the same legal weight. It is a parliamentary opinion which the government has to 'take into account' (Article 23(3) GG) by using it as a 'basis for its negotiations' (section 5 Bundestag-EU-Act).[43] According to these rules the *Bundestag* may – in contrast to the *Bundesrat* – not formally mandate the government to follow a certain line of argument during the negotiations or vote in a specific way. The government is obliged to take the parliamentary opinion into account and may be politically well advised to follow an opinion supported by a parliamentary majority. However, legally it holds the ultimate responsibility to decide the German position and may depart from the parliamentary opinion as a result of general political considerations or in reaction to the course of the negotiations.[44] Some commentators argue that the *Bundestag* may theoretically mandate the government to take a certain position beyond the special procedure foreseen in Article 23 GG by adopting a 'mandating law' (*Mandatsgesetz*) in accordance with the regular domestic legislative procedure.[45] It is however very unlikely that the latter conflict scenario will ever materialize, since the German parliamentary system is founded upon a close co-operation between the government and the parliamentary majority.

The effective exercise of the parliamentary control powers by the *Bundestag* is at the normative level of constitutional rules facilitated by various procedural and organizational instruments laid down in the *Bundestag*'s Rules of Procedure. They partly specify Article 45 GG which was introduced at the same time as Article 23 GG and provides for the possible empowerment of the *Bundestag*'s EU Committee to exercise the powers of the parliament vis-à-vis the government. This constitutional option for the EU Committee to speak on behalf of the *Bundestag* without later involvement of the plenary is unique in the German constitutional order.[46] However, Article 45 GG leaves it to the discretion of the *Bundestag* whether the EU Committee is generally authorized to speak on behalf of the plenary or whether the authorization can only be given on a case-by-case basis. In Rule 93a(2) of its Rules of Procedure, the *Bundestag* opted for a case-

43 Insofar as the Bundestag-EU-Act may be read as differing from the constitutional rule of Art. 23(3) EU by limiting the governmental obligations to the initial stages of the debate in Brussels it has to be interpreted in the light of the hierarchically supreme constitutional rule; see Kokott (1996) 942.

44 That view is in principle uncontested in legal literature; see among others Hölscheidt (2001) 123; Dann (2004) 197; Pernice (1998) at para. 105 and the comprehensive analysis of Article 23 GG in König (2000) 460.

45 See Rath (1995) 114 et seq. whose argument it supported by Hölscheidt (2001) 124; Pernice (1998) at para. 105, and the majority view among commentators counter that Art. 23 GG prevents recourse to the regular legislative procedure in matters of EU decision-making as a *lex specialis*.

46 Its originality is highlighted, among others, by Peter Badura (1994) 887 et. seq. at 901. In practice, most plenary decisions of the *Bundestag* are prepared in its powerful committees, but formally the eventual decision is in all other cases taken by the plenary on the basis of a committee proposal.

by-case authorization 'in respect of specifically designated EU items,' whose activation requires a vote in the plenary – in contrast to the original ambition of more streamlined parliamentary decision-making in EU affairs. Indeed, this cumbersome and time-consuming procedure has not been used a single time; the authorization of the EU Committee to speak on behalf of plenary therefore remains a theoretical and untested option.[47] However, the EU Committee may also issue an opinion on its own behalf under the second sentence of Rule 93a(3), which the government is legally similarly obliged to take into account, but which politically does not carry the weight of a parliamentary position adopted on behalf of the *Bundestag* plenary under the constitutional privilege of Article 45 GG.[48]

In any case, the EU Committee has to co-ordinate its position with the specialized parliamentary committees.[49] This co-ordination requirement is not the only situation of overlap. Indeed, any issue of European policy is first filtered through a complex allocation procedure in accordance with Rule 93(1)-(4), which results in allocation to either the EU Committee or a specialized committee. There are certainly good reasons for such a division of labour, since specialized committees hold the necessary knowledge to debate EU proposals within their area of competence and are also responsible for the drafting of the corresponding national legislation. However, they do not often have the EU expertise of EU Committee members, a deficit that shall be remedied by a privileged amendment right for the EU Committee for the specialized committee's EU opinions under Rule 93a(5) and the exceptional double committee membership of all EU Committee members in one specialized committee. It ideally results in the cross-fertilization of debate and the dissemination of expertise, which are further enhanced by the asymmetry of committee working hours with Wednesday afternoon sessions of the EU Committee after the parallel meetings of the specialized committees in the morning to allow double attendance.[50] In the same vein, the potential membership of MEPs in the EU Committee shall make inter-parliamentary cross-fertilization possible[51] and the option of special meetings outside the usual working period of the *Bundestag*[52] allows national parliamentary control of EU decision-making in line with the political calendar in Brussels.

---

47 See *infra* notes 52-54 and accompanying text.

48 For more details on the different alternatives, see Hölscheidt (1998) 130 and Janowski (2005) 91.

49 See the first two sentences of Rule 93a(3).

50 On the practical aspects of inter-committee relations, see Janoswki (2005) 91-5.

51 See Rule 93a(6) for the exceptional membership of a non-MP in a *Bundestag* committee. MEPs have a right to participate in the debate, but may not vote; see also Hofmann (2003) 48: 'unique composition' with the additional note that MEPs usually do not participate in practice.

52 Rule 93a(3), sentence 3 of the *Bundestag*'s Rules of Procedure, which theoretically also allows formal EU Committee meetings, including decision-making, outside the regular seat of the *Bundestag* in Berlin, *e.g.* in Brussels.

5.2 Practice and Problems

The examination of the normative concept of parliamentary control of EU affairs by the *Bundestag* illustrates the 'good intentions' of the legislative drafters. The practice does however look quite different. The *Bundestag* and its EU Committee may well be an important player in EU affairs, but the constitutional norms described above play almost no role in this respect. The special authorization procedure under Rule 93a(2) implementing the constitutional privilege to take decisions on behalf of the plenary has not been used a single time in the 12 years of its existence.[53] The complexity of the case-by-case authorization procedure instead of a general empowerment is one reason for this practical irrelevance.[54] Another reason is consideration of intra-parliamentary prestige with specialized committees eagerly defending their grip of EU laws within their area of competence, even if they do not debate or scrutinize them in their meetings.[55] In practice, the EU Committee is mainly given the lead function in 'horizontal issues' of European affairs, which in the past years included – admittedly important – issues such as Treaty reform (Amsterdam, Nice and the Convention process), the elaboration of the Charter of Fundamental Rights, the enlargement process or budget negotiations.[56]

Another reason for limited parliamentary activities in the EU field is the general nature of relations between the *Bundestag* and the federal government. Under the German parliamentary system, which was designed to prevent the rapid change of government which had characterized the Weimar years, the German government usually enjoys a water-proof parliamentary majority. In contrast to many northern European countries, the German parliamentary democracy has no experience with minority governments or changing majorities during one legislative term, which would reinforce the parliamentary practice of scrutinizing the government in domestic and EU affairs alike.[57] Moreover, the government is on a personal level firmly embedded in the *Bundestag* and the political parties supporting it. Cabinet and junior ministers are usually recruited among the MPs whose nomination before the elections is controlled by political parties. Any MP of a majority party, who wants to succeed within this system, would usually try not to be a stumbling block for the government. The exercise of the parliamentary control powers by the *Bundestag* and its committees (whose composition corresponds to the plenary) does however require a majority vote

53 See Janoswki (2005) 90 and the information on the homepage of the EU Committee <www.bundestag.de>.

54 See Hölscheidt (2001) 129.

55 See Sterzing & Tidow (2001) 279, and the former federal defence minister and law professor Rupert Scholz, in Scholz (2005) 279: 'egotism of specialized committees'.

56 See the description of its parliamentary profile by its former President Friedbert Pflüger, in Plüger (2002b) 326-9.

57 This difference is pointed out in Maurer & Kietz (2004) 11-2.

in either the plenary or a committee to exercise the control powers.[58] Many participants report that the usual alignment of the parliamentary majority with the government is one major reason for the remarkable self-restraint of the *Bundestag* in controlling the government in EU affairs.[59]

Even the most efficient procedural tools will not translate into an effective exercise of parliamentary control powers, when they are contrary to the overall constitutional structure and institutional dynamics. Members of the governmental majority will usually prefer indirect channels of contact to the government instead of publicly criticising the government by adopting an opinion against the government's will in EU affairs. Members of the opposition may prefer the adoption of a formal position, but do not have the necessary majority to do so. Thus, they have to rely on the various control powers, which the constitution gives the parliamentary minority to scrutinize government action. They were not specifically designed for the exercise in matters of EU decision-making, but may of course nonetheless be applied. In some cases, they may even result in a wider debate in the media and among the public. In the past years, the opposition had recourse to its general constitutional control powers on two occasions which touched upon EU affairs.

In 2002, the opposition filed a complaint with the German constitutional court in a protracted dispute over the purchase of the Airbus A400M military transport aircraft by Germany as a member of a European consortium in which the government had originally agreed to the purchase of more aircrafts than the parliament was eventually willing to finance. The lawsuit was later abandoned after an agreement had been found, but for two weeks the political dispute featured prominently in the public debate.[60] Three years later, a parliamentary committee of inquiry scrutinized the German practice of issuing 'Schengen visa' which almost resulted in the resignation of foreign minister Joschka Fischer. The committee was, *inter alia*, given the explicit task to evaluate 'whether the new visa rules (introduced by the red-green government in 1999) violated international obligations of the Federal Republic of Germany, in particular Schengen obligations,' which had been incorporated into the EU legal

58 Art. 42(2) GG, 48(2), 74 Rules of Procedure.

59 Pflüger points at the contrast between the German system of 'control through co-operation' and a constitutional system of 'checks and balances', which is particularly pronounced in the US, in Pflüger (2002a) 17-8 and Pflüger (2002b) 325; see also Sterzing & Tidow (2001) 279-80; Maurer & Kietz (2004) 6, and the general distinctions between the different types of parliaments with a view to national parliaments and the EP by Dann (2002) 19-23. Traditionally, the EU Committee has so far always been an 'opposition committee' on the basis of a well-balanced distribution of committee chairmanships among the different parliamentary parties. This would reinforce the anti-government stance of any formal opinion voiced by the EU Committee.

60 See Carstens (2002). Formally, the purchase was co-ordinated outside the EU framework within the European Armament Organization OCCAR; politically, it is however closely associated to the realization of European defence policy and was widely regarded as an European undertaking in the public debate.

framework by the Treaty of Amsterdam.[61] The committee hearings were shown live on television, but its final report of 492 pages came largely unnoticed due to the election campaign after the surprise dissolution of parliament.[62]

The scarcity of the formal exercise of control rights is not limited to formal authorizations of the EU Committee to act on behalf of the plenary in accordance with Rule 93a(2), which has so far never been used. Also, opinions in its own rights without the involvement of the plenary under Rule 93a(3) are rare and were adopted on only five occasions between 1993 and the end of the last legislative term in autumn 2005. The topics under debate confirm the focus on horizontal EU issues beyond the nitty-gritty of individual legislative measures; only on one occasion did the Committee formally voice an opinion on a specific legislative proposal concerning the European Centre for Monitoring Racism and Xenophobia.[63] Another opinion dealt with combating fraud (where the *Bundestag* did not aim at changing the government's view, but rather reinforced its negotiation position by means of parliamentary backing).[64] The remaining opinions concern issues of Treaty change during the Amsterdam IGC and the European Convention drafting the Constitutional Treaty and regarding the Charter of Fundamental Rights.[65] These opinions are of particular interest, since they reveal the underlying political motivation of the *Bundestag* not to engage in the scrutiny of individual legislative proposals.

German parliamentarians tend to point at their colleagues in Brussels and Strasbourg when it comes to the control of individual European laws. Two examples: During the Amsterdam IGC the German parliament (!) explicitly called upon the government not to institutionalize the role of national parliaments at European level through a reinforced COSAC[66] or by other means as had been proposed, *inter alia*, by France. Instead, the *Bundestag* wanted COSAC to remain a rather loose framework of inter-parliamentary co-operation without a formal role within the institutional architecture of the European Union.[67] In its opinion on the Constitutional Treaty, the *Bundestag* was even more explicit by unconditionally supporting the European Parliament in its call for equal co-legislation, while at the same time rejecting proposals for new parliamentary fora at European level which could have given a greater role to national parliaments: 'We support a reasonable parliamentary division of labour between the different levels of government. The Committee emphasizes that control and scrutiny

---

[61] See Bundestags-Drucksache 15/4552 of 17 December 2002.

[62] Bundestags-Drucksache 15/5975 of 2 September 2005.

[63] Opinion on the European Centre for Monitoring Racism and Xenophobia (Bundestags-Drucksache 13/6638 of 18 December 1996).

[64] Opinion concerning combating fraud (Bundestags-Drucksache 13/5209 of 3 July 1996).

[65] Opinion on the IGC preparing the Treaty of Amsterdam (Bundestags-Drucksache 13/6891 of 27 February 1997); the Charter of Fundamental Rights (Bundestags-Drucksache 14/1819 of 19 October 1999) and the European Constitutional Convention (Bundestags-Drucksache 15/1163 of 12 June 2003).

[66] The Conference of Community or European Affairs Committees of EU Parliaments.

[67] See *ibid.* Bundestags-Drucksache 13/6891.

through national parliaments must be a constructive contribution to the advance of European integration which shall not undermine the EU's capacity to act.'[68] The members of the German *Bundestag* regard the European Parliament to be the best forum for democratic control and scrutiny, with their subsidiary control powers being a supportive supplement.

5.3 Way Ahead

Against the background of the *Bundestag*'s support for the European Parliament as the primary subject of control of EU law, it seems logical that the EU Committee concentrates on horizontal issues of European affairs. Indeed, the *Bundestag*'s EU Committee focuses on subject matters where the European Treaties explicitly foresee a national parliamentary consent requirement. Treaty change (Article 48 EU), enlargement (Article 49 EU) and the own resources of the Union (Article 269 EG) are the primary examples in this respect – while fields where the European Parliament scrutinizes European draft laws as co-legislator are largely left for the MEPs to control. Recent developments do however indicate that the *Bundestag* may in the future pay more attention to two additional dimensions of EU decision-making: Police and judicial co-operation in criminal matters and control of respect for the principle of subsidiarity.

In co-operation in criminal matters under the EU's third pillar, closer scrutiny by national parliaments is arguably particularly important as the European Parliament plays only a marginal role in the EU legislative process.[69] In its judgement on the European Arrest Warrant, the *Bundesverfassungsgericht* emphasized the role of national parliaments in this respect. Its decision declares the German implementation legislation void on grounds of insufficient exercise of implementing discretion and will be remembered by future parliamentarians whenever they debate third pillar law and its implementation in the national legal order – even if one contests the *obiter dictum* of the *Bundesverfassungsgericht* that national parliaments may decide not to implement at all a third pillar framework decision, which it explicitly qualifies as regular international law in juxtaposition to supranational Community law, in particular directives.[70]

When it comes to better scrutiny of respect for the principle of subsidiarity, the *Bundestag* would – for the first time – position itself in potential contrast to the European Parliament. But this should not necessarily be understood as a contradiction to the earlier conclusion of 'supportive scrutiny.' The principle of subsidiarity does primarily concern the allocation of competencies between

68 *Ibid.* Bundestags-Drucksache 15/1163 in section 1, indent 5 of the annex (own translation).

69 According to Art. 39(1) EU it is only consulted.

70 *Bundesverfassungsgericht*, Judgement of 18 July 2005, Case 2 BvR 2236/04, at para. 81: 'national legislatures preserve their political regulatory freedom during the implementation phase, since they may refuse implementation if necessary'; available online, together with an English release, at <www.bverfg.de>.

the different levels of government and does not touch upon the constitutional rights of the institutions in accordance with the respective decision-making procedures. Thus, the *Bundestag* would be concerned with the extent of Union action (shall the EU legislate?), while the substantive direction of Union action would still be primarily controlled by the European Parliament, whenever the principle of subsidiarity does not hinder European action. Here, the rules of the Constitutional Treaty do of course considerably extend the weight of the opinions of national parliaments.[71] But there are already calls to bring their application forward, regardless of the fate of the Constitutional Treaty.[72] The *Bundestag* could then reposition itself as a supportive scrutinizer without interfering with the institutional rights of the European Parliament in areas where it deems the Member States should maintain regulatory powers.

6 *Bundesrat*: Preserving Federalism

The original motivation underlying the regulation of regional involvement in EU affairs has already been mentioned at the outset. Regional politicians had the impression that they were the object of twofold centripetal tendencies towards Brussels and Bonn/Berlin. Following earlier examples of compensating the loss of regional power by the involvement in the decision-making processes at federal level, they argued successfully for the introduction of Article 23 GG (see section I). It should be underlined again that the *Länder* were primarily concerned with the preservation of their own regional powers in contrast to the usual democratic motivation of calls for greater involvement of national parliaments in EU affairs. Indeed, the *Bundesrat* is composed of regional governments supported by regional civil servants.[73] They derive their democratic legitimacy from regional parliaments which have only a very limited say in EU affairs. Only some of them exercise basic scrutiny of the regional government's European activities, while the others remain largely silent.[74]

---

71 See in particular the Protocol (No. 2) on the Application of the Principles of Subsidiarity and Proportionality and its analysis, among the German authors, by Mager (2003) 471-484; practical consequences for national parliaments, in particular the *Bundestag*, are analysed by Maurer & Kietz (2004), and Kietz (2005).

72 *Supra* note 11. Legally, the application of the rules would not require Treaty change, since Art. 7 of the said Protocol, *supra* note 71, leaves the monopoly of initiative of the Commission legally intact. Even a parliamentary right of access to the ECJ could be foreseen in national constitutional law, see *infra* note 85.

73 In the *Bundesrat*, each *Land* is represented by the regional government in accordance with Art. 51 GG.

74 Further details may be found in Pahl (2004) 291-8, König (2000) 370-4 and Hofmann (2003) 57-8; for corresponding rules in some regional constitutions see Scheuing (1997) 7 et seq. at 31 and the recent debate to reinforce the powers of regional parliaments in federal and EU affairs alike in Grimm & Hummrich (2005) 280-289.

6.1 Normative Concept

Article 23(4) GG summarizes the principle of regional involvement in EU affairs: 'The Bundesrat shall be involved in the decision-making process of the Federation in so far as it would have to participate in a corresponding internal measure or in so far as the Länder would be internally responsible'. This basic rule results in three different categories of regional participation defined by the internal delimitation of competencies between the federal and the regional level under the *Grundgesetz* and always concern the legislative process as a whole. It should be born in mind that the *Bundesrat* is no classic parliamentary chamber and may therefore not only control, but effectively replace the federal government due to its executive composition and working methods. Regional representatives sometimes point out that the governmental infrastructure of some *Länder*, which includes offices in Brussels,[75] does not lag behind the institutional backbone of some smaller Member States.

A first degree in regional participation concerns areas 'in which the Federation has exclusive legislative jurisdiction' and where the interests of the *Länder* are nonetheless affected, *e.g.* most aspects of environmental and planning law. Here, the federal government has to 'take the opinion of the Bundesrat into account' (Article 23(5), sentence 1 GG). Such an opinion has the same legal weight as an opinion of the *Bundestag* under the rules governing its participation; the federal government therefore has to include the *Bundesrat*'s position in its internal decision-making process, but may depart from it without violating its constitutional obligations.[76] While the formal powers of the *Bundestag* under Article 23 GG do not reach beyond this obligatory grade, the regions have two more powerful levels of influence.

In accordance with Article 23(5), sentence 2 GG, the opinion of the *Bundesrat* 'shall be decisively taken into account (*maßgeblich zu berücksichtigen*) where essentially the legislative powers of the Länder, the establishment of their authorities or their administrative procedures are affected.' The federal government may only present a different view in Brussels under the 'responsibility of the Federation for the country as a whole.' The implementing legislation specifies that the decisive influence stipulated by Article 23(5) GG means, in cases of conflict between the federal government and the *Bundesrat*, that the latter's opinion prevails, if it confirms its view with a majority of two thirds of its weighted votes (Section 5(2) Bundesrat-EU-Act).[77]

Whenever the opinion of the *Bundesrat* prevails under the said conditions, the opinion is presented within the Council by the German government representative. But even this final prerogative shall be handed over to the *Bundesrat*

---

75 On regional representations in Brussels *supra* note 39 and accompanying text.

76 See *supra* note 44 and accompanying text.

77 Legal doctrine is unsure how to define the actual field of application of the norm and the conditions under which the government may divert from the opinion of the *Bundesrat*; for more details see Pernice (1998) at para. 112-6; Pahl (2004) 310-21, and the comprehensive analysis in Lang (1997).

'in the areas of education, culture and broadcasting.'[78] In such a situation, 'the exercise of the rights of the Federal Republic of Germany as a Member State of the European Union shall be transferred by the Federation to a representative of the Länder designated by the Bundesrat' under Article 23(6) GG, which also provides for close involvement of the federal government. Section 6 Bundesrat-Rat-Act specifies the modalities for the change of seats in the Council and its working groups and for the co-operation between the federal government and the *Bundesrat* in this respect.[79] The hand-over of executive privileges in the Council to a representative of a regional government illustrates perfectly that the constitutional norms on the involvement of the *Bundesrat* in EU affairs are not motivated by the desire to control executive activity by democratic parliamentary means, but to preserve the domestic federal balance of powers.

6.2 Practice and Problems

It may not be surprising that the implementation of the constitutional norms described above has met practical difficulties. Observers even speak of a 'German vote,' which refers to situations where Germany effectively abstained, since the government and the regions could not agree on the distribution of competencies among them.[80] This may be an exaggeration at a time when the extent of regional participation in EU affairs was again under review in the Commission on the Reform on German Federalism.[81] But the underlying difficulty of the constitutional norms cited above remains. They were largely designed against the background of the domestic division of competencies between the federal and the regional level under the German constitution. Indeed, the rules make sense from the isolated perspective of German federalism, of which to preserve is their major purpose.

The European decision-making process is however not modelled on the domestic delimitation of powers under the German constitution. Individual European laws and much more the agendas of individual Council meetings do in many cases defy the categorization of Article 23(4)-(6) GG. On some subject matters, the German position may be decisively defined by the *Bundesrat* but presented by the federal government, while on other agenda items the *Länder* may have the privilege to let a regional representative speak. One easily understands the frustration of many participants complaining about internal quarrels

[78] The reference to specific policy areas was introduced on the occasion of the 2006 constitutional reform package, replacing the rather opaque reference to areas 'where essentially the exclusive legislative jurisdiction of the Länder are affected'. The new wording takes up recognized areas of regional competence under the German constitutional system, whose substantive reach differs from the corresponding EU terminology and must be interpreted autonomously.

[79] Again, more details may be found in the thorough analysis by Pahl (2004) 321-336.

[80] Scholz (2005) 275.

[81] A few years earlier, the former Europe minister of Berlin gave a much more positive practical report; see Wartenberg (1998).

being costly in terms of negotiation power.[82] The fact that these problems materialized in practice does however illustrate that the *Länder* are ready to stand up for their interests and rights and are willing to confront the federal government in this respect. Self-esteem as powerful federal states certainly plays a role in this respect, but it also illustrates a degree of political independence from the federal government, which the parliamentary majority in the *Bundestag* does not have.

6.3 Way Ahead

The German *Länder* have tried to shape European decision-making in their interest by various means during the past 15 years. The Committee of the Regions was an attempt to get directly involved in EU decision-making through a 'third chamber', an attempt which has largely been abandoned in the meantime. In a similar vein, the detour of Article 23 GG with its concept of influencing European law-making through the official German position in the Council has also showed mixed results. This might explain the recent tendency of preserving original fields of autonomous action by limiting the extent of powers of the federal and European level. One may observe this tendency towards both the European Union and the domestic German situation alike and determined their stance in the European Convention drafting the Constitutional Treaty and the Commission on the Reform on German Federalism debating a revision of the German *Grundgesetz*. In both arenas, the *Länder* pleaded passionately for a restriction of supra-regional regulatory powers.[83]

They credit themselves for being important sponsors of the Early Warning Mechanism giving national parliaments, including their second chambers, a more formal say in the European supervision of respect for the principle of subsidiarity.[84] Article 8 of the new Protocol on the Application of the Principles of Subsidiarity and Proportionality, which explicitly authorizes the Member States to give national parliaments the power to demand the initiation of an infringement proceeding before the Court of Justice, may even be modelled on a similar clause, which the *Bundesrat* had already obtained in domestic law on the occasion of the Maastricht Treaty.[85] Most recently, the *Bundesrat* has moreover taken the initiative to give the *Länder* a greater say in the nomination of judges and advocates general for the ECJ and the ECtHR, a measure which was originally agreed upon during the debate on the ratification of the Constitutional

---

82 See the highly recommended and balanced account by Hrbek (2005) esp. at 261-7.

83 For the reform of German federalism, see again Hrbek (2005) 267-70; for the European Convention the former prime minister of Baden-Württemberg and *Bundesrat* representative in the Convention, see Teufel (2003).

84 On the Early Warning Mechanism *supra* note 71.

85 Section 7 Bundesrat-Rat-Act obliges to federal government to initiate proceedings in areas of regional competence, if the *Bundesrat* so requests.

Treaty, but which shall now be brought forward independent of its fate, since it is conceptually not linked to its entry into force.[86]

7 Conclusion

Parliamentary control of EU decision-making in Germany rests upon two distinct pillars reflecting the federal structure of the German constitution and its parliamentary system. Both follow a different motivation and establish different means and channels of control corresponding to the respective composition and functions of the two chambers of parliament. While the directly elected members of the *Bundestag* are primarily expected to hold the federal government responsible for its action at the European level, the regional governments represented in the *Bundesrat* aim at preserving the federal balance of power against the background of European law restricting their regulatory freedoms.

The detailed rules on the flow of information and the involvement in the decision-making reflect these differences. They were however designed at the academic drawing table and have largely failed the reality check in the eyes of many observers, albeit for different reasons. Only the constitutional norms on the flow of information may be qualified a success. The *Bundestag* in particular is, at least in theory, an omniscient European actor with complete and timely information on all matters of potential interest. No subject areas are excluded from the parliamentary information right with the government having the additional information to provide 'insider' information on the course of the negotiations. Complaints about an avalanche of information have recently resulted in a new rule giving the *Bundestag* the option to pre-select certain areas in which it forgoes its information right voluntarily. The *Bundesrat* with its executive composition and working methods, on the contrary, is better prepared to handle extensive quantities of information.

Substantive control powers of the *Bundestag* illustrate the good intentions of the legislative drafters, which established various procedural mechanisms to facilitate parliamentary scrutiny of EU decision-making. But even the most efficient procedural tools will not translate into an effective exercise of parliamentary control powers in practice, when they are contrary to the overall constitutional structure and political dynamic in parliamentary systems. Intra-parliamentary considerations of prestige between the EU Committee and specialized committees as well as desire of the parliamentary majority not to be a stumbling block to the government, which it supports, are two major reasons why the existing control powers have hardly been exercised despite procedural facilitation. The *Bundestag*'s EU Committee instead focuses on decisions which require its original involvement in EU affairs, such as Treaty change or the implementa-

[86] See the legislative initiative extending the nomination procedure for federal judges to EU nomination in Bundesrats-Drucksache 915/05 of 10 February 2006.

tion of directives and framework decisions. Here, its scrutiny does not overlap with the respective powers of the European Parliament, which it has repeatedly supported as the main source of democratic legitimacy of European law.

Constitutional norms on substantive involvement of the *Bundesrat* mirror the original domestic arrangements for compensating the *Länder* for loss of regulatory powers by involvement in decision-making at the federal level. The ultimate option to hand over German representation in the Council to a representative of a regional government, speaking on behalf of the *Bundesrat*, illustrates perfectly their aim of preserving the domestic federal balance, not to control executive action by democratic parliamentary means. The different degrees of regional involvement in EU affairs are closely modelled on the domestic distribution of powers between the federal and regional level, but without due regard to the idiosyncrasies of EU decision-making. Frustrated with the limited effectiveness of these rules, the *Länder* seem to follow a new strategy of preserving original areas of regulatory freedom for themselves vis-à-vis Berlin and Brussels instead of compensating their loss of powers by involvement in decision-making.

References

Peter Badura, "Das Staatsziel 'Europäische Integration'", in: Johannes Hengstschläger et al. (eds.), *Für Staat und Recht,* Festschrift für Herbert Schambeck (Duncker & Humblot: Berlin, 1994).

Sandra Bartelt, "Die Europafähigkeit des Grundgesetzes und die Föderalismuskommission – Ein Abgesang", *Die Öffentliche Verwaltung* (2005) 894-902.

Peter Carstens, "Ein Lehrstück deutschen Haushaltsrechts", *Frankfurter Allgemeine Zeitung* of 2 May 2002, p. 6.

Philipp Dann, "Looking Through the Federal Lens: The Semi-Parliamentary Democracy of the EU", *Jean Monnet Working Paper* 5/2002 <www.JeanMonnetProgram.org> which also provides an English summary of his German monograph *Parlamente im Exekutivföderalismus* (Springer: Berlin, 2004).

Charlotte Gaitanides, et al. (eds.), *Europa und seine Verfassung, Festschrift Manfred Zuleeg* (Nomos: Baden-Baden, 2005).

Christoph Grimm/Martin Hummrich, "Zum Einfluss der Landesparlamente auf die Stimmabgabe im Bundesrat im Falle der Übertragung von Länderkompetenzen", *Die Öffentliche Verwaltung* (2005) 280-289.

Konrad Hesse, *Der unitarische Bundesstaat* (Müller: Heidelberg, 1962).

Sven Hölscheidt, "The German Bundestag", in: Andreas Maurer, Wolfgang Wessels (eds.), *National Parliaments and their Ways to Europe: Losers or Latecomers?* (Nomos: Baden-Baden, 2001) 117-46.

Rudolf Hrbek, "Der deutsche Bundesstaat in der EU", in: Charlotte Gaitanides, et al. (eds.), *Europa und seine Verfassung, Festschrift Manfred Zuleeg* (Nomos: Baden-Baden, 2005) 256-273.

H. Hofmann, "Parliamentary Representation in Europe's System of Multi-Layer Constitutions – A Case Study of Germany", *Maastricht Journal* 10 (2003) 39-65.

Cordula Janowski, *Die nationalen Parlamente und ihre Europa-Gremien* (Nomos: Baden-Baden, 2005).

Hendrick Kafsack, "Wissen ist Macht", *Frankfurter Allgemeine Zeitung* of 12 May 2005.

Daniela Kietz, "Der Bundestag in der Europapolitik – bestehende Potentiale und vom Verfassungsvertrag eröffnete Möglichkeiten besser nutzen", *SWP-Aktuell* 19 (2005) <www.swp-berlin.org>.

Paul Kirchhof, "The Balance of Powers Between National and European Institutions", *European Law Journal* 5 (1999) 225-242.

Juliana Kokott, "Kontrolle der auswärtigen Gewalt", *Deutsches Verwaltungsblatt* (1996) 937.

Doris König, *Die Übertragung von Hoheitsrechten im Rahmen des europäischen Integrationsprozesses* (Duncker & Humblot: Berlin, 2000).

Ruth Lang, *Die Mitwirkungsrechte des Bundesrates und des Bundestages in Angelegenheiten der Europäischen Union gemäß Artikel 23 Abs. 2 bis 7 GG* (Duncker & Humblot: Berlin, 1997).

Ute Mager, "Die Prozeduralisierung des Subsidiaritätsprinzips im Verfassungsentwurf des Europäischen Konvents", *Zeitschrift für Europarechtliche Studien* (2003) 471-484.

Andreas Maurer/Daniela Kietz, "Die neuen Rechte der nationalen Parlamente – Umsetzungsprobleme und Empfehlungen", Stiftung Wissenschaft und Politik, Diskussionspapier März 2004 <www.swp-berlin.org>.

Andreas Maurer, "National Parliaments in the European Architecture: From Latecomers' Adaptation towards Permanent Institutional Change", in: Andreas Maurer/Wolfgang Wessels (eds.), *National Parliaments and their Ways to Europe: Losers or Latecomers?* (Nomos: Baden-Baden 2001) 27-76.

Marc-Oliver Pahl, *Regionen mit Gesetzgebungskompetenzen in der Europäischen Union* (Nomos: Baden-Baden, 2004).

Friedbert Pflüger, "Die Beteiligung der Parlamente in der Europäischen Verfassungsentwicklung", in: Walter Hallstein-Institut (ed.): *Die Konsolidierung der europäischen Verfassung: von Nizza bis 2004* (Nomos: Baden-Baden, 2002) 9-26; also available online <www.whi-berlin.de/pflueger.htm>.

Ingolf Pernice, "Artikel 23 GG", in: Horst Dreier (ed.), *Grundgesetz-Kommentar, Band II* (Mohr Siebeck: Tübingen, 1998).

Friedbert Pflüger, "Der Europaausschuss des Deutschen Bundestages in der 14. Legislaturperiode", *Integration* (2002) 325-330.

Christian Rath, "Die 'unionswärtige Gewalt' des Deutschen Bundestages. Zur verfassungsrechtlichen Legitimation des gemeinschaftlichen Rechtsetzungsprozesses", in: Winfried Steffani/Uwe Taysen (eds.), *Demokratie in Europa: Zur Rolle der Parlamente* (Westdeutscher Verlag: Wiesbaden, 1995) 114 et seq.

Markus Rau, "Subsidiarity and Judicial Review in German Federalism", *German Law Journal* 4 (2003) 223-6.

Fritz W. Scharpf, "Politikverflechtungsfalle", *Politische Vierteljahresschrift* 26 (1985) 323-356. In English: Fritz W. Scharpf, "Joint-decision Trap: Lessons from German Federalism and European Integration", *Public Administration* 66 (1988) 239-68.

Dieter Scheuing, "Deutsches Verfassungsrecht und europäische Integration", *Europarecht*, Beiheft 1/1997.

Rupert Scholz, "Zur nationalen Handlungsfähigkeit in der Europäischen Union", in: Gaitanides (2005) 274-287.

Christian Sterzing/Stefan Tidow, "Die Kontrolle der deutschen Europapolitik durch den EU-Ausschuss des Deutschen Bundestages – Bilanz und Reformpotentiale", *Integration* (2001) 274-288.

Erwin Teufel, "Konturen der Europäischen Verfassung", Speech at Humboldt-University, 23 April 2003 <www.whi-berlin.de/teufel.htm>.

Daniel Thym, "Beyond Parliament's Reach? The Role of the European Parliament in the Common Foreign and Security Policy", *European Foreign Affairs Review* 11 (2006).

Klaus Vogel, *Die Verfassungsentscheidung des Grundgesetzes für eine internationale Zusammenarbeit* (Mohr Siebeck: Tübingen 1964).

Gert Wartenberg, "Praktische Erfahrungen bei der Bund-Länder-Koordinierung in Angelegenheiten der Europäischen Union", Speech at Humboldt-University, 15 June 1998 <www.whi-berlin.de/wartenberg.htm>.

CHAPTER 4

EU Affairs before the United Kingdom Parliament

A Case of Scrutiny as Substitute Sovereignty?

Adam Cygan

1 Introduction

One of the features of the Constitutional Treaty is the increased prominence and the new role it would give to national parliaments in the Union's legislative process. The Amsterdam Treaty required copies of all proposals to be sent to national parliaments and for six weeks to elapse before any decision could be taken at Union level.[1] The Constitutional Treaty would go further and provide for national parliaments to express a view on the compatibility of legislative proposals with the principle of subsidiarity. Though currently on hold, the Constitutional process provides an excellent 'jumping off point' from which to consider further what specific norms are required to address the issue of the EU's democratic deficit. Rather than viewing the process as being terminated, this paper adopts the standpoint that the rejection by the French and Dutch of the Constitutional Treaty makes the search for shared norms and objectives in relation to activities of national parliaments even more imperative.

A Protocol[2] annexed to the Constitutional Treaty provides that if a sufficient number of parliaments raise objections, the proposal has to be reviewed. The Constitutional Treaty also envisages challenges against adopted measures being brought on behalf of national parliaments in the European Court of Justice on the grounds of subsidiarity. One positive result of these potential changes is to have focussed the attention of all national parliaments on how they might give effect to the Protocol on subsidiarity.

From the outset, a number of Member States' parliaments have sought to monitor and exercise a measure of control over their governments' agreement in the Council to decision-taking and law-making at the European level. Initially, at least in the case of the United Kingdom, the reason for domestic parliamentary scrutiny of Community legislative action was to try to compensate in some measure for the loss of or shift of power from the State to the Community institution and can be expressed as a form of substitute sovereignty. After Maastricht and the creation of the European Union, as the areas of activity and responsibility have enlarged, parliamentary scrutiny has had to develop and adapt, in particular to European Union matters not falling under the EC Treaty. However, keeping Parliament informed and requiring Ministers to be accountable remain at the core of the UK regime.

The purpose of this paper is to explain how the system of parliamentary scrutiny of European legislation works in the United Kingdom (UK) Parliament by considering the practice and procedures within the House of Commons and House of Lords. Where appropriate any overlap between the work of the two Houses will be highlighted. The paper will also attempt to evaluate the experience of scrutiny to date within the UK Parliament and assess the constitutional importance and impact of parliamentary scrutiny in the UK.

---

1 Protocol on the role of national parliaments in the European Union.

2 Protocol on the application of the principles of subsidiarity and proportionality.

2 The Legal, Political and Constitutional Context of Scrutiny

Parliamentary sovereignty is the key constitutional provision which has underpinned UK constitutional law and practice.[3] The idea that there is no law that Parliament cannot make and that parliament cannot bind its successors are defining features of the UK's unwritten constitution.[4] Since the UK joined the EU in 1973, there have undoubtedly been legal and political developments which challenge this orthodox constitutional view that Parliament is sovereign. Wade has argued[5] that section 2 (4) of the European Communities Act (ECA) 1972 has a 'constitutional quality' that entrenches this Act of Parliament in to UK law and consequently provides an enduring guarantee of supremacy in UK law. Section 2 (4) states that all UK law to 'is to be construed and take effect subject to directly enforceable Community rights'. The House of Lords in *Factortame*[6] interpreted this section purposively:

> 'The words 'is to be construed and take effect subject to directly enforceable Community rights' are to be understood *as having the same effect as if a section were incorporated in to the Merchant Shipping Act 1988* (emphasis added), which enacted that the provisions with regard to the registration of British Fishing Vessels were to be 'without prejudice to the directly enforceable Community rights of nationals of any member state of the EC.'

This is the 'new' constitutional order within which Parliament participates in EU affairs. The interpretation of this section by the House of Lords in *Factortame* is entirely consistent with the view of Wade that EU law has a special binding characteristic upon Parliament, which is different to when Parliament acts in a wholly domestic context. EU law binds Parliament and requires that it acts consistently with the objective of the Treaties and section 2 (4) of the ECA 1972 provides for this. The constitutional concept of parliamentary sovereignty has undoubtedly altered following the ECA 1972, but this provision also has significant implications for procedure within the UK Parliament when it seeks to enforce ministerial accountability for decisions, which are made at the EU level. Not least is that Parliament has no constitutional right to amend EU legislation.

In the context of EU decision-making, it is the Commission which occupies the role of primary initiator of European legislative proposals. Consequently, the position of the UK Parliament is weaker to that when it scrutinises wholly domestic legislation. For over thirty years, the Scrutiny Committees of both Houses have not been brought within the Community method of decision-making. During this time, neither Committee has developed a formal relationship with the Commission, primarily because the objective of scrutiny is to

---

[3] See in particular A.V. Dicey, *Law of the Constitution* (ed. E.C.S. Wade), 10th edition (London 1959).

[4] See I. Jennings, *Law and the Constitution* 5th edition (London 1959).

[5] W. Wade, "Sovereignty – Revolution or Evolution", *Law Quarterly Review* 112 (1996) 568

[6] Case C-221/89 *R* v *Secretary of State for Transport ex parte Factortame* [1991] ECR I-3905.

influence the Executive and not the Commission.[7] Likewise the Committees have no formal working relationship with the European Parliament other than the loose framework of COSAC, though since 1999, there exists a permanent UK Parliamentary office in Brussels. As the task of scrutiny has remained focussed on the need to influence the minister, the Commons in particular has not always appreciated that through the co-decision procedure, the lack of a formal working relationship with the European Parliament has, on occasion, hampered their scrutiny activities. The Commons' European Scrutiny Committee[8] and the European Parliament[9] have acknowledged that this is a weakness, yet there is no immediate prospect of institutionalising the working relationship between the European Parliament and national parliaments beyond the existing arrangements for COSAC. In 2002, the European Parliament passed a resolution which stated that national parliaments and the European Parliament have complimentary and not competing roles and that jointly they may contribute to what was referred to as the 'parliamentarisation' of the EU.

From a constitutional perspective, the scrutiny process is a complete reversal of traditional law making procedures within the UK. Parliament is neither the initiator of nor does it take the final decision on the content of a legislative proposal. The scrutiny process does not offer Parliament any opportunity to amend the substance of the legislative proposal. Parliament can express its view to the minister and hope that this view receives some support within the Council. In addition to carrying out scrutiny, which fits within the broader constitutional role of parliament ensuring accountability of decision-makers, the role of Parliament is limited to the passing of enabling legislation which has the specific purpose of incorporating the Directives into domestic law. St JN Bates has argued that the role of the Westminster Parliament in the European legislative process can be categorised in the following manner:

> 'To put it in more negative terms, Westminster, in respect of the European Community, finds itself in the unaccustomed and uneasy, although perhaps not unique role of lobbyist.'[10]

---

7 Though regularly invited to attend the debate in the European Standing Committees, the Commissioners rarely attend.

8 See HC 152-xxx (2001-02) at paragraph 107 where the Committee proposed a regular six-monthly meeting with all UK MEPs to discuss the Commission's Annual Work Programme and Presidency priorities. Other national parliamentary committees have their own individual relationships with MEPs, for example German MEPs have a right to attend all meetings of the Bundestag's EU Affairs Committee. See Bundestag Rules of Procedure, Section 93a, paragraph 6.

9 See the European Parliament's resolution of 7 February 2002 on relations with national parliaments (P5-TA (2002) 0058) and the *Napolitano Report* of January 2002 which considered how a closer working relationship may be developed with domestic legislatures (A5-0023/2002).

10 T. St. J.N. Bates, "European Community legislation Before the House of Commons", *Statute Law Review* (1990) 109.

This is an accurate constitutional assessment of the position of the UK Parliament within the EU. For St JN Bates, the overriding change in Parliament's constitutional status as supreme law maker arises from the legislative process within the EU. In the light of the broad consultation procedure undertaken by the Commission with a variety of pressure groups at the pre-legislative stage, Parliament (together with other national parliaments) is a part of this consultation process. Scrutiny can therefore be viewed as part of this lobbying process. This is why Parliament must have effective procedures to influence the minister before he goes to give final approval in the Council.

A prevailing view within especially the Commons Committee, particularly since the Maastricht amendments to the legislative process, has been that the European Parliament is a competing institution with its own role in the legislative process. In this regard, the European Scrutiny Committee has viewed the European Parliament as part of the accountability problem within the EU and not the sole solution. From a Commons perspective, the European Parliament is part of the problem because it can amend the Council's common position, which had been subject to prior review by the Scrutiny Committee. The Commons (and Lords for that matter) can only exercise influence over the UK minister in Council, and in the light of existing Treaty provisions for co-decision, there is no time included for automatic review of European Parliament amendments. It is not unsurprising that the Commons commits most of its time and energy to scrutinising the legislative activities of the Council, as this remains the primary influence which it retains.

Both Houses of the UK Parliament have tried to compensate for the limited influence which they can exert over the EU institutions through seeking to maximise the effectiveness of their own internal procedures. Most notably this has been through the introduction of the Scrutiny Reserve Resolution.[11] The Reserve, though significant in domestic parliamentary terms, because it provides control over ministerial action, cannot place a complete brake on the overall legislative process. The demise of the veto and the norm of qualified majority voting have altered significantly the EU's decision-making processes, and raise problems for the Committees which were not wholly anticipated in 1974, though both Houses did acknowledge at the time that procedures would need to evolve in parallel with the development of European integration.

The Committees are continually aware of their scrutiny function, but practical arrangements have not always secured this objective. Exerting influence over the minister and receiving an ever-increasing volume of paperwork in good time to enable the requisite scrutiny to be completed remain significant challenges for the Committees. Since the Maastricht Treaty, the work of the Committees has been dominated by one additional question, namely, what is the most appropriate mechanism through which to monitor the application of the subsidiarity principle? The growth of EU competence, which has been brought about by successive Treaty amendments, has challenged the position of domestic legis-

[11] HC Debs. 17 November 1998 Col. 779.

latures across the EU and raised the uncertainty of how and by whom should subsidiarity be policed.

3 Brief History of Parliamentary Scrutiny in the United Kingdom

The history and work of both the European Scrutiny Committee (in the House of Commons) and the Select Committee on the European Union (in the House of Lords) can be traced back to the mid 1970s.[12] They predate references to national parliaments in the Treaties. What is noteworthy is that the current systems in both Houses still remain largely consistent with those 1973 Reports with many of the same problems facing the scrutiny Committees today as they did 30 years ago. Procedures have inevitably been adapted in the light of experience and Treaty developments and mandates have been enlarged, but no fundamental change has taken place. That said, three important recent developments should be noted.

First, the process of parliamentary scrutiny has been the subject of very detailed and critical reviews in both Houses.[13] Procedures have been adapted in the light of experience and events and mandates have been enlarged. Specifically, this means a more systematic review of Second and Third Pillar activities.

[12] In December 1972, both Houses appointed Select Committees to consider what procedures should be established to scrutinise legislative proposals and other Community documents emanating from the Communities. In the Commons the Committee was chaired by Sir John Foster. The Committee laid down the basis for scrutiny in the Commons as described below. Lord Maybray-King chaired the Lords Committee. The principal recommendation of its report (1972-73, HL 194). presented in July 1973, was to set up a sessional select committee. The Select Committee on the European Communities was set up on 10th April 1974. It was reappointed at the beginning of each Parliamentary session until it was superseded, in December 1999, by the Select Committee on the European Union.

[13] In 1998, the scrutiny of European legislation in the Commons came under review by the Select Committee on Modernisation of the House of Commons. Reports on the scrutiny process in the Commons were prepared in 1996 and 1997, by the Select Committee on European Legislation (Twenty-seventh Report 1995-96) and the Select Committee on Procedure (Third Report 1996-97) respectively. The upshot of the review was a redrawing of the terms of reference of the Commons committee, significantly by extending its remit to Second and Third Pillar matters. Its Scrutiny Reserve Resolution (the effect of which is explained below) has also been amended to include references to texts requiring a decision of the Council of Ministers under the Second and Third Pillars. The Committee was also renamed the European Scrutiny Committee. Shortly after those changes in the Commons, the terms of reference of the Lords Scrutiny Committee were revised and the House adopted its own Scrutiny Reserve Resolution. This was done essentially to bring the terms of reference into line with those of the Commons Committee, to reflect the extension of the Scrutiny Reserve to Second and Third Pillar matters and to make clear, by adoption of its own resolution, the operation of the Scrutiny Reserve in the context of procedures in the House of Lords. The Lords Committee was renamed the European Union Committee.

In the House of Lords, a number of reforms were effected following the Select Committee's review and Report in 2002.[14] The reform process is continuing. One area that remains problematic for the Committees is the review of decisions taken via the comitology procedure and soft law processes such as the open method of coordination.

Second, the UK National Parliament Office has been established in Brussels. This is an important point of contact between the two Houses and the Union's institutions, especially the European Parliament. The Office provides a valuable source of direct information for the two Scrutiny Committees.

Third, the Modernisation Committee of the House of Commons has recently proposed that a Joint Committee of the two Houses be established to consider matters related to the European Union (the Parliamentary European Committee).[15] This proposal, which has been regularly discussed since the late 1980's, is considered further at the end of this paper. A number of the Modernisation Committee's other recommendations concerning the scrutiny process are set out in the description of the work of the Commons' European Scrutiny Committee immediately below.

A key feature of scrutiny activities in both Houses is that the task is delegated to specialist committees and sub-committees. No review of European Union legislative proposals is undertaken by the specialist departmental select committees in the Commons or Lords. That is not to suggest that such committees are not interested in European Union matters. They will consider legislative proposals as part of wider policy investigations which their Standing Orders require of them. However, the mechanics of scrutiny are left to the specialist committees. Though this has allowed for the development of expertise within the Committees, it has relegated EU affairs from the mainstream of parliamentary activity perhaps reinforcing an impression that European Union affairs are peripheral to governmental activity.

4 The Heterogeneity of National Scrutiny Procedures

Parliamentary scrutiny of proposed European Union legislation is a well-established fact in many Member States, including the United Kingdom. The extent to which national parliaments monitor the legislative processes of the EU, and their governments' participation in it, varies from Member State to Member State. The precise methodology differs and reflects the constitutional, cultural and political situations in the different Member States and it is beyond the scope of this paper to explain such differences in detail. In some Member States, scrutiny is written into the national constitution and governments may not act in the Council without prior and specific authority from the

[14] *Review of Scrutiny of European Legislation* (1st Report 2002-03 HL Paper 15).

[15] Select Committee on Modernisation of the House of Commons Second Report, *Scrutiny of European Business*, (2004-05, HC 465).

national parliament (or one of its committees). A good example of this is the Danish model of scrutiny.

In the United Kingdom the process is essentially a political rather than a legal or formal constitutional one, though the wider objective of these activities is to ensure the constitutional principle of ministerial accountability. Both Houses of Parliament are given the opportunity, on the basis of documents and information provided by the Government, to examine and express their views on proposals for Community legislation and other important documents, and to debate them where appropriate. The procedures for doing this are devised by each House in accordance with its own practices and conventions. Both Houses have delegated this task to specialist select committees though and ultimately share the objective of improved ministerial accountability in the context of EU decision-making. The Government undertakes, subject to limited exceptions, not to agree to any proposal until each House has completed scrutiny – the so called 'Scrutiny Reserve'. This unique reserve, applicable to both Houses, is the key to effective scrutiny and is perhaps the closest that UK Parliament procedure has developed to include a written code of practice for ministers. The operation of the Scrutiny Reserve and the constitutional issues surrounding it are discussed in more detail below.

5 Scrutiny of European Union Legislation by the Westminster Parliament

The work of the two Select Committees, the European Scrutiny Committee in the House of Commons and the Select Committee on the European Union in the Lords ("the Scrutiny Committees"), has as its core two *essential* common features:

- the deposit of EU documents and accompanying explanatory memoranda;
- the scrutiny reserve resolution.

Information remains central to effective scrutiny and both Committees use internal parliamentary procedures to ensure a consistent and efficient flow of information. In this context, the primary target of the Committees is Her Majesty's Government. However, if documentation is delayed from Brussels, this can seriously inhibit the opportunity for effective scrutiny and no amount of internal reform to parliamentary procedure can compensate for this. In both Houses, European Union matters are delegated to specific committees who undertake scrutiny activities on behalf of the whole House. This delegation to a specialist Committee undoubtedly makes the scrutiny process more efficient and effective.

(a) European Union documents

The two Committees scrutinise "European Union documents".[16] The term is given a broad meaning and covers proposals for Community legislation and a large variety of other documents issuing under the Treaties. They include the Commission's annual work programme, green and white papers, reports and communications, reports of the Court of Auditors and, importantly, Second and Third Pillar documents (draft common strategies, joint actions or common positions in the former case and draft common positions, framework decisions, decisions or conventions in the latter case).[17] When in the course of legislation a new text is produced, such as an amended Commission proposal or a Council common position, a new document is thereby generated and the scrutiny process begins again.[18]

European Union documents are deposited in Parliament by the Foreign and Commonwealth Office, which is the lead department for EU affairs, within two working days of their receipt in London. Within ten days of deposit the lead Department is expected to provide an Explanatory Memorandum signed by a Minister. As a public document it is the Minister's evidence to Parliament and is the start of the ministerial accountability process.[19]

---

16 This term is defined in the House of Commons Standing Order No 143. The definition is reproduced, in identical terms, in the Motion appointing the House of Lords Committee, which is renewed at the start of each parliamentary session.

17 Second and Third Pillar documents were brought within the terms of reference of the Commons Committee as a result of the 1998 recommendations of the Modernisation Committee, mentioned above. This followed reports on the scrutiny process in the Commons prepared in 1996 and 1997, by the Select Committee on European Legislation (Twenty-seventh Report, 1995-96) and the Select Committee on Procedure (Third Report, 1996-97) respectively. The Lords Committee has historically had wider terms of reference, which enabled it to examine Second and Third Pillar instruments prior to the amendment of the definition of depositable documents in the Commons Standing Order.

18 A practical example of this can be seen in the scrutiny of the draft Directive on minimum standards for granting in Member States and withdrawing refugee status. The publication and debate of the European Union Committee's Report, *Minimum Standards in Asylum Procedures* (11th Report 2000-01 H.L. Paper 59) was not the end of the story by any means. Subsequent versions of the Directive or of particular articles were furnished to the Committees for scrutiny. Each was subjected to a rigorous critical examination by Sub-Committee E (Law and institutions). There was correspondence with the Government and two further meetings between the Sub-Committee and the Minister and her officials in which the Committee raised questions and sought further clarification of a number of issues, not least on draft articles affecting the rights of the individual and the level of standards being proposed. See *Evidence by Caroline Flint MP on Asylum Procedures* (1st Report, Session 2003-4, HL Paper 8) and *Further Evidence by Caroline Flint MP on Asylum Procedures* (18th Report, Session 2003-4, HL Paper 106).

19 In the case of a legislative proposal, it should include *inter alia*: a description of the subject matter; details of the legal basis, a legislative procedure proposed for the measure and any reservations or comments the Minister may have about them; assessment as to whether the proposed legislation accords with the principles of subsidiarity and proportionality; the impact on United Kingdom law; the

The requirement to provide an Explanatory Memorandum is an important and valuable feature of the system. It enables the two Scrutiny Committees to assess the documents quickly, and it establishes at the outset the constitutional imperative of scrutiny, namely, the accountability of Ministers to Parliament and its Committees for their conduct with regard those documents.

The document-based nature of the activity has recently come in for criticism. It is said that by the time a proposal formally emerges from Brussels, opinions in the Commission have already been set and it may be difficult to budge them.[20] It is argued that there needs to be more information sharing on what is in the pipeline. The attention of such critics should be drawn to the emphasis already placed by both Committees (and in the Lords, the Sub-Committees, as explained below) to "upstream scrutiny". The Committees undertake scrutiny of the Commission's annual work programme. Furthermore, both Committees are increasingly engaged in examining strategic decisions and recommendations of the European Council (*e.g.* the recent Hague Programme), Action Plans, Green and White Papers and Staff Working documents. This would become increasingly important if the provisions of the Constitutional Treaty came in to force. National parliaments will want to highlight (even if they cannot formally flourish the "yellow card" – see below) at the earliest opportunity that the principle of subsidiarity may be offended.

It should also be recalled that the Committees of both Houses have representatives based in the UK National Parliament Office in Brussels. This Office is an important point of contact between the two Houses and the Union's institutions, especially the European Parliament. The Office provides a valuable source of information for the two Scrutiny Committees. The Office is a key part of the Committees' eyes and ears and acts as an unofficial bridge between the EU Institutions and Parliament. There is nevertheless a case for saying that engagement between Parliament and interested parties (industry, consumers, civil society, etc.) could be improved, though the onus for interested parties to provide an input in to the deliberative work of the Committees remains on them, and they must bear some responsibility for communicating their concerns promptly to Parliament.

In its recent Report, the Modernisation Committee of the House of Commons has accepted that there is a case for establishing a system for examining legislative proposals before the Commission has produced its first formal document. The Committee has recommended that the Government give an undertaking to alert the European Scrutiny Committee by letter at an early stage of consultation exercises on important proposals in which it is involved. The Scrutiny Committee could then decide whether to ask for an unnumbered explanatory memorandum on the proposal from the Government, or to supplement the information supplied by the Government with information from

Government's policy towards the document; the financial implications; and the likely timetable for the Council's consideration of the proposal.

20 Digby Jones, *UK Parliamentary Scrutiny of EU Legislation* (the Foreign Policy Centre April 2005).

interested parties. The Scrutiny Committee might then decide to take evidence and produce a report on the proposal itself, to recommend a standing committee debate, or to draw the attention of the relevant departmental select committee to the proposal.[21]

(b) The Scrutiny Reserve Resolution

The cornerstone of the UK system of scrutiny is the Scrutiny Reserve Resolution. Both Houses share the same Resolution.[22] The key point is that the Resolution restricts the freedom of ministers to give agreement to a legislative proposal in Council until parliamentary scrutiny is completed. The Resolution provides that no Minister of the Crown shall give agreement to any proposal for European Community legislation, or for one of the specific instruments of Title V or Title VI of the Treaty on European Union (TEU), which is still subject to scrutiny. In practice this means one on which the Scrutiny Committee has not completed its scrutiny, or which is awaiting consideration by the House in that it has been recommended for debate and the debate has not yet taken place. The Resolution has a saving for any proposal which is "confidential, routine or trivial, or is substantially the same as a proposal on which scrutiny has been completed". The Minister may also give agreement to a proposal still subject to scrutiny "if he decides that for special reasons agreement should be given". In such circumstances, the minister is required to explain his or her reasons to the Committee or the House at the first opportunity. However, such an explanation will by its very nature always be *ex ante* and this remains the weak link in the chain of ministerial accountability.

It has been contended that Ministers are increasingly reluctant to override the scrutiny reserve.[23] Certainly there is much more transparency about the process of overriding scrutiny. The Government/Cabinet Office now provides the Scrutiny Committees with statistical information about how many times scrutiny has been overridden. This information is published in the annual reports of both Committees. Overriding scrutiny is a matter to which both Committees pay careful attention. Occasionally a Minister may be called to give evidence to explain the need to override scrutiny.[24]

There is no one clear reason why the Government overrides the reserve, though there is no overt evidence to suggest that the Government is seeking to marginalise Parliament. It is important to remember that the EU legislative process is one which is outside the scope of control by the UK Government.

---

[21] Select Committee on Modernisation of the House of Commons Second Report, *Scrutiny of European Business* (2004-05, HC 465), at paragraphs 48 and 49.

[22] Resolution of the House of Commons of 17 November 1998 modifying the resolution of 24 October 1990, which replaced a 1980 Resolution, which in turn replaced successive ministerial undertakings to similar effect. Resolution of the House of Lords of 6 December 1999.

[23] Digby Jones, *UK Parliamentary Scrutiny of EU Legislation* (The Foreign Policy Centre April 2005) 5.

[24] House of Commons European Scrutiny Committee, *The work of the Committee in 2004* (6th Report 2004-05), at para 14.

Time is arguably the crucial issue given the fast moving nature of co-decision once a final proposal is jointly agreed upon by the European Parliament and the Council. That is not to suggest that overriding the scrutiny reserve does not occur. A recent report by an independent think tank, OpenEurope, states that the government has overruled the scrutiny reserve 346 times since 2001 and that the increased the use of 'copyout' by the Government as an implementing technique for EU legislation further limits the impact of scrutiny.[25] The chairman of the Commons Scrutiny Committee has rejected the view of the OpenEurope Europe that the current Government ignores the Reserve more frequently. Previously, in evidence given to the Joint European Committee on European Affairs of the Irish Parliament, the chairman stated that:[26]

> '...we have made it perfectly clear to Ministers that if they ignore the scrutiny reserve they will have to come back and explain to us and to the people, in front of television cameras, why they did this. It is good discipline, but there are times when Ministers, in view of all those considerations, must make a decision and stand by it. There are occasions when they will override a scrutiny reserve but when they do they must come back with some good answers.'

Implicit in this statement is a recognition that the Committee is focused on ensuring that there is effective *ex post* accountability of the Government but also that Ministers in Council need flexibility to make decisions when it is in the UK's interest. Arguably, in the absence of any legal enforcement of the Reserve there are few other options available to the Committee. It is important to remember that scrutiny is a *political,* not a legal, process and that any sanction comes within the scope of parliamentary practice and procedure. If Government abuses parliamentary procedure, it is then a matter for parliament to resolve. The difficulty in the UK remains that Government is in *prima facie* control of Parliament. For the Scrutiny Committees of both Houses, their response to this ebbing of influence has been to do more of what they are already doing – namely, reviewing documents and holding inquiries and where possible bolstering their own working procedures.

6 The House of Commons – European Scrutiny Committee

(a) The European Scrutiny Committee

The scrutiny system in the House of Commons has two main components:

- the weekly meeting and report of the European Scrutiny Committee

---

[25] OpenEurope *Getting a Grip: Reforming EU Scrutiny at Westminster,* p. 17. The Report states that the Government ignored the Reserve on 77 occasion in 2005. the Report is available at: http://www.openeurope.org.uk/scrutiny.pdf.

[26] Evidence of 11 December 2003.

(ESC); and
- debates either in one of three European Standing Committees, or on the floor of the House.

The ESC examines approximately 1200 documents per year and aims to produce rapidly a short report on all significant documents, with approximately 600 reports each year. The purpose is to extract the main elements and bring the contentious features of each such document to the attention of the House and recommend whether or not it should be debated and, if so, whether on the floor of the House, or by a Standing Committee. On average, each year the Committee recommends 30 documents for debate. Of these, only a handful takes place on the floor of the House, the remainder in Standing Committee. Scrutiny is essentially an activity which has been delegated to Committees by the parliamentary chamber and is not part of the mainstream activities of the House.

(b) The Weekly Report

The Committee usually meets on Wednesdays when the House is sitting. A brief on every document on the agenda for the meeting will have been prepared by the Committee's staff and circulated to members before the meeting. The standing orders of the ESC require it to consider documents that appear to raise *questions of legal or political importance*. The ESC staff also circulates draft reports for the consideration of the Committee. The drafting of these reports, by four Clerk Advisers, usually retired civil servants who are familiar with the working of the EU and with the subject matter of the legislation, is the engine-room of the ESC. Documents are put on the Committee's agenda as soon as possible after the Explanatory Memorandum has been received. In relation to each document, the Committee may decide as follows.

a) The document is not legally or politically important, so there is no need to report substantively on it to the House or for the Committee or the House to give it any further consideration. About half the documents are disposed of in this way.
b) The document is of political or legal importance and so merits a substantive report for the information of the House, but there is no need for it to be debated.
c) The document is legally or politically important, but the decision whether there should be a debate should be deferred until later. For example, if, in the case of a proposal for legislation, the Government has gone out to consultation, the Committee may wish to see the response before deciding whether a debate would be appropriate. If the Explanatory Memorandum, in important respects, is unclear or incomplete, the Committee may wish to seek further information from the Minister before recommending a debate.
d) The document is legally or politically important and should be recommended for debate either in a European Standing Committee or on the floor of the House. When the Committee recommends a debate, it has been the practice to help to focus the debate by listing the main issues in the Committee's report.

The key point to note about these options available to the Committee is that the matter of what option to take is one which remains exclusively for the Committee to decide. Neither the Government nor Parliament can require the Committee, or ask it to refrain from an inquiry in to a particular document.

When considering documents, the Committee meets privately. The Modernisation Committee has recently recommended that the Scrutiny Committee conduct this part of its business in public as a way of raising awareness both within the Parliament and the public more generally.[27]

(c) European Standing Committees

These innovative Committees were introduced in 1990 to provide a more suitable forum for debate than the late night debates on the floor of the House, which had until then been the practice. To improve the quality of debate, the Procedure Committee recommended[28] that five European Standing Committees be established, which would take the debate away from the floor of the House of Commons and enable a degree of specialist knowledge to develop for MP's who are interested in European affairs.

Primarily due to problems securing sufficient membership, the number of Committees is today reduced to three, each specialising in particular areas of Union activity. Each Committee has thirteen permanent Members, but any other Member of the House may attend and participate in the proceedings, but not vote. The proceedings, which are public, last for up to two and a half hours. The first hour is set aside for questions to the responsible Minister attending the debate and this reinforces the principle of ministerial accountability. For the rest of the time, the Committee debates the document on the basis of a draft resolution (to which amendments may be tabled) moved by the Minister. The question time followed by debate format provides an effective means of requiring Ministers to explain and defend the Government's policy in relation to Community proposals.

The Modernisation Committee of the House of Commons has recently recommended that the number of European Standing Committees be increased from three to five, that the Committees be designated by names, which indicate clearly their functional ambit, rather than letters and that the core membership of each Committee be reduced from 13 to nine. Each European Standing Committee would be given a permanent chairman.[29] This proposal is aimed at increasing the prominence of the work done and seeking to involve more MPs in the House's European activities, though it is unclear whether the interest among MPs exists for this move.

The Standing Committees provide for focussed and informed debate on the document at hand and undoubtedly are an improvement upon the pre-1990

---

[27] Second Report Select Committee on Modernisation of the House of Commons Second Report, *Scrutiny of European Business* (2004-05, HC 465) at para 92.

[28] See HC 622- I (1988-89) at paragraph 65.

[29] *Ibid* at para 96.

arrangements for debating legislative proposals. The characteristic of the late night debates is that the turnout of MPs was confined to the 'usual participants'. Generally, this would include those MPs that were either pro or anti-European integration and who would be inclined to rehearse existing arguments, rather than actually debate the document at hand. From this perspective, the establishment of the Standing Committees has been a positive development and added to the quality of the scrutiny which takes place and ultimately the influence exercised over the Executive.[30]

7 The House of Lords – Select Committee on the European Union and its Sub-Committees

Since its inception in 1973, the work of the Lords Committee has had two distinguishing characteristics from the Select Committee in the House of Commons and reflects the individual scrutiny role of each Chamber. These are its very broad terms of reference (which do not inhibit the Committee from examining in detail the merits of proposals or restrict its activities to examination of deposited EU documents) and its ability to appoint permanent specialist Sub-Committees and, when necessary, *ad hoc* Committees for inquiries, which transcend many policy areas, or into major strategic issues such as a forthcoming IGC.[31]

The Committee has about twenty members.[32] Its Chairman[33] is appointed as a salaried Officer of the House, the Principal Deputy Chairman of Committees. The Committee has a Clerk and a Legal Adviser.[34] It meets regularly (at least fortnightly) when Parliament is in session. Much of the work of the Select Committee, in particular its detailed enquiries into current legislative proposals or other topical matters, is effected by its Sub-Committees. There are currently seven (A-G), each having particular sectoral responsibilities, and their policy remit varies depending upon European Union priorities and the expansion of European Union competence. The flexibility which the Select Committee has to re-structure its sub-committees or appoint *ad hoc* ones is a key strength and allows it to be a reactive committee which can organise inquiries efficiently.[35]

---

30 The full procedure for debate in Standing Committee can be found in Standing Order No.16.

31 The last time was in 1994 when a committee was appointed to examine the possible agenda for the 1996 Inter-Governmental Conference:*1996 Inter-Governmental Conference.* 21st Report, 1994-95.

32 Appointed by the House, on a proposal from the Committee of Selection.

33 Presently Lord Grenfell.

34 Second Counsel to the Chairman of Committees. The Legal Adviser, who is aided by the Legal Assistant, provides legal advice to the Select Committee and each of its Sub-Committees, especially Sub-Committee E.

35 The current composition of the sub-committees includes: Economic and Financial Affairs, and International Trade (A); Internal Market (B); Foreign Affairs, Defence and Development Policy (C); Agriculture

Each of the Sub-Committees is made up of usually two or three members of the Select Committee and other peers who are co-opted. Sub-Committees normally meet weekly. Each Sub-Committee is chaired by a member of the Select Committee and has its own Clerk.

Before considering the impact of the scrutiny work of Parliament, it may be useful to recall what the Lords Committee itself considers to be the purpose of national parliamentary scrutiny of EU legislation. In its 2002 Report reviewing the scrutiny process, the Committee emphasised the constitutional importance and purpose of the scrutiny of EU legislation which once adopted may not be reversed by national parliaments, even if the measure in question has to be given effect by means of domestic primary or secondary legislation. The Committee stated:[36]

> 'We accordingly stress that national parliamentary scrutiny of EU legislation has a clear constitutional purpose. Scrutiny at an early stage is therefore essential and must be effective as possible. To that end, scrutiny should include:
>
> - The accumulation, presentation and summary of relevant material, including information, statistics, explanation and analysis.
> - The provision of information to the House and the public as a contribution to transparency.
> - Drawing the attention of the House, the Government, European institutions and the public to significant matters contained within that information and in particular making recommendations – "focusing the debate".
> - Contributing to the law-making process by detailed analysis of draft texts, by exposing difficulties and proposing amendments.
> - An examination of the Government and its role in agreeing European legislation and, as part of that process, compelling the Government not only to think through what it is doing or has done but sometimes to account for it.
> - An examination of the Commission and the policies it formulates.'

At the core of these activities is improved executive accountability when participating in EU decision-making.

The Procedures and Range of Scrutiny in the Lords

(a) The Sift

The Select Committee has delegated to the Chairman the task of conducting a first sift of all the documents formally deposited for scrutiny. (The process of deposit of documents and submission of explanatory memoranda is described above.) The Chairman examines each document and its explanatory memorandum and decides whether it should be referred to one or more of the Sub-

---

and Environment (D); Law and Institutions (E); Home Affairs (F); Social Policy and Consumer Affairs (G).

[36] *Review of Scrutiny of European Legislation* (1st Report 2002-03 HL Paper 15), at para 13.

Committees or retained for exanimation by the Select Committee itself (this is relatively rare but is important for dealing with matters affecting all the Sub-Committees, such as the Commission's Annual Work Programme) or cleared from scrutiny. The Clerks and the Legal Adviser aid him in this process.

There are no formal criteria defined either by the Select Committee, the Chairman or the Clerk to the Select Committee for determining which documents should be cleared on the sift (and which should not). In broad terms, the political, practical or legal implications of the document are examined. There are several factors which may be considered relevant, in the light of experience, by the Legal Adviser when advising the Chairman whether to sift a document to a Sub-Committee for further examination.[37]

In practice, the sift is undertaken once a week when the House is in session. The results, in particular the identity of those documents cleared by the Chairman from scrutiny, are circulated to Sub-Committee Chairmen. Approximately one third of all documents submitted for scrutiny are sifted to a Sub-Committee. Just over a half of those sifted for further examination are formal legislative proposals.

(b) Detailed Inquiries and Reports – Debate

On receipt of a document, a Sub-Committee has three basic options, the choice depending largely on the degree of importance of the document, the information already available and the time factor. A Sub-Committee may, at one end of the spectrum, undertake a detailed inquiry into the proposal. This will entail the Sub-Committee taking written and oral evidence from the relevant Government Department, Union institutions (usually including the Commission), other experts and interested parties. A Specialist Adviser may be appointed to assist the Sub-Committee in a particular enquiry.[38] The outcome is a Report on the matter from the Select Committee to the House. Reports conclude with a recommendation whether the Report should be "for debate" or "for information". Copies of the Report are sent to the responsible Minister who

---

[37] These include *inter alia*: the nature of the document (a Green or White paper, draft legislative proposal or routine report); Scope (including geographic) of application of proposal, including degree of UK interest; Policy implications (usually identified and assessed by Government – any acknowledged problems of which the Committee should be aware and/or might have a view); Legal problems (*vires*, subsidiarity, extension of competence, implementation issues); Broad political/public impact; Reactions of European Parliament or other national parliaments; Advice from reputable NGO or other interested party; Previous involvement of Select or Sub-Committee, whether in relation to an earlier sifted document or an earlier (general or focused) Report; Completeness of the documentation/EM (in particular the absence of a Regulatory Impact Assessment where the measure could have substantial implications for producers, suppliers, users, consumers or taxpayers); Particular interest/expertise of members in the Sub-Committee.

[38] This is extremely rare in the case of Sub-Committee E but is standard practice for the other Sub-Committees.

responds on behalf of the Government within two months of publication.[39] Such transparency is considered as being integral to bring European Union affairs to the notice of the House more generally and also fulfils the function of ministerial accountability.

The Select Committee may itself conduct inquiries. It did so recently, for example, in relation to the application of the principle of subsidiarity under the Constitutional Treaty.[40] The Select Committee also publishes, in report format, its regular meetings with the Government's Minister for Europe (current issues and developments), representatives of the Presidency (its six month programme), and the Commission (annual work programme).

(c) Ministerial Correspondence

In practice only a very few proposals are subject to such detailed examination. The same number of documents is deposited in the House of Lords as is the case in the Commons, requiring the Committee to be very selective as to which documents it recommends for further debate. European Union policy priorities or documents containing controversial legislative proposals are more likely to be selected. On average, each Sub-Committee will conduct three inquiries each year/parliamentary session. What of the rest? The Sub-Committee may, having looked at a particular proposal, decide to write to the Minister seeking further information on it or recording its views on the matter. Sometimes that letter may be written with the benefit of written evidence volunteered or solicited from interested parties. All such and other significant correspondence from the Select Committee and its Sub-Committees to the Government is reproduced in twice yearly Reports entitled *Correspondence with Ministers.*[41]

At the other end of the spectrum, the Sub-Committee may simply note the document and clear it from scrutiny. Even in this case the Committee may write to the Minister asking to be kept informed of developments and reserving the right to conduct a detailed inquiry at a later stage.

9 Impact of the Scrutiny Process within the UK Parliament

It is difficult to assess what effect parliamentary scrutiny has in practice and perhaps only Ministers and civil servants can give a meaningful answer to the question. However, three observations may be offered regarding the work of both Select Committees within the UK Parliament. First, the disci-

39 Formerly it was the practice to publish Government responses in Correspondence with Ministers reports, described below. They are now published in a separate Government Responses report. See, for an example, 26th Report 2003-04.

40 *Strengthening national parliamentary scrutiny of the EU* – the *Constitution's subsidiarity early warning mechanism*. 14th Report Session 2004-05. HL Paper 101.

41 This relatively unknown series of Reports contains a mass of varied information about the work of the committees.

pline of Ministers having to submit Explanatory Memoranda and to respond, in writing and sometimes in person, to questions raised by the Scrutiny Committees should not be dismissed. This is a more subtle form of ministerial accountability. There can be little doubt that it is an important and efficient means of keeping the Government of the day accountable to Parliament. Though, as mentioned, there have been a substantial number of occasions when the scrutiny reserve has been over-ridden by the Government, it remains a real and effective check on Ministers. In particular the requirement that they must explain their actions in public ensures that any decision to bypass Parliament is not taken lightly. In this context, ministers cannot rely on the support of their own party members who are appointed to the Committees. In the Commons, though the composition of the Committee is in proportion to the number of MPs elected and thus favours the party in government, the Committee tends to act with a high degree of collegiality and consensus, and this is also the case in the House of Lords. This behaviour reinforces the constitutional convention of ministerial accountability which in such circumstances the Committee secures on behalf of Parliament. Such a consensus is an undoubted strength, and one which is generally lacking within the Chamber of the House of Commons where adversarial politics are the norm.

Second, parliamentary scrutiny can contribute substantially to the transparency and openness of the Union's legislative process and arguably help to aid citizen's understanding of European Union activities. Perhaps the best examples of this can be seen in the scrutiny of Third Pillar measures. The House of Lords' work on Europol is a good instance of bringing to the wider attention of both Parliament and the media the development of policy under the third pillar. The Select Committee has issued a number of Reports concerning the European Police Office.[42] The first Report, *Europol* (published in 1995), examined the Convention in draft form. The later Reports considered some of the detailed rules and regulations made under the Convention, those on the Confidentiality Regulations and the Joint Supervisory Body taking further the interests identified in the first Report (especially the need to monitor the exchange of personal data and to protect individual rights) and, significantly, placing in the public domain the detail of the rule-making under the Convention. A later Report (published in 2003) assessed Europol's role in fighting crime and made a number of recommendations relating to its remit and practices.[43] Most recently Europol was one of a number of bodies whose work was assessed by the Committee in its Report, *After Madrid: the EU's response to terrorism*.[44]

Third, the work of the Scrutiny Committees can have a direct impact on the progress or content of legislation. It is frequently said that Commission officials

---

[42] *EUROPOL* (10th Report. 1994-95. HL 51), *EUROPOL: Confidentiality Regulations*.(1st Report. 1997-98. HL 9), *EUROPOL: Joint Supervisory Body* (13th Report. 1997-98. HL 71), *EUROPOL: Third Country Rules* (29th Report 1997-98. HL 135).

[43] *Europol's Role in Fighting Crime* (5th Report. 2002-03. HL. 43).

[44] 5th Report 2004-05 HL 53.

read House of Lords Reports assiduously. Whether or not that is true, there have been instances where the Select Committee's recommendations have led to change in the measure being negotiated. An example can be seen in the 1999 Comitology Decision.[45] At the outset of its inquiry into the (then) draft decision, the Committee asked to be supplied with a complete list of comitology committees. The Community institutions contended that this was not possible, but the fact that the Select Committee required and the UK Government produced a list, showed that it was not impossible, and the Select Committee's recommendation that there should be a published list of comitology committees was taken into the final text of the Decision.[46] Despite this, it remains very difficult to measure accurately circumstances where Committee Reports lead to direct changes in legislative proposals.

10 Scrutiny as Substitute Sovereignty?

After thirty years of European Union membership, the primary objectives for the Scrutiny Committees in both Houses remain the *ex ante* review of legislative proposals and to influence the minister prior to attending the Council. With the development of the Scrutiny Reserve, the Committees have acquired a closer monitoring function of Council decision-making with ministers being subject to *ex post* accountability if they breach the Scrutiny Reserve. Through such scrutiny, the Commons and Lords are seeking to transfer to European legislative proposals those traditional constitutional principles, collectively referred to as Executive accountability, which are readily apparent when reviewing domestic legislative measures. At the core of this is the requirement of government ministers to come to the despatch box and explain their actions. In this context the two Houses, and perhaps the Commons more specifically, have attempted to maintain the same rigorous review of Executive action in relation to the European legislative proposals as are applied to domestic ones.

Executive accountability is dominated by the adversarial system of politics within the Parliament. Yet in the context of EU affairs, and in particular the work of the Select Committees of both Houses, there are identifiable elements of consensual politics which undoubtedly have improved the quality of scrutiny. The Committees of both Houses have recognised that, within the EU decision-making process, Parliament is constitutionally redundant. It has no specific role in the decision-making procedure and has no direct control over the Council of Ministers. By focussing their activities on the UK minister through seeking to establish prior influence, the Committees accept their narrow parliamentary centric role. Through operating in a cross-party consensual manner, MPs and

45 Council Decision 1999/468/EC of 28 June 1999 laying down the procedures for the exercise of implementing powers conferred on the Commission. [1999] OJ L184/23.

46 *Delegation of powers to the Commission: Reforming Comitology* (3rd Report 1998-99).

peers recognise that their influence over the minister will be far greater than if the Committees were to split on party lines. The Committees operate on a principle that a committee divided is a committee whose influence is lost.

The form of scrutiny undertaken by the both Houses can be categorised as substitute sovereignty – the more scrutiny that occurs, the more that MPs and Peers may consider that this operates as a counterbalance for legislative sovereignty that has been transferred to the EU level. The goal of executive scrutiny should not be understated and the work of the Committees must be considered a crucial task, as it remains to this day the only direct control over the UK Government throughout the entire EU decision-making procedure.

In 1974, the aim of the Foster and Maybray-King Committees was to put forward a framework for scrutiny that would secure both Houses of Parliament the maximum influence over the executive. One issue raised within the Foster Committee was that the Commons would only be able to maintain influence if legislative proposals were in the form of directives rather than regulations.[47] This misconception demonstrates not only how the perception of scrutiny within the Commons has been dominated from the outset through a desire to uphold parliamentary sovereignty, but also how political actors have over the years misunderstood the impact of European law within the UK legal system.[48]

The European Scrutiny Committee in the Commons has through time come to appreciate that the function it performs on behalf of the Chamber is different to that which is performed when the Commons reviews domestic legislative proposals. Most significantly the European Scrutiny Committee cannot propose amendments to a legislative proposal, making the directive/regulation distinction redundant with regard to content of a proposal. In an omni-competent and enlarged EU the task of the European Scrutiny Committee should not be to claw back sovereignty through excessive domestic scrutiny which ultimately has minimal impact within the Council. Rather, given that the objective of scrutiny is to influence the minister *ex ante*, scrutiny procedures should be seeking to employ effective and targeted mechanisms to achieve this. The Scrutiny Reserve is paramount to achieving this. The need for functioning scrutiny reserves is the primary conclusion which emanated from Working Group IV as a fundamental and common principle to which all national parliaments can adhere, irrespective of their other domestic scrutiny arrangements.

Both Houses in the UK have made it clear that some form of new EU institution representing national parliaments at the EU level and performing this scrutiny function is not required.[49] It would also be inappropriate for any EU Institution to seek to influence or determine how any national parliament undertakes its scrutiny activities. However, the difficulty facing all national

---

47 See HC 463-II (1972-73) paragraphs 723-725.

48 Evidenced clearly through the *Factortame* litigation and the UK's failure to appreciate the impact of the Merchant Shipping Act 1988 on the rights contained in Article 43 EC.

49 See HL 48 (2001-2) *A Second Parliamentary Chamber for the EU: an Unreal Solution to some Real Problems* and HC 152 xxxiii-I (2001-2) *Democracy and Accountability in the EU and the Role of National Parliaments.*

parliaments lies in the fact that it is the progress of the decision-making process itself that ultimately governs when, and to what extent, such scrutiny will occur. The present lack of co-ordination between the EU institutions and domestic parliaments over issues such as the legislative timetable or providing sufficient time for scrutiny goes to the heart of the unease that exists in the relationship between them.[50] This in part, is one explanation why, in the past, the Commons has compensated for the transfer of competence with over rigorous scrutiny. For the House of Commons, problems of transparency and efficient provision of documentation with their roots firmly in the EU must first be addressed before any progress can be made to resolve the wider problem of direct disconnection between the EU institutions and citizens.[51]

Scrutiny remains effective if it is pre-legislative and based upon the timely provision of all available documentation. The Committees seek to achieve this through enforcing the Scrutiny Reserve which reinforces the argument that parliamentary scrutiny procedures amount to substitute sovereignty. The Reserve, which seeks to maximise executive accountability, is primarily intended for domestic parliamentary consumption to reassure sceptical MPs that the views of the UK Parliament do matter and are relevant to EU decision-making. Consequently, the introspective nature of Reserve leads it to operate independently of the Council timetable. Working Group IV recognised that this is unsatisfactory and that scrutiny reserves require greater prominence in the Treaty if national parliaments are themselves to believe they have not become peripheral to the process of European integration. The Constitutional Treaty Protocols and related provisions would go part of the way, at least, to addressing this.

Connected to these arguments of substitute sovereignty is the fundamental question of which level of governance should have competence to legislate in a given policy area. The House of Commons would like to see more subsidiarity in practice as decision-making at the national level suggests increased executive accountability. Through the transfer of competence to the EU level, the view is reinforced that domestic scrutiny compensates for the loss of actual legislative sovereignty. Both Committees have, to this end, made it clear that they would need to review their existing procedures in the light of the Constitutional Treaty provisions relating to national parliaments to ensure ministerial influence is maintained and if possible enhanced.

---

50 Though in his statement of February 11 2004, the Foreign Secretary stated that from April 2004 and then subsequently every January the government will seek to aid the Committee in its task by laying before the House a White Paper looking at the year ahead for the EU's legislative and other activities. The objective of the Paper will be to set out the government's priorities in the light of the Commission's legislative and work programme for the year ahead, as well as the operational programme for the forthcoming EU presidencies agreed each December by the European Council. See HC Debs. February 11 2004, Col. 1416.

51 HC 63-xxiv, (2003-03), p. 7, paragraph 8.

11 Future Reform of the UK Scrutiny Process

As mentioned above, the process in the United Kingdom has recently come under criticism, notably for the lack of awareness of MPs and, more generally, the public about legislative proposals emanating from Brussels. The good work of the two Scrutiny Committees has been acknowledged but there remains, it is strongly argued (by the Government and such bodies as the CBI), a failure of MPs to engage with and in the European legislative process. One solution promoted in the Parliament which sat from 2001-2005 was the creation of a Joint Grand Committee for Europe (described above).[52] It is envisaged that the Committee would meet about four times a year, two of which would be devoted to considering the Foreign Secretary's regular six monthly White Papers on Europe. MEPs would be allowed to attend. Commissioners and Commission officials might also participate in meetings of the new Committee but, the Report makes clear, would not be subject to scrutiny by the Joint Committee. Their role would be to share information, to inform the debate and to foster dialogue between the Commission and Parliament. What seems clear is that the new Joint Committee would not take over or displace the regular detailed scrutiny work undertaken by the two Scrutiny Committees. The CBI has commented: "clearly such an infrequently-meeting committee could not launch an inquiry, or examine an issue in any detail, and thus would not contribute significantly to the scrutiny process".[53] Such criticisms deserve careful examination. For example, the Joint Committee might well have to be selective but one cannot rule out the possibility that a well-prepared meeting might examine a Minister or Commissioner on a particular proposal (*e.g.* the controversial draft Services Directive) in some detail. How it might strengthen Parliamentary awareness and scrutiny of European legislation and policies is to be seen. Whether, and how best, the Grand Committee might complement and supplement the detailed work of the Scrutiny Committees needs further consideration.

Any future development in relation to the work and practical arrangements of both Committees remains subject to the future prospects for the Constitutional Treaty. In practice this will mean what, if any, parts of it can be salvaged, perhaps in the form of some new Treaty. The provisions of the Constitutional Treaty which relate to national parliaments would improve their ability to conduct scrutiny and arguably could be introduced without the need for a specific Treaty but through a change to the Council's rules of procedure and the Commission making documents available more efficiently. Though piecemeal reform it would assist Committees, such as those in the UK Parliament, to ensure ministerial accountability is upheld, EU legislation is more transparent and that ultimately citizens are better informed of their rights and obligations.

---

[52] Select Committee on Modernisation of the House of Commons Second Report, *Scrutiny of European Business*, (2004-05, HC 465).

[53] Digby Jones, *UK Parliamentary Scrutiny of EU Legislation*, at p 5.

CHAPTER 5

Belgian Parliaments and EU Decision-making

"In the Government We Trust"

Hendrik Vos, Sofie Staelraeve, Carl Devos, Jan Orbie, Hilde Van Liefferinge, An Schrijvers

1 Introduction

This paper consists of two main parts. Firstly, we will look at the organisation of parliamentary control of EU decision-making in Belgium. We will discuss the functioning of the Federal Advisory Committee, as well as its role in the flow of information about EU decision-making in the Belgian Parliament. The decisive moments at which parliamentary control of EU decision-making is or could be exercised will be explored. Special attention is paid to divergences between the actual situation of parliamentary control on the one hand, and the formally laid down provisions on the other. Being a highly federalised country, an analysis of the Belgian situation cannot be confined to the federal level. Thus, the paper will also look at the role of the regional parliaments, with the Flemish Parliament as a case study. The second major part of this contribution gives more contextual information of the Belgian system at large. We will discuss which characteristics of Belgian society and politics contribute to explain how parliamentary control in EU decision-making takes place in Belgium.

We will demonstrate that (federal and regional) governments dispose of a relatively large discretion in the Belgian political system. In this elite-driven, consociational democracy with several political cleavages, many political parties and broad coalitions, the governments and the political parties are the centres of power. Furthermore, the complexity of the federal state makes it difficult to assess who is responsible for what elements of decision-making. Parliaments are rather weak in the Belgian political context. This is all the more so in EU matters. In this contribution we will put forward the hypothesis that a permissive consensus under the elite contributes to a lack of political will to scrutinize EU affairs. European topics are never really contested among the elite, leading to an indifferent attitude in the parliaments vis-à-vis European issues.

2 How Parliamentary Control of EU Decision-making is Organised in Belgium

2.1 A Uniquely Composed Federal Advisory Committee

To enhance the Belgian, federal parliament's involvement in the control of EU decision-making, an Advisory Committee on European Affairs was established in 1985.[1] It is a unique Committee, compared to other parliamentary bodies.

The very name is uncommon: it is called an "Advisory Committee" and not a "Standing Committee" like the other committees parties in the parliament. However, its composition especially makes this Advisory Committee rather exceptional: it is composed of ten members of the House of Representatives

[1] For an overview of the precursors to this Committee, see De Winter & Laurent (1996).

(henceforth: House) and ten members of the European Parliament (MEPs), elected on a Belgian list. Being involved on an equal basis, this means that the MEPs do have full voting rights and that they can even be appointed as rapporteur. The political groups are represented on a proportional basis.

The close involvement of MEPs in the Advisory Committee has as its main objective facilitating the flow of information between the EU-level and the Belgian, federal level. However, if the House decides to have a plenary session on an advice, resolution or recommendation of the Advisory Committee, the MEPs are not entitled to take part in this debate.[2]

The rules of procedure of the House require that the presidency of this Advisory Committee be exercised by the Chair of the House or a Deputy-Chair, appointed by the Chair.[3] The rules of procedure of both the House[4] and the Senate[5] also establish a "Federal Advisory Committee on European Affairs" composed of the members of the Advisory Committee plus ten members of the Senate. Actually, the Advisory Committee is usually meeting in the latter composition (Federal Advisory Committee), the members of the Senate included.

2.2 The Functioning of the Federal Advisory Committee

The Federal Advisory Committee is frequently meeting (almost on a weekly basis) but does not have ample administrative support (only 1 FT employee). This is all the more remarkable since the list of its tasks, as detailed in the rules of procedure of the House, is long.

The first aim of the Federal Advisory Committee is to co-ordinate and to stimulate the parliamentary control of EU decision-making and to watch over the follow-up of its own resolutions and recommendations. Another explicitly mentioned task of the Federal Advisory Committee is to give recommendations on EU Treaty revisions. The Federal Advisory Committee is also supposed to keep an eye on the implementation of European laws into Belgian laws. On a regular basis, the Deputy Minister for European Affairs must submit a report on the current situation.

The Federal Advisory Committee made it a rule to invite the Belgian Prime Minister before and after every meeting of the European Council (approximately four times a year). At this occasion, the Prime Minister gives an overview of the points on the agenda, the Belgian point of view and, at the post-briefing, a summary of the conclusions. This is mostly a listening exercise for the members of the Committee, but being an opportunity to catch first hand information, these pre- and post-briefings are heavily attended, also by the MEPs who tend to be absent during the 'ordinary' meetings of the Federal Advisory Committee.

---

2 Stuk Kamer nr. 1149/1, 27.02.1985, 23.

3 Article 68, 1.2.

4 Article 68, II.

5 Article 85.

Finally, it must be said that the Federal Advisory Committee is also involved in the follow-up of 'other' European organisations and activities, such as the Council of Europe or the Western European Union.

The discussions in the Federal Advisory Committee can be concluded with a proposal for a resolution, a recommendation or another intervention which can be discussed during a plenary session of the House or, where appropriate, the Senate. Other 'traditional' parliamentary procedures apply as well, such as the right to organise hearings or to submit oral and written questions to the members of the government. It is important to stress that the government is not required to ask the Federal Advisory Committee or any other Standing Committee for an opinion before taking a stance in the Council meetings at EU-level. There is an agreement, however, to pass on information to the Federal Advisory Committee on the running EU-programme and the Belgian standpoints before and after Council sessions (see below).

2.3 The Standing Committees and European affairs

The follow-up of EU-related affairs by the Standing Committees of the House is covered in the rules of procedure of the House as well. There are about a dozen Standing Committees in the House, such as the Standing Committee for Social Affairs, for Justice, for Public Health and the Environment, etc. Many topics that are discussed in these Standing Committees do have a European dimension.

Article 36 of the rules of procedure says that at least once a month every Standing Committee has to organise an internal discussion on relevant issues on the agenda of the EU institutions (Council and European Parliament). Since the 1999-2003 legislature, Article 37 of the same rules of procedure stipulates that within each Standing Committee a 'Europromotor' shall be appointed. This Standing Committee member is responsible for the follow-up of recommendations, resolutions and other texts of the Federal Advisory Committee with a relevance to his Standing Committee. Thus, the Europromotor is the link between his Standing Committee and the Federal Advisory Committee.

Up until now, the Senate does not have a similar procedure, but a proposal for establishing such an arrangement has been submitted on May 24th 2005. This proposal states that every Standing Committee in the Senate shall appoint a "European facilitator". This proposal is still under scrutiny.

To improve the flow of information between the European Parliament and the thematic Standing Committees of the House, the rules of procedure of the House make it possible for a MEP to participate in a Standing Committee meeting. However, this requires prior permission of the Chair of the Standing Committee.[6] Contrary to the Federal Advisory Committee for European Affairs,

6 The Standing Committee for External Affairs is the exception. No prior permission is required; MEPs do have a right to attend these meetings at all times.

where MEPs do have full rights, they are only members in an advisory capacity in the Standing Committees.[7]

As we shall see later, MEPs do not make use of this opportunity: they do not attend thematic Standing Committee meetings. More generally, the follow-up of EU-related affairs in the legislative and pre-legislative phase of the decision-making process by the Standing Committees is rather limited, not to say marginal. There is little or no proactive attitude vis-à-vis European affairs and attempts to influence the decision-making process can hardly be discovered.

2.4 The Flow of Information

Information about EU decision-making flows via several paths to and from the national parliament. One issue is explicitly mentioned in the Belgian Constitution: the revision of the European Treaties. Article 168 of the Belgian Constitution says that the parliament has to be kept informed, right from the beginning of any negotiation on the revision of the founding Treaties of the European Communities and the Treaties and Acts amending these Treaties.

In reality, these matters are indeed discussed by the Federal Advisory Committee, which is kept informed by the federal government on a regular basis during, *e.g.* an intergovernmental conference (IGC) aimed at amending the Treaties. However, it is mainly a one-way transfer of information: in the delicate negotiations preceding a Treaty revision, the government keeps the freedom to act on its own discretion. A strict mandate has never been defined and neither has the Parliament ever given precise instructions to the government negotiators.

When discussing the flow of information on EU-proposals, we must look at three other aspects as well. First, there is the aforementioned composition of the Federal Advisory Committee and the Standing Committees of the House. By allowing MEPs as full members (Federal Advisory Committee) or in an advisory capacity (Standing Committees of the House), the parliamentary bodies are composed in a way that is facilitating the flow of information to and from the EU-level. In reality, however, we see that MEPs are not participating in the activities of the Federal Parliament, apart from attending a couple of meetings of the Federal Advisory Committee.

Second, there are the European Commission documents. Proposals for legislative acts (directives, regulations, and decisions) and other documents (communications, the working program, green and white papers) find their way to the Federal Advisory Committee secretariat. A selection of these documents is sent to the chair and the Europromotor of the relevant Standing Committees. Receiving such a Commission document, the Standing Committee has two options: it can take note of it without further discussion or it can make a recommendation for the government. If time allows, a plenary debate can be held on this recom-

7 Devuyst (1992) 469.

mendation. When a minister is given such a parliamentary recommendation, he is supposed to keep the Standing Committee informed on the follow-up of its suggestions. In principle, a Standing Committee has to inform the Federal Advisory Committee about what happened with the forwarded Commission documents within one month. Not being a part of the rules of procedure of the House, this procedure is agreed upon by the Bureau of the Parliament. As practice shows, however, this agreement is not followed. It is very rare for a Commission document to be discussed by a Standing Committee.

Third, there is a flow of information coming from the federal government. Federal ministers are supposed to report on European Council of Ministers' activities. The Belgian Permanent Representation at the EU does submit the agendas of Council meetings to the Federal Advisory Committee, which forwards these agendas to the relevant Standing Committees. There is also an engagement by federal ministers to give an overview of the discussions and the positions taken by them. However, in reality, only a few ministers do report on Council sessions. The Parliament itself, however, does not seem to insist on keeping the engagement.

2.5 Control of EU Decision-making by the Federal Parliament – an Evaluation

As practice shows, the control of EU decision-making by the Belgian Federal Parliament is simmering. Standing Committees scarcely discuss EU-related affairs and they are certainly not intending to give 'instructions' to the ministers.

The Federal Advisory Committee is much more active, but it is mainly focused on the 'history-making' and institutional aspects: Treaty revisions, European Council meetings, etc. This becomes clear when we look at the Committees reports and documents. These are classified into four categories: reports on Treaty revisions, reports on interparliamentary meetings,[8] reports on European Council meetings of Heads of State and Government, and so-called 'initiative-reports'. These initiative-reports (approx. 40 in the 1985-2005 period) sometimes do cover very specific proposals, such as the directive on cocoa and chocolate products (1997-1998) or the renegotiation of the Lomé Convention (2000). In most cases however, it is again the 'big' issues which are discussed: a resolution on the Charter of Fundamental Rights, a report on the European Asylum and Migration Policy, a resolution on Security and Defence Policy, etc.

The Federal Advisory Committee is first and foremost a meeting place for members of the House and the Senate and (at the occasion of European Council meetings) MEPs to exchange ideas on the major European topics. But it is certainly not an instrument for controlling the government's policy actions or for giving instructions or recommendations on specific, day-to-day issues that

8 Especially concerning the COSAC.

are discussed at the EU-level, such as proposals for directives or regulations (secondary legislation).

Generally speaking, we can say that there seems to be an implicit trust in the ministers: they are not held accountable to the parliament for their actions at the EU level. No minister has ever been confronted with a threat of sanction because of neglecting the parliaments' position in the Council, since specific European issues (secondary legislation) are simply not debated in parliament. When it concerns EU decision-making, ministerial accountability is not an issue in Belgium.

Thus, the Belgian parliament is not very proactive in dealing with EU decision-making. Procedures do permit a parliamentary input and several provisions (should) guarantee a smooth flow of information. However, it seems that a lack of political will by the members of the Parliament themselves is responsible for an insufficient use of these provisions. Moreover, there is no protest if government engagements are not kept. In other words, the government gets *carte blanche*, at least implicitly. These findings are in line with the conclusions of studies by Vandevivere[9] or Maurer, speaking of a weak parliamentary involvement in EU decision-making in Belgium.[10]

2.6 The European Role of Regions and Communities

During the last decades, the Belgian state has moved far in the direction of a federal state. In 1993, a unique system was established granting the Regions and Communities foreign responsibilities in the fields for which they are domestically competent. This means they can even conclude Treaties and Agreements with other regions and states around the world.

Different governments within Belgium have to consult each other, but Communities or Regions are able to conclude 'exclusive treaties' with other countries in policy fields like education or housing, for which the federal government is not competent anymore.

If competences are shared between the federal and the regional level, 'mixed treaties' must be concluded. This means that ratification can only take place after endorsement by all parliaments involved. European treaties do fall into this category and need approval by the federal parliament *and* the five regional parliaments prior to ratification.

Since the regions have competences in the field of foreign policy, the federal government is no longer solely responsible for Belgian positions in a Council of Ministers session at the EU-level.

When studying parliamentary control of EU decision-making in Belgium, one cannot confine the analysis to the federal level. The governments of both Regions and Communities are far beyond Federal Parliament's control, but they do play a European role directly as well as indirectly.

9 Vandevivere (2001).

10 Maurer (2001) 24.

First, they play a *direct* role because ministers of Regions or Communities do participate in meetings of the Council of Ministers at EU level if the topics being discussed largely or exclusively belong to their domestic competences in the Belgian context.

The Maastricht Treaty created a procedure which makes it possible for a regional minister to be a member of the Council (and replace a national minister). Thus, regional ministers are allowed to participate in the meetings of the Council, but only on the condition that they can commit their state as a whole. In Belgium, a Cooperation Agreement between the federal government and the subnational governments provides a system by distinguishing six categories of EU Councils: [1] those with an agenda consisting only of issues belonging to the exclusive competences of the federal government (*e.g.* Ecofin, the budget, justice), [2] those with an agenda of issues belonging to the competences of both federal and subnational governments, with a dominant federal share (*e.g.* internal market, public health, social affairs), [3] those with an agenda of issues belonging to the competences of both the federal and subnational governments, with a dominant subnational share (*e.g.* industry, research, environment) and [4] those with an agenda of only issues belonging to the exclusive competences of the subnational governments (*e.g.* culture, education). Category [5] and category [6] only contain the Fisheries Council and the Agriculture Council respectively.

In the first case (respectively fourth case), the leader of the delegation and his assessor[11] will both be members of the federal government (respectively subnational governments). In the second and in the third cases, the delegation is headed by a member of the government with a dominant share, with the assessor being a member of the government which has the non-dominant share. A simple rotation system regulates which subnational government will represent Belgium in the different Councils (this rotation system applies to both the leader of the delegation and the assessor). Flanders is representing Belgium in category five, and for category six, the delegation is headed by a member of the federal government, with the Flemish and Walloon ministers in assistants' roles.

Second, the fact that ministers of the regions and the communities also play an *indirect* role in EU decision-making is at least as important. It so happens they are highly involved in the establishment of a Belgian position. The decision-making process for the Belgian position to be defended in the Council is coordinated by the Federal Foreign Ministry: all issues that will be dealt with in the different Councils are discussed within the Directorate for European Affairs, the so-called Directorate General (DG) E.[12] Every decision on the Belgian position is reached in DG E by representatives of the federal prime minister and deputy prime ministers, of the minister-presidents of the different subnational governments and of those ministers (both federal and subnational) who are responsible

---

11 The assessor assists the leader of the delegation and he consults the governments that are not present in the Council negotiations.

12 Sometimes after an *ad hoc* consultation procedure in an inter-ministerial conference, mostly concerning technical aspects.

for the subjects on the agenda. The Permanent Representation of Belgium in the EU is represented as well. It is important to stress that the decisions have to be reached in consensus. In other words, the regions have the right to demand a say in the Belgian position on all matters, but particularly when it concerns regional affairs. However, all regions *and* the central state have to agree on this position. Differences of opinion must be overcome within this framework, since it is not possible to split up the Belgian votes at the European level. This sometimes leads to difficult situations since opposite interests between the regions or between the regions and the central state may be involved. If no agreement is reached on a common position, the Belgian representative has to withhold his vote in the Council.

2.7 Regional Parliaments and EU Decision-making: The Case of Flanders

In practice, few European topics have no regional dimension in Belgium. In the Belgian political system, it is unconceivable for the federal parliament to instruct (or even advise) the ministers of the regional level. Therefore, it is important to look at the way the regional parliaments deal with European decision-making. This will be illustrated by the situation of Flanders, where one Flemish parliament is competent for Regional as well as for Community matters.

Surprisingly, no separate Europe Committee exists as is the case in the federal parliament. European issues are discussed in the Committee for Foreign Policy, European Affairs, International Co-operation and Tourism. This implies that this Committee, which meets three times per month, also deals with topics that barely have any connection with European politics, such as the withdrawal of American nuclear weapons, development policy or tourism.

Just like all other 'policy committees' (Standing Committees), it disposes of a monitoring function. Its members are entitled to ask ministers for explanations, they have a right of interpellation and they can propose a motion. The commission can also hold hearings, adopt resolutions, etc.

This Committee discusses the 'big European topics' (financial perspectives, treaty revisions) as well as subjects that receive a lot of attention in the media (*e.g.* directive on liberalization of services, impact of enlargement). However, the follow-up of these specific issues leaves much to be desired. Just like the federal parliament, the Flemish parliament rarely takes a proactive attitude in the consideration of EU affairs. In the course of 2005, the Flemish parliament had decided to assign 'Europromotors' in the Standing Committees.[13] Officially, this Europromotor should 'stimulate discussions within his/her specialist policy committee about Europe and, more specifically, about the European impact on subjects that are covered by this committee. The Europromotor should inform his/her colleagues about evolutions and initiatives at the European level that are

---

[13] Decision of the Bureau of the Flemish Parliament, 4th July 2005.

important for his/her committee. This should lead to debates and hearings in his/her committee. The committee or sub-committee should be aware of preliminary work at the European level and on the basis of this information he/she should be able to take action.' It remains to be seen whether this will be put into practice. In this respect, experiences at the federal level are not encouraging.

With regard to the flow of information, it should again be stressed that members of parliament who want to scrutinize European issues can (at least theoretically) make use of several channels.

Firstly, just like in the federal parliament, Flemish members of the European parliament are allowed to participate in the meetings of the Flemish parliaments committees.[14] However, in practice this has rarely been the case.

Secondly, there are the documents from the European Commission. Proposals for regulations, directives and decisions that concern competences of the regional governments should be sent from the federal level to the parliaments of their regional governments. This was laid down in the 'bijzondere wet' (special law) for institutional reform' of 8th August 1980.[15] In practice, the Flemish parliament indeed receives these documents, but just like in the federal parliament, there is hardly any follow-up.

Thirdly, since June 2005, the Flemish parliament has established an administrative 'Europe Service' which coordinates the distribution of European documents (green and white papers, communications, and working programme) and draft legislation to the competent committees (and especially to the Europromotors). This Service has at least the intention to monitor whether this information is effectively integrated in the activities of the Standing Committees. For the time being, this service is still in its infancy, so the result has yet to be seen. Experiences in the federal parliament, in this respect, are not really convincing.

Fourthly, the Flemish government has recently committed itself to deliver a six-month report about current European issues to the Flemish Parliament. However, this is only a one-way communication, which basically concerns information that members of parliaments could also find via other channels (*e.g.* EU databases such as eurlex, prelex or oeil).

The conclusions with regard to the Flemish parliament are thus similar to its federal counterpart. Arrangements and mechanisms which provide the flow of information from the European level to the parliaments have been established. But given that this information is scarcely scrutinized, especially if it concerns concrete topics, there is no two-way traffic. The parliament does not communicate its concerns to the European level because a common position with regard to EU affairs is not being developed. In other words, the political will is lacking to make use of the European information, to integrate it in the parliamentarian activities, and thus to participate in the different levels of the European decision-making process.

---

14 Art. 28 (4) of the regulations of the Flemish parliament.

15 Art. 92 quater, added by the *'bijzondere wet'* of 5th May 1993.

3 Why Parliamentary Control of EU Decision-making in Belgium is Weak

From the first part of this paper, it may be clear that Belgium does not lack institutional provisions to enhance parliamentary control on EU decision-making. However, we have also stated that Belgian MPs do not control the government proactively in European affairs and that they in fact almost give the government carte blanche in European decision-making.

In this second part of our contribution, we will go even further and state that Belgian parliaments are not only weak when it comes down to control in EU matters, we will argue that the weakness of parliaments is a permanent feature of the Belgian political system at large.[16] In order to make this clear, we will examine some relevant historical and political backgrounds of the Belgian system. We will explain that the consociational and complex federal nature of the Belgian state forces the government(s) to play first fiddle and to crowd out the role of parliament(s) in decision-making. But before that, we briefly discuss the normative aspect of the organization of parliamentary control in Belgium. Indeed, the Belgian parliament does have normative instruments for a powerful legislative control.

3.1 Normative Signs of a Powerful Parliament

Basic legal norms for parliamentary control of the national as well as the regional governments in Belgium are found in the Belgian constitution. Article 101 of the Belgian Constitution states that Ministers are accountable to the House of Representatives. Since the Belgian federalization of 1993, Ministers are no longer accountable to both the House of Representatives and the Senate. The House has become the one and only 'political' room of the parliament. It gives trust to the government and uses most of the controlling instruments. The Senate only owns a right to ask written or oral questions, and to hold a parliamentary inquiry. Interpellations, votes of confidence, and ministerial accountability are aspects of political control, which belong uniquely to the lower chamber. The constitutional article stipulates that ministers are accountable to parliament, that their presence can be claimed by parliament and that parliament approves the budget on an annual basis.

The rules of parliamentary control are further specified in the rules of procedure of the House and the Senate. Written questions of members of parliament have to be answered within twenty days; the answers are published and may lead to a parliamentary debate.[17] For the oral questions, the rules of procedure make a distinction between oral questions in plenary session, a debate on actual news and urgent questions. All of them are also possible in committees. They should

---

16 See also: De Winter & Brans (2003).

17 Article 123 of the Rules of Procedure of the House of Representatives.

fit within time limits and should follow specific procedures.[18] Also interpellations can be held in plenary session or in committee. The interpellations are held within two weeks after their submission.[19]

The Belgian federal parliament discerns two types of controlling motions:[20] a so-called 'structural' motion of non-confidence and a motion of non-confidence. Both motions can only be submitted in specific circumstances: to conclude the parliamentary debate on the government policy statement after a new government came into office, changes in the government program or in the government team, or following on a statement of the government to ask parliamentary support. The structural motion of non-confidence declares to take away confidence from the entire government, while immediately proposing a new prime minister. A structural motion cannot declare distrust towards an individual minister, and should be supported by one third of the members of parliament.[21]

The Government, on her part, can propose a motion of confidence to the parliament.[22] This motion (re)declares trust of the parliament in the government or in an individual minister. A motion of confidence is submitted by the prime minister and, logically but interestingly, has priority above all other motions. An approved motion of confidence runs out all other motions.

Next to these instruments of control, the rules of procedure of the Belgian House also provide a special controlling commission on two specific policy fields: police services[23] and arms traffic.[24]

Regional parliaments in Belgium control the regional governments. Norms for regional parliamentary control are based on the federal constitution and are worked out in detail in the regional parliaments' Rules of procedure. Regional MP's are able to ask written or oral questions, hold interpellations, and parliamentary inquiries, but they cannot bring the government to resign. Regional parliaments do have the power to introduce a motion of non-confidence towards a minister or the regional government, but the motion should immediately propose a successor and thus should always be a structural motion of non-confidence.

Although Belgian parliaments in comparative perspective[25] have average controlling powers and although the use of controlling instruments – mainly parliamentary questions – has become more popular every year,[26] parliaments in Belgium do not have a large decision-making impact. Aspects of political culture and the federal constitutional structure offer explanations for this weakness.

---

18 Article 124-129 of the Rules of Procedure of the House.

19 Article 130-131 of the Rules of Procedure of the House.

20 Article 133 of the Rules of Procedure of the House.

21 Article 137 of the Rules of Procedure of the House.

22 Article 135 of the Rules of Procedure of the House

23 Article 149 of the Standing Orders of the Chamber of Deputies.

24 Article 151 of the Standing Orders of the Chamber of Deputies.

25 Von Beyme (2000) 83-84.

26 Belgian Chamber of Deputies, Annual Report of the Chamber activities.

3.2 Belgium: "The Most Thorough Example of Consociational Democracy"[27]

According to Arend Lijphart, Belgium is a typical, probably the most typical, example of consociational democracy with executive power-sharing in broad coalitions, several mechanisms aimed at the balance of power and proportional representation, neo-corporatism and a multiparty system.[28] The dominant consociational nature of Belgium runs through all its political vessels. As Belgian society is – or in many cases, was – deeply divided along religious, ideological, linguistic, regional and cultural lines with the status of political cleavages, power had to be shared, dispersed en restrained in several ways. Social segmentation and a high degree of pillarization via the organizational penetration, incorporation and encapsulation of religious, ideological-philosophical segments, is one dominant way of consensus building.[29] The reconstruction of the unitarian Belgian state, since the end of the 1960s, into a federal state is another. An underlying principle of all mechanisms of conflict management in Belgium is the construction of consensus through formal, overt and mainly informal, closed consultation and cooperation between the top management – in other words the elite – of the institutionalized segments (such as pillars, regions, unions and employer organizations, etc.). This implies elite-driven political decision-making with low levels of political participation. Parliament is dominated by government and the political parties. Partitocracy would be the best term to describe the Belgian political system. It refers to the disproportional and dominant power of political parties. They control government and parliament.[30]

In contrast to what the constitution declares, parliament is not the most powerful institution in Belgian political decision-making.[31] Constitution and political behavior are clearly divergent. Parliament only introduces about 15% of the voted laws in Belgium; 85% are produced by the government.[32] Research by political scientists about the most powerful political decision makers in Belgium confirms the confined power position of members of parliament: the most important decision makers are the prime minister, ministers, party chairmen, and the leaders of the trade unions. Members of parliament are only in the seventeenth position.[33]

As the legislative work of parliament is less effective, Belgian parliaments have become more and more active as institutions of control, rather than of rulemaking, mainly by using the instrument of parliamentary (written and

[27] Lijphart (1981) 1.

[28] Lijphart (1999) 34-42.

[29] Deschouwer (1999).

[30] Walgrave, Caals et al. (2004).

[31] Dewachter (2001) 17.

[32] Dewachter (2001) 19; Staelraeve (2005) 333.

[33] Dewachter & Das (1991).

oral) questions and interpellations in committees.[34] The Belgian federal parliament provides various relatively powerful instruments for control, compared to other democracies[35] and there are few procedural restrictions on the use of these instruments. But that does not mean that control is effective. Overall, control results in acquisition of government information and parliamentary debate rather than effective influence on governmental decision-making.

The consociational nature of Belgian democracy is one reason for governmental dominance and parliamentary weakness in decision-making. Another reason is the federal nature of the Belgian state.

3.3 Belgium: An Ever Further Federalizing State

Officially Belgium became a federal state – so it was written in the constitution – since the fourth constitutional reform of 1993. The process of moving away from a unitary to a federal state was initiated in 1970, when the regions (economic and territorial competences such as environment) and communities (cultural and person related competences such as education) were installed. But even before 1970, as a result of the deeply divided nature of Belgian society, several arrangements, *e.g.* language laws, were introduced in order to pacify the territorial-linguistic cleavage that became the dominant cleavage at the end of the 1960s. At that time, most of the other cleavages were already pacified or at least they lost most of their regime threatening impact. The management of the capital-labour cleavage resulted in an elaborated system of collective bargaining (corporatism) and an extended welfare state. The philosophical-religious cleavage led – through several 'School Wars' (the Belgian version of the '*Kulturkampf*') to a general pact that regulated the relations between the state and the catholic segment. So at the end of the 1960s, the regional-territorial cleavage remained the last and most important political issue to deal with that had the potential of disrupting the entire political system. After World War II, burning issues such as the collaboration with the German occupiers, the 'Royal Question', the protest against the Single Act of the Eyskens Government, '*Leuven Vlaams*' and other crises, had overwhelmingly illustrated that something needed to be done to deal with the increasing tensions between the Flemish speaking Northern part and French speaking Southern part of Belgium. In 1970, the first step towards the reconstruction of Belgium was set.

In 1993, Belgium was declared 'a federal state, composed of (three) Communities and (three) Regions',[36] each with its own government, parliament and administration. The Flemish Region and Dutch speaking Community fused into one political structure (next to the Brussels Region, Walloon Region, French speaking Community, German speaking Community and a complex of Community institutions on the territory of the bilingual Brussels Region).

---

34 Staelraeve (2005) 350-351.

35 Von Beyme (2000) 81-88.

36 Witte (2000).

Complexity is an understatement, but it keeps the system running, despite all the malfunctions of the *sui generis* Belgian federalism. They are the price for peace and the Belgian holding-together federalism.

The last constitutional reform dates from 2001 and shifted policy fields with major European and international relevance and impact to the level of the regions: foreign trade, development co-operation, and agriculture. This increases the joint decision trap problems associated with a large number of actors in decision-making in a policy field where the objective is often the conclusion of one single position, namely the Belgian position in the Council.[37] The international competences of the Regions and Communities were, compared with other federations, already well developed. As a general rule, the states are externally competent (international competences, *e.g.* the conclusion of treaties) in all policy fields in which they are internally competent (the so called *in foro interno, in foro externo* principle). Education is a competence of the Communities, so the Communities are empowered to conclude international treaties concerning education. Since 2001, Regions and Communities do not only have the competence to make international agreements on their own policy themes, but they also become more important players in policy fields with major European aspects, such as agriculture.

We agree with Börzel[38] that highly decentralized or federal states have more difficulties adapting to the European Union than more centralized states. In addition, Börzel differentiates between more competitive regionalism and co-operative federalism, claiming that the latter will have less difficulty to adapt. Although Belgium has some procedures and institutions of co-operative federalism, according to Bursens,[39] it can be characterized more by competition than by co-operation: "with respect to European policies, especially the Flemish Region puts a lot of effort in strategies to by-pass the federal level and to become a player of its own right in the European and international arena". Bursens[40] refers to 'institutional jealousy' since regional levels are very keen to protect the acquired competencies.

Besides the institutional complexity and rivalry, and the lack of interest in EU affairs, the support of the Belgian political elite for crucial EU policies should be understood as the result of combined ideological, economic and domestic political factors.[41] For example, the struggle for EMU membership by the Dehaene-government was partly understood as a tool to ease tensions between the Flemish and Walloon community.[42] This indicates that Belgian government 'uses' the European Union and European decisions when suitable

37 "The joint-decision trap (...) explains the low capacity for institutional reforms when high-conflict constellations must be resolved through compulsory negotiations." See for example: Scharpf (1997) 31.

38 Börzel (1999).

39 Bursens (2002) 577.

40 Bursens (2002) 595.

41 Coolsaet (1998).

42 Bursens (2002) 580.

for domestic issues. The EU is often used for internal use, at least as much as the other way around. The focus on Belgian domestic political problems and the federalization process has resulted in only marginal attention for European politics,[43] as is illustrated by the low degree of attention that is given by parliamentary bodies to the control of the different governments' European policies. Therefore, it is not surprising that comparative analyses of the role of national parliaments in European policy-making have classified the Belgian federal parliament as 'weak'.[44] Moreover, Belgian parliaments are weak all together.

During the reorganization of the Belgian state, European or international considerations were of no importance, not even with respect to reforms in highly European-relevant sectors. The growing importance of the European level was only used as a second order argument.[45] The complex co-ordination mechanisms and the division of competencies between the federal and the regional levels are focused on the management of internal tensions. Moreover, competition between regional and federal competencies is possible, as there is no hierarchy of norms. Norms from the federal level cannot repeal regional norms and vice versa. For example, norms about the sound volume of air traffic can be different in every region, and could be equal or more severe than the European norms. National or federal parliament cannot oblige the regions on taking the same (European) norm and cannot control the European decision-making process on this theme. The absence of a hierarchy of norms and a not-homogeneous spread of competences constrain powerful parliamentary control on EU decision-making. If it is a hard task to establish which government (and therefore parliament) should be held accountable for which parts of the national EU decision-making process, if information is dispersed and responsibilities are shifted over and back again, true parliamentary control becomes an unrealistic objective.

4 Conclusion

In this paper, we initially discussed the main peculiarities of the Belgian case concerning the organisation of parliamentary control on EU decision-making. Firstly, there is the membership of Members of European Parliament to the Federal Advisory Committee and the possibilities for MEPs to participate at the meetings of the Standing Committee, both at the federal and at the regional level. In practice, these mechanisms, which were established to facilitate the flow of information, prove to be insufficient. Secondly, the involvement of regional governments in the follow-up of concrete EU issues is quite large, as a result of which the determination of a position takes place between governments of the different levels, rather than between the parliament(s) and the government(s). Thirdly, the governments have relatively large discretion.

43 Bursens (2002) 581.

44 Maurer (2001) 24.

45 Bursens (2002) 587.

In practice, if specific topics are dealt with, they have *carte blanche*. Before the parliament, they barely have to account for decisions in EU matters. There are no indications that members of the parliaments are asking for a structure which allows for a systematic follow-up of EU politics. Existing mechanisms are scarcely used and the parliament generally takes an indifferent attitude vis-à-vis Europe. As an exception, the 'big topics' (treaty revisions, subjects of the European Councils) are discussed in the parliaments, but not with an intention to influence the decision-making process. Finally, the observation that members of parliament are hardly involved is remarkable, given that it concerns a country which has asserted itself as an outspoken supporter of European integration since the end of the seventies. This particularity has been noticed before,[46] but the causes for the lack of political will to scrutinize European issues have never been examined. One hypothesis would be to look at the influence of the permissive consensus that has long characterised Belgium's policy towards Europe. Under this permissive consensus, which has only recently started to erode, European topics were never really contested. In European negotiations, Belgian ministers were expected to argue for a more extensive EU role, and Belgium's diplomacy mostly confirmed this image. European issues have seldom been a controversial subject in Belgian politics because they were usually approached from one single perspective: the dimension of (more or less) European integration. In this respect, all political parties were situated on the same side, namely in favour of 'more Europe'. In the absence of political conflict, members of parliaments have difficulties creating a distinct profile in EU matters; so European issues were largely brushed aside. Only in recent years has the political establishment realized that other dimensions also play a role in EU politics, such as the socio-economic left-right perspective. This is becoming clear in a number of specific dossiers (such as the liberalization of services), which gradually increase the awareness of members of parliament for European issues.[47] It remains to be seen whether this will ultimately lead to more parliamentary debate and to the integration of European topics in the activities of the parliaments.

As a second part of this paper, we looked at the underlying reasons why parliamentary control of EU decision-making is relatively weak in Belgium. A large part of this political weakness can be explained by referring to the deeply divided nature of Belgian society, which resulted in a concentration of power in non-parliamentary actors and meetings. This made it very difficult for parliament(s) to play a major role in decision-making since government and political parties were/are the centers of power. So the minor importance of national parliamentary control on EU decision-making in Belgium must be understood in the context of a general limited importance of parliaments in this consociational democracy, a partitocracy where power is strongly concentrated in the elite of government and political parties and in the context of a complex federal state structure with often unclear divisions of competences.

46 See Vos (2004).

47 See also: Vandevivere (2001).

This complexity, a necessary price for the peace and stability of the Belgian *sui generis* federalism, makes control more difficult, even by parliament(s). It also means that accountability in EU matters is low. The complexity of the federal system and associated joint decision traps make it rather difficult to assess who is responsible for what elements of the Belgian parts of EU decision-making.

Belgium surely is no exception to the general rule that in many countries internal political issues dominate mass and elites' attention. Tensions between the two main communities, *i.e.* the Flemings and the Walloons, dominated other policy areas and led to successive state reforms, which transformed the country from a unitary into a federal state. In reforming the Belgian state, the Belgian Regions and Communities have acquired large competences on the international level according to the *in foro interno, in foro externo* principle. That makes the state governments, and in theory the state parliaments, important EU players. However, while rebuilding the Belgian political structure, there never was a clear, pronounced vision or strategy in function of the EC or EU. In other words, the state reforms did not take the EU as a relevant criterion or element into consideration. Reforms were mainly a*d hoc* solutions and the results of long negotiations aimed at reaching a special majority in the federal parliament.

Since the establishment of the European institutions, the transfer of competences to a supranational level has been a big issue in many – especially highly centralised – European countries. In Belgium, however, thanks to the gradual federalisation, Belgian politicians and people are 'used to' the re-scaling of competences. This in turn 'eases' the transfer towards the EU, which is not the subject of thorough debate in Belgian parliaments and politics in general. As a founding member of the EU, European integration is by most people seen as an evidence.

This lack of debate does not only reflect the general, silent positive attitude towards the integration process; on the other hand, it also reflects – and both are not contradictory – a lack of interest in European affairs, by members of parliament as well as by Belgian voters.[48] However, how can voters show more interest in a decision-making level if they feel that their representatives have no significant influence on that level? We cannot but conclude that there clearly is a lack of accountability of Belgian parliament members regarding the European Union.

[48] See for example: Verlet & Blomme (2005).

References

K. von Beyme, *Parliamentary democracy: democratization, destabilisation, reconsolidation, 1789-199*, (Houndsmills: Macmillan Press Ltd. 2000) 83-84.

T. Börzel, "Towards convergence in Europe? Institutional adaptation to Europeanization in Germany and Spain", in: *Journal of Common Market Studies* 37 (1999) 573-596.

P. Bursens,, "Belgium's adaptation to the EU. Does federalism constrain Europeanisation?", in: *Res Publica* 54:4 (2002).

R. Coolsaet, "Continuïteit en discontinuïteit in het Belgische Europa-beleid", in: *Res Publica* 40:2 (1998) 179-191.

K. Deschouwer, "From consociation to federation. How the Belgian parties won", in K.R. Luther, K. Deschouwer, (eds.), *Party elites in divided societies. Political parties in consociational democracy* (London: Routledge, 1999) 74-107.

Y. Devuyst, "De Adviescomités voor Europese Aangelegenheden van het Belgisch Parlement", in: *Tijdschrift voor Bestuurswetenschappen en Publiekrecht* 47:7 (1992).

W. Dewachter, *De mythe van de parlementaire democratie. Een Belgische analyse* (Leuven: Acco, 2001) 17.

W. Dewachter, E. Das, *Politiek in België: geprofileerde machtsverhoudingen* (Leuven: Acco, 1991).

A. Lijphart, (ed.), *Conflict and coexistence in Belgium. The Dynamics of a Culturally Divided Society* (Berkeley: University of California, Institute of International Studies, 1981).

A. Lijphart, *Patterns of democracy: government forms and performance in thirty-six countries* (New Haven: Yale University Press, 1999).

A. Maurer, "National Parliaments after Amsterdam: Adaptation, Re-Calibration and Europeanisation by Process", Paper for Working Group Meeting XXIVth COSAC, 8-9 April 2001.

F. Scharpf, *Games Real Actors Play. Actor-Centered Institutionalism in Policy Research* (Colorado: Westview Press, 1997) 31.

S. Staelraeve, "Staatsvormen en parlement", in C. Devos, (ed.), *Politicologie. Inleiding tot de politieke wetenschappen* (Gent: Academia Press, 2005) 333 e.v.

C. Vandevivere, "The Federal Parliament of Belgium: Between Wishes, Rules and Practice", in: A. Maurer, W. Wessels, (eds.), *National Parliaments on their Ways to Europe: Losers or Latecomers?* (Baden-Baden: Nomos Verlagsgesellschaft, 2001) 77-97.

D. Verlet, W. Blomme, "The influence of increasing European integration on political parties. Case study: How do the Belgian political parties come to term with Europeanisation?" Paper presented at '2nd Global Conference – Redefining Europe: Federalism and the Union of European Democracies', Prague, April 29th – May 2nd 2005.

H. Vos, "Het Vlaams Parlement en Europa: over democratie en de Europese rol van regionale parlementen", in: N. de Batselier, (ed.), *Levende Democratie – de kracht van een parlement in de 21ste eeuw* (Tielt: Lannoo, 2004) 194-228.

S. Walgrave, T. Caals, M. Suetens, K. de Swert, *Ministerial cabinets and partitocracy. A career pattern study of ministerial cabinet members in Belgium* (Antwerp: University of Antwerp, PSW Paper 2004/7, 2004).

L. de Winter, T. Laurent, "The Belgian Parliament and European Integration", in: Ph. Norton, (ed.), *National Parliaments and the European Union* (London: Frank Cass, 1996) 75-91.

L. de Winter, M. Brans, "Belgium: Political Professionals and the Crisis of the Party State" in: J. Borchert, J. Zeiss, *The Political Class in Advanced Democracies* (Oxford: Oxford University Press, 2003) 45-66.

E. Witte, "Increasing tension between the communities and the creation of a federalized Belgium", in: E. Witte, J. Craeybeckx, A, Meynen, (eds.), *Political history of Belgium. From 1830 onwards* (Antwerpen: Standaard Uitgeverij, 2000) 239-259.

CHAPTER 6

Control of EU Decision-making in the Hungarian National Assembly: the Experience of a new Member State

Klára Szalay and Angéla Juhász-Tóth

1 Introduction

The Hungarian Republic is a unitary state governed constitutionally as one single unit, with a unicameral legislature. In order to facilitate a peaceful political transition to a constitutional state, parliamentary democracy and a social market economy, the Constitution was to a large extent re-written in 1989.[1] The relationship between the executive and the legislature rests on important principles such as the rule of law, democratic legitimacy, the separation of powers and accountability of the government to the Parliament.[2] In general, the majority of Hungarian Acts are adopted by the Parliament with a simple majority vote. However, there are a number of subjects enumerated in the Constitution which can only be regulated by an Act adopted with a two-third majority vote of the MPs in attendance. The list includes Acts on courts, prosecution, the constitutional court or some fundamental rights as well as the Act on the relationship of the Parliament and the Government in matters connected with EU integration.[3] It is important to note that the Acts of qualified majority do not have a higher status in the hierarchy of norms. On the other hand, the Constitution is given supremacy over ordinary law.[4] Therefore, if there is a conflict between a legal provision and the Constitution, all or part of the Act can be declared *ultra vires* by a Constitutional Court and struck down as unconstitutional.

The National Assembly (the *Országgyűlés*) is the supreme body of state power and people representation. National parliamentary elections are held every four years. The President of the Republic of Hungary is elected by the Parliament every five years. He has a largely ceremonial role, but his powers also include that of recommending the person of the Prime Minister. The Parliament formally votes on the election of the Prime Minister and the Government programme with one single vote.[5] The Prime Minister selects the ministers and has the exclusive right to dismiss them. Formally, ministers are nominated by the President of the Republic on the proposal of the Prime Minister. Each nominee appears before one or more parliamentary committees in an open hearing. Finally, the whole Government (the Prime Minister and the ministers) takes an oath of office in front of the Parliament.

The key aspect in the relationship of the Parliament and the Government is that of *political confidence*. If the Parliament loses its confidence, the Government may be forced to resign by means of a so-called 'constructive motion of censure'. According to this latter principle, which was a very important safeguard for maintaining democratic stability after the political changes in

1 Preamble of the Constitution; Act XX of 1949.

2 Act XX of 1949, Article 39.

3 Act XX of 1949, Article 35/A.

4 The Constitution is an Act adopted by the Parliament with a two-third majority vote of *all* the 386 MPs – the strongest form of qualified majority is legislature.

5 Act XX of 1949, Article 33 (3).

1989, MPs can only take a vote of confidence against the Government if, at the same time, they designate the person of the new Prime Minister.[6] A motion of censure can be initiated only against the Prime Minister, *i.e.* against the whole Government. The ministers individually cannot be held politically responsible on the basis of this principle; in this respect, the Parliament must rely on interpellation. If the minister's response to an interpellation is not accepted by the MP posing the question, the plenary takes a vote. If the response is voted down, the issue is further examined by the relevant standing committee.[7] Accordingly, the political accountability of the individual ministers is not regulated in legal norms; it is usually up to the Prime Minister or the particular minister to determine the consequences.

The two main constitutional functions of the National Assembly are legislation on the one hand, and supervision and control over Government on the other. We shall currently be dealing with this latter function. We may distinguish between three levels of parliamentary control: that exercised by the plenary, by the committees and by specialised institutions (*e.g.* Court of Auditors or the Ombudsmen). The control function of the plenary and the committees is based on the constitutional provisions on the Government's responsibility towards its Parliament. The tools of control are laid down in the Rules of Procedure of the Parliament, which distinguishes the record, the report, the information, the political debate, the interpellation and the question. On top of this, committees of the Hungarian National Assembly all have broad controlling rights. They can hold hearings and submit opinions in connection with the nominations to major posts defined by public law. The obligatory appearance of members of the Government is deduced from the Constitution[8] stating the Government's responsibility towards the Parliament. This responsibility includes the obligation of furnishing information to the Parliament and the obligation of attendance in front of standing committees on their request. All state institutions and civil organisations are subject to this obligation. One further important guarantee of control over Government activities is the fact that none of the ministers or state secretaries can become a member of a parliamentary standing committee at the same time.[9]

The above introduction helps visualize the context of parliamentary control in Hungary, and more particularly what the principle of Government accountability means in Hungarian constitutional law. In the following, the study shall be specifically focusing on the tools and methods of control of *EU decision-making* in the Hungarian National Assembly. Apart from the traditional parliamentary means of control, a new procedure was established with the accession of Hungary to the EU: scrutiny of EU legislation. In this procedure, the parlia-

---

6 Act XX of 1949, Article 39/A.

7 Interpellation is a tool frequently used in the Hungarian parliament, although it is not necessarily a tool for making a minister resign.

8 Act XX of 1949, Article 39.

9 Ministers and state secretaries can be MPs as well, but it is not a condition.

mentary Committee on European Affaires (further referred to as the Committee) is the major actor. The Committee is given the right to adopt a position on a European draft and the related government position in the name of the whole National Assembly. The role of the Committee is unique; none of the other Committees possesses the right to form a position in the name of the whole Parliament. We shall be exploring the reasons behind this mode of operation. Once the system of control of EU decision-making is described, we will move on to outline some of the problems and challenges of the regime of control. Finally, in the conclusion, we shall give a possible explanation to the interrelation between the control of EU decision-making and the general constitutional system, and shall open up ideas or further questions worth examination.

As far as terminology is concerned, in the context of this study we understand *scrutiny in the broad sense*[10] (further referred to as *parliamentary control*) as a complex set of tools of parliamentary control over EU decision-making applied vis-à-vis the Government in order to affect the outcome of the EU decision-making process in Brussels. On the other hand, *scrutiny in the narrow sense* (further referred to as *scrutiny*) is a specifically regulated process of discussion resulting in an opinion on either the EU proposal and/or the government position. The primary aim of the process is to influence, control or hold to account the Government for its legislative activities in the Council of Ministers of the EU.

2 Norms and Powers Regulating National Parliamentary Control of EU Decision-making

The logic of Hungarian legislation dictates a three-layer legislative frame for parliamentary control of EU decision-making. Firstly, a constitutional modification (eventually passed 17 December 2002) was required for the Hungarian legislative system to accept the legitimacy of the EU legal instruments. Article 2/A,[11] often referred to as the 'Europe-clause', establishes the legal ground by stating that the Union derives its competence from the Member States.[12] The extent to which the EU may exercise constitutional powers is broadly defined as 'to the extent necessary in connection with the rights and obligations conferred by the Treaties' of the EU. The limit of the transfer of powers is described as 'certain constitutional powers'. This wording leaves space

10 Szalay (2005).

11 (1) By virtue of the treaty, the Republic of Hungary, in its capacity as a Member State of the European Union, may exercise certain constitutional powers jointly with other Member States to the extent necessary in connection with the rights and obligations conferred by the treaties on the foundation of the European Union and the European Communities (hereinafter referred to as 'European Union'); these powers may be exercised independently and by way of the institutions of the European Union.

12 Somogyvári (2001).

for the Constitutional Court to further interpret the notion of national sovereignty.[13]

Articles 2/A and 35/A of the Constitution specify that the Government is obliged to provide the Parliament with information. The latter article also contains two major statements in relation to the controlling powers of the Parliament in EU Affairs. Firstly, it states the fact that *detailed* rules concerning the controlling powers of Parliament, the cooperation between the Parliament and the Government, and the informational obligations of the Government shall be elaborated in a law passed by two-third majority of MPs in attendance. Consequentially, the right of parliamentary control is unquestionable, but its scope and limits are to be defined by the law.

Secondly, the Constitution mentions the controlling powers of the Parliament in general *and* the more specific cooperation mechanism between the Parliament and the Government.[14] This wording already signals a conscientious differentiation between control of EU decision-making in general and scrutiny more specifically, which is reflected in our distinction between a broad and a narrow sense of our definition of scrutiny.

As far as the informational obligation of the Government towards its Parliament is concerned, the Constitution explicitly states that the Government shall send the Parliament all the proposals being on the agenda in the decision-making procedures of the institutions of the European Union functioning with government participation.[15] Furnishing Parliament with information is a prerequisite of control.

By and large, we may state that the Constitution attributes both the *right* – unquestionable right of control of the executive by the Parliament – and the *means* of parliamentary control – information, and the cooperation methods between the Parliament and the Government in EU affairs – to the Parliament. It clearly defines the distinction in roles between the Government and the Parliament. Parliament has the right and the means of control, but the Government is the actor, the body representing the Republic of Hungary in the institutions of the European Union that require government participation.[16]

Parliamentary scrutiny is more explicitly regulated in Act LIII of 2004 (further referred to as the Act). Based on Article 35/A (1) of the Hungarian Constitution, on 17 May 2004, the National Assembly adopted the Act on the cooperation of the Parliament and the Government in European Union affairs. It is clear from the subtitles of this Act[17] that scrutiny and other forms of parlia-

[13] Vörös (2002).

[14] '... detailed rules governing the supervisory powers of Parliament or its committees, the cooperation between Parliament and the Government (...) shall be enacted by a two-thirds vote of those Members of Parliament present'. Constitution of the Republic of Hungary, Article 35/A (1).

[15] Constitution of the Republic of Hungary, Article 35/A (2).

[16] Act XX of 1949, Article 35 (k).

[17] The main subtitles are: general provisions, procedure of consultation (scrutiny), other informational obligations of the Government (other forms of parliamentary control), the control of the principle of subsidiarity and the closing provisions.

mentary control, although both are meant to be tools of control, are considered to be different in nature. Drawing on what has been said above we may identify the following *three main assets of control* of EU decision-making:

1) *Traditional parliamentary supervisory assets, e.g.* interpellations and questions in plenary, political debates, reports and records. These are the long established tools of parliamentary control we have referred to in the introduction. Since neither the Constitution, nor the Act exclude using these tools in controlling the executive in EU decision-making, they form part of the armour of parliamentary control.
2) *Scrutiny of EU affairs*: specified by the Act, is a procedure mainly focusing on EU legislative activities. The process is based on selection; it requires a government position to be sent to Parliament and Government's intense participation in the discussions. The result of scrutiny is a standpoint adopted by the Parliament. Scrutiny is conducted with the aim of influencing the standpoint of the Government during the EU negotiation process.
3) *Other forms of parliamentary control,* also specified by the Act, include such supervisory assets as hearings before and after the European Council meetings, regular reports on Government related activities in EU matters and hearings of government-delegated nominees.

We shall be discussing scrutiny and other forms of parliamentary control below in order to unfold details of this new method of control established as a part of Hungary's integration in the European Union.

Finally, to complete the three-layer legislative frame we have started describing in this chapter, we shall take note of inter-institutional rules of operation within the Parliament set out at the level of the regulation. On the basis of the law, the Standing Orders of the National Assembly were modified (Resolution No. 47/2004 (V.18.) to give further detail and guidance to the process of scrutiny within the National Assembly.

All the above-mentioned legal means regulating scrutiny (the Constitution, the Act and the Resolution) had been adopted by a qualified majority. We have explained in the introduction that this qualified method of adoption of legal norms is meant to serve as a strong guarantee for the stability of the system. However, as these rules are difficult to modify, they must be flexible enough to follow the hectic agenda of EU decision-making. In the following, we aim at describing how the need for flexibility, the controlling purpose and the stability of the system were met in the scrutiny procedure of the Hungarian Parliament.

3 Scrutiny of EU Affairs in the National Assembly

In the introduction, we have already referred to the fact that the Committee on European Affairs is given a quite unusual role in parliamentary control of EU decision-making in Hungary. The Committee is the decision-maker in the scrutiny of EU affairs: '...the parliamentary standing committee dealing with European Union affairs shall have the power to decide matters in the procedure concerning drafts of the European Union specified in this act'.[18] This scope of power is unprecedented within the National Assembly, however, not unprecedented in the scrutiny systems of other countries. A similar structure of delegation of decision-making powers to the Committee level exists in Estonia, Latvia, and Poland from the new Member States, and Denmark and Finland from the old Member States.[19] This probably has a very simple explanation. Parliamentary decision-making tends to be slow, and preparatory work is conducted by the committees anyway before the plenary takes its decisions. In order for parliamentary control of EU decision-making to be effective, a body capable of reacting to the events and happenings at the EU level is needed. Therefore, the committee is an ideal decision-maker: flexible and responsive. While it only seats a limited number of MPs (currently 20 from the total of 386 MPs), it is formed in proportion to mandates allowing for representation from all parliamentary factions and opinions. From a functionalistic point of view, therefore, the choice of the Committee adopting a standpoint in the name of the whole National Assembly with such safeguards as the involvement of other standing committees and the possibility of raising the items in plenary has its advantages. The Committee is also involved in traditional legislative activities within Parliament, which basically allows it to see an EU decision through: before decision-making at the European level through the scrutiny process; and, after decision-making, during the implementation of legislation at the national level.

3.1 Scope of Information

One of the basic elements of successful national parliamentary control is receiving information. Transparency of the work carried out in the EU was an imperative in bringing to life the public databases of the EU such as PRE-LEX, EUR-LEX or the OEIL of the European Parliament. Many other public sources of information, especially news sources, NGO web-sites, etc. are available these days to gain information, monitor decision-making and explore different viewpoints on subjects in the pre-legislative phase. Furthermore, the

18 Act LIII of 2004, Article 1 (2) and Article 134/B (1) of the Standing Orders.

19 These are the countries where only the Committee on European Affairs is empowered to adopt the parliamentary standpoint. There are a number of countries among the new Member States where both the Committee and the plenary may form the final opinion of Parliament. See: Szalay (2005); and Juhász-Tóth (2005).

Hungarian National Assembly actively seeks alternative ways of receiving information, *e.g.*: through a delegated official who works in the European Parliament and through using such networking channels as COSAC, the Conference of Community and European Affairs Committees of Parliaments of the European Union.

The informational obligation of the Government as defined in the Constitution called for designing Parliament's own database of official information, EUDOC. The corresponding Act specifies information as all draft legislation, proposals and documents put on the agenda in the decision-making procedures of the institutions of the EU operating with governmental participation.[20] Thus, the definition covers all COM proposals (directive, regulation), documents of intergovernmental conferences, communications, invitations, agendas, nominations, etc. As for the interpretation of the expression 'institutions operating with governmental participation', the definition covers institutions such as the European Council, the Council, COREPER, other preparatory committees of the Council and working groups of the Council as well.

As a result of the informational obligation of Government, the National Assembly receives all material forwarded to the Republic of Hungary through the Council extranet service immediately after their receipt. Records of these documents are kept with the Committee on EU Affairs in the EUDOC database and are accessible for MPs, staff of parliamentary factions and the Office of the Parliament.[21]

This automatic transfer of Council documents is – at the beginning of each presidency – supplemented by a so-called 'indicative list'. In it, the Government indicates those documents that it believes belong to the legislative authority of the Parliament, and particularly those which:

a) refer to a subject that is provided for by an act passed by qualified majority by virtue of the Constitution or by a special act;
b) refer to the definition of the contents of fundamental rights and obligations and the essential guarantees of their enforcement, or
c) include any provision conflicting with legislation in force.[22]

The indicative list also marks those documents that are of extraordinary importance for the Republic of Hungary.[23]

The information on a scrutinized EU draft becomes complete once the Government prepares the position it intends to take in the decision-making procedure of the European Union.[24] The proposed position to be sent to the Parliament has certain obligatory elements defined by the Act. It shall include:

a) a summary of contents of the draft of the European Union;

---

20 Act LIII of 2004, Article 2 (1).

21 Article 134/A (1)-(2) of the Standing Orders.

22 Act LIII of 2004, Article 2 (3).

23 Act LIII of 2004, Article 2 (4).

24 Act LIII of 2004, Article 3 (1).

b) an indication of the decision-making process applicable in the course of the decision-making by the European Union;
c) the expectable schedule of the adoption of the draft of the European Union and possibly the starting date of the discussion of the draft by the Council;
d) the position of the Government concerning the draft of the European Union, the objectives to be achieved in the decision-making process of the European Union and their reasons, and
e) the presentation of possibly legislative tasks stemming from the draft of the European Union.[25]

What seems to be a unique feature of Hungarian scrutiny is the possibility of the Parliament to request an extended version of the proposed government position if it thinks this may be necessary or if the proposal is of extraordinary relevance. In this case, the government position shall also include effective regulation applicable in Hungary and in the European Union; a brief presentation of the expectable economic, budgetary and social impacts; and the opinions of institutions of the European Union and Member States.[26] So far, Parliament has not asked for an extended version of the government position (from 1 May 2004 to 30 May 2006). However, it did receive impact assessments from the Government concerning some of the EU drafts under scrutiny.

3.2 Process of Discussion

Scrutiny regarding specific EU drafts is started on the proposal of the chairman, by the decision of the Committee on European Affairs.[27] On the motion of two-fifths of the committee members, consultation on a specified EU draft shall also begin.[28] In practice, the staff of the Committee and the experts of the factions play an important role in the selection process. They continuously scan the database for new information and closely study the indicative list provided by the Government. Colleagues of the secretariat also examine the annual legislative work program of the Commission and the planned agenda of the Council Presidency. Proposals of seeming importance are examined in more detail, and a short summary is prepared for each. The strategic importance of the proposals is then assessed. At the same time, the chairman consults the vice-chairmen of the committee and the experts of the factions. Finally, the chairman of the Committee hands in his list of documents that are susceptible to scrutiny, and MPs of the Committee vote on the items of the list.

Once a draft is selected for scrutiny, the Speaker calls upon the appropriate standing committee (sometimes even more than one) to develop an opinion on

[25] Act LIII of 2004, Article 3 (3).

[26] Act LIII of 2004, Article 3 (4).

[27] Article 134/B (2) and (3) of the Standing Orders.

[28] Article 134/A (3) of the Standing Orders.

the selected EU draft with the indication of a deadline: this ensures channelling in the sector specific knowledge. In practice, the standing committee is nominated at the commencement of the procedure when the vote on initiating scrutiny is taken in the Committee. The chairman of the Committee makes his proposal on the involvement of one standing committee and the factions can propose other standing committees too. A standing committee, however, may ask to be nominated for the development of an opinion on its own initiative. In this case, it is obligatory to nominate the committee.[29] Experience shows that the readiness of a standing committee to get actively involved largely depends on the personality and interest of its chairperson. Standing committees may invite representatives of national interest groups and social organisations to their open sittings.[30]

Whereas the Committee on European Affairs puts strong emphasis on the involvement of the standing committees, due to the unpredictability of EU decision-making, the Committee may eventually adopt its standpoint in the absence of the opinion of the standing committee as well.[31] Obviously, this serves the purpose of both flexibility and accountability. It is better to have a stated opinion of the Committee without awaiting the opinion of the standing committee in order to make Government accountable for its actions in Council. As a result of this *modus operandi*, there seems to be a clear difference evolving between how an EU draft is dealt with in the standing committees and the Committee on EU Affairs. Whereas the standing committee deals with consulting representatives of national interest groups and social organisations, NGOs, experts in open meetings, the Committee prefers working with the results of these consultations forwarded to it in writing, attached or embedded in the final opinion of the standing committee.

The Committee on EU Affairs, while continually keeping the EU draft on its agenda, awaits the opinion of the appointed standing committee. Prior to the Council meeting deciding on the adoption of the EU draft, the responsible minister or state secretary appears before the Committee on EU Affairs to expound the final position the Government intends to represent at the Council meeting.[32] After hearing the responsible minister or state secretary and usually in light of the opinion of the standing committee, the Committee on European Affairs develops its standpoint in an *in camera* meeting.[33] The standpoint of the Committee is a summary by the chairman included in the minutes that the Speaker of the House and the Government receive in writing within 24 hours following the Committee meeting.[34]

29 Article 134/B (4) of the Standing Orders.

30 Article 134/B (5) of the Standing Orders.

31 Article 134/B (9) of the Standing Orders.

32 Act LIII of 2004, Article 4 (3).

33 Article 134/B (6) of the Standing Orders.

34 Article 134/B (10) of the Standing Orders.

As far as the timing of scrutiny is concerned, neither the Act nor the Standing Orders of the Parliament specify a timeframe for the scrutiny procedure. Aiming for maximum flexibility, the Act only states that Parliament may adopt a standpoint 'within reasonable time' considering the EU agenda for decision-making.[35] Moreover, there is no time limit specified for the Government to forward its position to the Committee. The only event that is linked to an explicit deadline is developing the opinion of the designated standing committee.[36] Therefore, in practice, timing of discussions largely depends on available information on the internet (OEIL and PRE-LEX), background information on decision-making from the Government and the information channelled in through the permanent representative in the EP.

3.3 Parliamentary Influence

In its final parliamentary standpoint, the Committee on European Affairs refers to the objectives of the European draft and its most important elements, the opinion of the involved standing committee, and the position of the Government. The Committee states whether it supports the government position or not. It may underline the national viewpoints that it considers necessary to enforce in the decision-making process of the EU.[37] At the same time, careful wording assures a flexible frame for the Government in its negotiations.

As far as the relative force of the standpoint is concerned, by studying the scrutiny systems of other Member States,[38] we discovered a difference in character between the consultative and the politically binding opinions. Therefore, we defined *'consultative'* opinions as positions of the national parliament that are taken into consideration or that serve as the basis of the final position of government. A *'politically binding'* opinion on the other hand means that if the position of parliament is not considered and represented by the Government in EU decision-making, this divergence is reported and must be justified in front of a designated body of parliament.

In Hungary, the standpoint of the Committee is politically binding. The Government elaborates its final position on the basis of the Parliament's standpoint.[39] It may however modify its proposed position in the course of the EU decision-making process. Consequentially, after a decision in the EU is made, the Government must give a verbal justification if its eventual position differs from that of the Parliament. This verbal justification is given to the Committee

35 Act LIII of 2004, Article 4 (1).

36 The time frame for the development of this opinion is not indicated either in the Act or in the Standing Orders, but determined by the Speaker of the House who considers both the recommendation of the Committee as well as the proposed agenda of EU decision-making when deciding on this deadline. Standing Orders, Article 134/B (4).

37 Act LIII of 2004, Article 4 (2).

38 Szalay (2005).

39 Act LIII of 2004, Article 4 (4).

of EU Affairs in general. However, if the decision concerns a 'qualified majority issue' in Hungarian constitutional law, justification should be given to the plenary.[40] This explains why it is more important to compose a standpoint in the Committee rather than to await the opinion of the standing committee. *Ex post* control over the Government is always stronger if a standpoint in the Committee has been adopted.

The Hungarian scrutiny system has not been operational for long. It started in September 2004 with a proposal for a directive on the patentability of computer-implemented inventions. At present, the Committee runs a total of about 30 active scrutiny procedures.[41] Committee meetings are generally held Mondays and Tuesdays. When an EU draft is discussed, there is a strong emphasis on political representation in front of the Committee. It is usually the Minister or the state secretary that is bound to appear during these meetings of the Committee. Whereas scrutiny is a tool of influence with marked rights, other forms of parliamentary control are a heterogeneous category of supervisory assets we shall briefly describe in the following.

3.4 Other Forms of Parliamentary Control

The Act established other forms of parliamentary control including hearings prior to the European Council meetings and oral information following the European Council meetings, regular reports on Government related activities in EU matters and hearings of government-delegated nominees.[42] Some of these tools may be exercised by the plenary and some by a committee where membership is determined by political status.

Prior to the *European Council meetings* and other events of strategic importance, and on the initiative of the Speaker of Parliament, the Prime Minister shall inform the Speaker of Parliament, the leaders of parliamentary factions, the members of the Committee dealing with EU Affairs, the chairman of the Committee dealing with constitutional affairs, the chairman of the Foreign Affairs Committee, as well as parliamentary officials, chairmen of standing committees and chairmen of the European integration subcommittees of standing committees invited by the Speaker of the Parliament on the position to be represented by the Government.[43] The Prime Minister shall orally inform the plenary session of the Parliament following the meeting of the European Council.[44]

---

40 Act LIII of 2004, Articles 5-6.

41 'Active' is used in the sense that the scrutinized EU draft is still at some level of the decision-making process in the EU, and Government has not yet officially informed the Parliament in writing on the decision taken.

42 Act LIII of 2004, Article 7-8.

43 Act LIII of 2004, Article 7 (1).

44 Act LIII of 2004, Article 7 (3).

It is clear from the wording of the Act that, contrary to scrutiny, the initiative lies within the hands of the Speaker and not the Committee of EU Affairs. Naturally, consultative meetings should always take place prior to the European Council meetings, which, in practice, usually means the week preceding it. The actual date largely depends on the Speaker of the Parliament, as she possesses the right of convocation. At these meetings, the Prime Minister is usually accompanied by the Minister for Foreign Affairs as well as other experts. Invitees specifically enumerated above have the right to pose questions and raise issues. It is clear however that this form of consultation comes at such a late stage of the procedure that influencing policy is highly unlikely, although politically this tool is of importance.

Feedback (or *ex post* control) following the European Council meeting is ensured in the traditional parliamentary mechanism. The Prime Minister requests to speak in plenary outside the order of the day following the event. He presents a speech on the conclusions of the European Council and the achievements of Hungarian diplomacy at the meeting. Then faction leaders are given time to react.

Another tool the Act mentions as a form of control is that of the *Government report*. The Government informs the plenary session of the Parliament annually on questions concerning the membership of the Republic of Hungary in the European Union and the status of European integration.[45] This written report is usually handed in at the end of March and it is handled like any other government report; *i.e.* before discussions in plenary it is discussed by a committee and following the debate in plenary the endorsement of the report is voted on. Consequentially, the report is firstly tabled in the Committee on EU Affairs that makes a recommendation for general debate to the plenary. It is then discussed in plenary and finally adoption of the report is recommended in the form of a parliamentary resolution. The annual report is an excellent political means to debate mainly the past actions of the Government, but also to orient the future of governmental EU policy.

Last, but not least, the Act also hints at the possibility of *hearing government delegated nominees* for certain posts in the EU. The Committee on European Affairs may conclude hearings of ministers and Government officials regarding European issues, and is obliged to do so upon the appointment of the ministers for European Affairs, Foreign Affairs and Justice. The Committee may also request a hearing from high-level Government-appointed European officials, namely, the EU Commissioner, the judge of the European Court of Justice and the Court of First Instance, and members of the Court of Auditors. However, while in some countries this is an obligation,[46] in Hungary the Act clearly states the right of the Government to make a proposal to the respective institutions of the EU. As far as Parliament is concerned, it '*may* hear the person proposed by

45 Act LIII of 2004, Article 7 (4).

46 *E.g.*: the Czech Chamber of Deputies and the Seimas of Lithuania.

the Government'.[47] So far, the Committee only organised one hearing, that of the future EU Commissioner after he had already been heard by the European Parliament.

4 Dilemmas Relating to the Practice of Parliamentary Control of EU Decision-making

Hungary has been involved in scrutinizing EU legislation for only a short period of time. Like all new systems, this form of control also needs time to evolve. It needs understanding not merely from the part of the officers, but also from the side of the politicians who often get carried away in day-to-day political struggles that attract more media attention.

So far, we have described the Hungarian system of parliamentary control as it is regulated in the norms. In the following, we wish to highlight questions of *implementation*. Examples are issues that have not been regulated in the norms at all, or turned out to be interpreted according to the understanding of one party, but not the other. Access to documents is a good example. This question has not been clarified either in the Act or in the Standing Orders, and the general rules concerning the secrecy of documents could not be applied. Eventually, it was the Speaker of the House who took political responsibility and made a decision on access to EU documents marked 'limited'. For the moment, only the staff of the Committee on European Affairs and staff of the Office for Foreign Relations have access to all the documents in the database. MPs may access public documents only. The reasoning behind this decision was the greater interest in assuring the secrecy of these EU documents as opposed to the access rights of MPs.[48]

Another sound example of what problems interpreting normative rules may raise concerns the argumentation over the term 'after a decision made by an institution of the EU' means. This event is crucial because it determines the moment when Government informs the Parliament in writing on the decision of the EU. The debate focused on the exact meaning of the word 'decision'. In the Committee's point of view, a decision marks the date when political agreement is reached in the Council. According to the Government, a decision formally happens when a vote is taken as an 'A' item agenda point in Council following the political agreement and the lawyer-linguist finalisation of the document. The compromise in this matter was to invite the competent minister

47 Act LIII of 2004, Article 8.

48 We must also note that the status of some of these documents may change from limited to public during the EU decision-making process and therefore become entirely or partly available from the register of the Council.

following the political agreement to present an oral report, and later, after the final vote in the Council, to receive the written report from the Government.[49]

Apart from questions of implementation, there is the *constant issue of equilibrium*. How to balance the political and the technical points during parliamentary control; what can be the centre of gravity in scrutiny: quality or quantity; and finally, how to balance diplomacy and transparency in this work?

As for the first aspect, we found that quite a number of scrutinised EU drafts are about technical details in legislation. Neither MPs in the Committee, nor its staff, or for that matter, EU experts of the factions, can compete with the technical expertise accumulated by ministries in the many fields scrutiny may embrace. It would be both unwise and a waste of money to double the work of ministries. However, what happens if we look at merely the political aspects? If politics rules scrutiny, the control function of the Parliament acting as a whole is lost, since MPs of the Government have majority in the Committee too. Therefore, the standpoint of the committee is a summary by the chairman aiming for voicing consensual points emerging during the discussions rather than bringing out those details that are picked up as issues of a conversation between the ruling party and the opposition. The standpoint is not voted on and its elaboration does not follow the ordinary logic of parliamentary work where a proposed piece of legislation or a report may be modified through proposed amendments.

The other huge dilemma in the scrutiny procedure is finding balance between quality and quantity. The Committee basically has two options: scrutinising less proposals in more detail or scrutinising as many proposals as it can handle in order to widen the scope of scrutiny. A more detailed scrutiny requires more technical expertise in several fields of science, while a quantitative scrutiny although more formal, yet provides a broader overview to politicians and is more likely to attract media attention.[50]

Last, but not least, the bigger scene is dominated by the delicate balance between successful diplomacy and the transparency of parliamentary work, an important principle of democracy. The work of national parliaments rests on transparency. It makes the work of politicians visible; it helps form their public image and is related to their media performance too. It is a means of democratic control. Diplomacy, on the other hand, requires good negotiating skills and a lot of discretion. Package deals are not uncommon in the EU. Therefore, openly discussing the negotiating position of the Government or the positions of other Member States in a given matter may eventually mean undermining a good deal in the EU.

---

49 By the way, this question was reopened after the parliamentary elections in 2006 and the Government accepted the original reasoning of the Parliament in its newly established Regulation.

50 To a large part this choice is made by the chairman of the Committee. His personality, interest and enthusiasm leave a strong mark on the operation of scrutiny.

5 Widening the Perspective

The Preamble of the Hungarian Constitution – cited in the introduction – clearly defines the aims of 1989: to facilitate a peaceful political transition to a constitutional state, parliamentary democracy and a social market economy. Undoubtedly, the Constitution's provisions on, for example, the constructive motion of censure or the election of the President of the Republic by any means, are safeguards of democracy. They were designed to prevent situations of power-vacuum, which may eventually lead to unwanted power concentration and may undermine the freshly established democracy of the Hungarian Republic. This was the political and normative frame into which EU issues needed to be embedded. Hungary submitted its application for EU membership in 1994 with broad political consensus. Ever since that date, reaching this aim was such an unquestionable goal that it was never exposed to political debate among the parties in Parliament. Parliamentary control in EU decision-making is also consensus driven as well as the elaboration process leading to the adoption of the legal means regulating it. The Constitution, the Act and the Resolution are all adopted by a qualified majority.

What we can draw as a conclusion from studying the normative background is that the roots of scrutiny and other forms of parliamentary control in the Hungarian legislature are different from one another. Consultative meetings before the EU Council, the activity report of the Government and the little rights parliament has in hearings of nominees precisely follow the logic of ordinary parliamentary life; documents and events are handled according to the 'usual' daily functioning of the House. The Committee does not possess the rights it has in scrutiny and it is not the final decision-maker either. The government report for example, is registered in the central database of the Parliament and not in EUDOC, and the parliamentary channels the report goes through are precisely those deducible from the general rules on how a report is handled according to the Rules of Procedure. Hearings of government-delegated nominees 'only' differ from hearings of proposed ministers or future ambassadors in the sense that Parliament actually has less power. There is no formal requirement for these hearings and no vote is taken on the eligibility and acceptance of the nominees, if the nominee decides to appear at all. Even the consultative meeting before the European Council meetings and other events of strategic importance described above fits this traditional parliamentary control mechanism. This consultative forum is not more than a committee itself, perhaps special in its composition. Membership depends on political status and the committee is chaired by the Speaker of the Parliament.[51] In summary, therefore, we may state that other forms of parliamentary control did not result in profound changes either in the parliamentary toolkit or in its normative grounds.

---

[51] The consultative committee has its roots in the former Grand Committee set up before accession as a forum to monitor accession negotiations.

European scrutiny, however, is different. Firstly, it is run by the Committee on European Affairs, equipped with the power to decide matters in the name of the whole Parliament.[52] To give one specific committee such a privilege is unique in the Hungarian parliamentary structure. The second unique feature of this system is the differentiation it makes between the standpoint of the Committee and the position of other parliamentary committees. A standing committee may discuss any matter within its competence – either in response to the request from the Parliament, or at its own decision – and take a position thereon.[53] However, only the standpoint of the EU Affairs Committee is considered as the opinion of the Parliament and sent officially to the Speaker of the Parliament and the respective Ministers of the Government.[54] The third distinguishing feature lies in the way EU documents and documents related to the scrutiny procedure are handled. The EUDOC database is separated from the parliamentary database and is maintained separately by the Committee. Documents are uploaded into the system according to a different logic than the 'normal' parliamentary database and users of the system are to a certain extent limited. Even the language variation is different as EUDOC is a multi-lingual database. Finally, the result of scrutiny is also something different from what one would expect from the logic of parliamentary work. It is not a normative document (an act or a resolution), it is not a political debate in plenary, but it is the standpoint of the Committee presented in the form of a summary by the chairman represented in the minutes of the meeting.

Before the current system of scrutiny was set up, the experience and systems of the old Member States was closely studied, especially that of the United Kingdom and Denmark. These two countries are the classic examples of the two major scrutiny systems, which literature refers to as *document-based scrutiny* and *mandating* (or Council based) *scrutiny*. Several articles were published describing the future Hungarian system as being a moderately strong, selective system where the Committee on EU Affairs plays the central role.[55] In June 2005, the Hungarian National Assembly initiated a comparative analysis of the scrutiny systems of the ten new Member States in order to see the similarities and differences between the – by that time – functioning scrutiny systems. Essentially, all the newly set up systems went back to the classic examples referred to above. The comparative analysis[56] showed that for historic reasons, the eight former communist block countries directed their attention more towards the mandating model.[57] They eventually set up systems of a mixed nature, taking

52 Act LIII of 2004, Article 1 (2).

53 Article 30 (3) of the Standing Orders.

54 Article 134/B (10) of the Standing Orders.

55 Among others Győri (2003).

56 Szalay (2005); and Júhász-Tóth (2005).

57 On the other hand, both Cyprus and Malta, also for historic reasons, as a result of strong British influence turned towards the UK document-based scrutiny model while implementing their scrutiny systems.

elements from both the document-based and the mandating systems, but their self-perception of strength is viewed from the angle of the mandate. The notion of 'mandate' implies clear and strict power structures: there is the one possessing power and rights (Parliament) who assigns part of this power to someone else (the executive), but only to the extent defined in the mandate itself. The expression 'mandate' inherently includes the unquestionable right of control, and control, for historic reasons, is a very dominant issue in these relatively new democracies.

The other observation worth mentioning concerns the importance systems of scrutiny attach to success and effectiveness. However, none of the systems we looked at[58] can really pinpoint what the criteria are that they use to measure success and effectiveness.[59] Both these terms are relative and difficult to measure in a political context anyway. It seems though that mandating systems focus more on the result of scrutiny, the extent to which Parliament is capable of binding its Government by means of a mandate. If concrete objectives are laid down in the mandate, checking becomes easier, thus *ex post* control is easier to exercise (but the negotiation capacity of a Government may be less successful). On the other hand, document-based systems focus more on the process. They concentrate on bringing in as many aspects as possible in order to exercise control, or rather influence Government behaviour this way.

6 Conclusion

In this study, we have focused on the national system of control of EU decision-making. However, we must not forget to look at scrutiny from another perspective, namely, that of the relation between national legislation and EU policy making. The question therefore is where does national legislation stand in the perspective of the European policy cycle? The following scheme represents the EU policy cycle: it is an endless circle of policy development (policy proposal and policy decision) and policy implementation (including rule making, application and evaluation). This is the widest perspective where national parliaments operate. There are many actors and interests involved in policy formulation at the European level of which national parliaments represent only one.

---

58 Including examples from the old Member States.

59 In this respect see: Mullally & Watts (2006) 26-31.

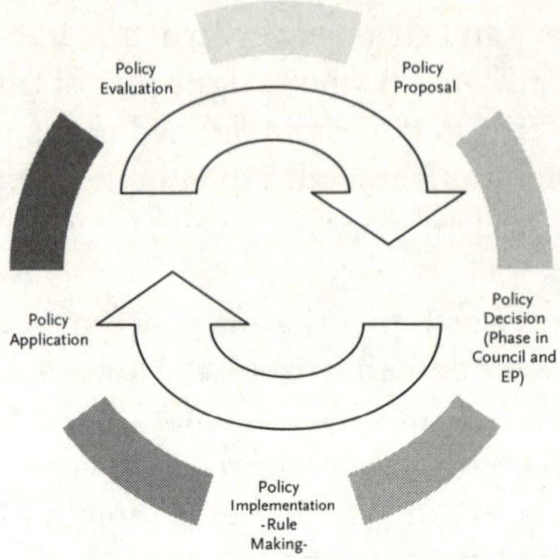

By looking at this wider, European perspective, would it not be more realistic to say that EU policy making influences national parliaments through the mechanism of parliamentary control in order to prepare national parliaments for playing their part in policy implementation at the later stage, thus contributing to the legitimacy of the political projects?

Nobody denies the fact that national parliaments contribute to the legitimacy of the European project at the political level. Their involvement in EU decision-making compensates for some of the democratic deficit of the EU. There also seems to be general agreement on the fact that although national parliaments could represent added value from a political and democratic point of view, this does not mean that national parliaments should be capable of blocking every European measure.[60] But, is the problem of democratic deficit really solved by giving certain controlling rights to the national parliaments? Can national parliaments successfully influence their Governments' activities in the EU? In the current, rather anti-political attitude, do national parliaments really have the means to get closer to their own citizens, let alone to the citizens of the EU? Do the citizens know anything about the work of the National Assembly in connection with the EU? Moreover, should they do so? How can you make MPs motivated in issues that do not necessarily give them the media representation they long for? And does it increase the acceptability of the whole European project to make EU issues part of national political games? Well, answers to some of these questions are inevitable to move the European project forward in the near future, but these answers do not seem to be deducible from the constitutional norms that currently govern parliamentary control of EU decision-making at the national level.

60 Vos (2005).

References

N. Chronowski, "Az országgyűlés és a kormány integrációs ügyekkel kapcsolatos együttműködésének szabályozásáról", *Magyar Közigazgatás* 9 (2003) 530-540.

A. Cserny, "A nemzeti parlamentek és az európai integráció", *Magyar Közigazgatás* (1999) 3. szám, 128-135.

E. Felföldi, "Az európai integráció magyar országgyűlést érintő alkotmányos vonatkozásairól", *Eu-csatlakozás* (Szeged, 2001) 67-132.

B. Fülöp, "A nemzeti parlamentek szerepe az EU-integrációban I.", *Európai Tükör* (1999) 6. szám, 37-62.

B. Fülöp, "A nemzeti parlamentek szerepe az EU-integrációban II.", *Európai Tükör* (2000) 2. szám, 55-74.

E. Győri, "A magyar országgyűlés részvétele az integráció folyamatában", *Európai Szemle* (1998) 1. szám, 32-56.

E. Győri, *Az Európai Parlament bizottsági rendszere és kapcsolatai a Magyar Országgyűléssel*, in: Izikné dr. Hedri Gabriella (ed.), *Magyarország úton az Európai Unióba* (Budapest: Aula Kiadó, 1995) 211-245.

E. Győri, "Hogyan őrizheti meg szuverenitását az Országgyűlés az EU csatlakozás után?", *Politikatudományi Szemle* 4 (2003).

A. Juhász-Tóth, *A nemzeti parlamentek és a kormányok együttműködése Európai uniós ügyekben Magyarországon és az Európai Unió többi új tagállamában* (Budapest: Magyar Országgyűlés, 2005).

A. Juhász-Tóth & K. Szalay, "Az európai uniós döntéshozatal kontrollja a nemzeti parlamentekben I.", *Európai Tükör* 2 (2006) 36-60.

L. Mullally & B. Watts, *Getting a grip: reforming EU scrutiny in Westminster* (London: Open Europe, April 2006).

Béla Pokol, "Az uniós csatlakozás és a magyar parlamentarizmus", *Politikatudományi Szemle* (1998) 1. szám, 87-98.

I. Somogyvári, "Az uniós csatlakozás alkotmánymódosítást igénylő kérdései", *Európai Közigazgatási Szemle* (2001).

K. Szalay, *Scrutiny of EU affairs in the national parliaments of the new member states – comparative analysis* (Budapest: Hungarian National Assembly, 2005).

K. Szalay & A. Juhász-Tóth, "Az európai uniós döntéshozatal kontrollja a nemzeti parlamentekben II.", *Magyarország Tükör* 3 (2006) 75-97.

J. Tóth, "Az európai integráció és az alkotmányosság kapcsolata", *Európai Tükör* (1998) 1. szám, 99-115.

H. Vos, *National/Regional Parliaments and the EU Decision-Making under the New Constitutional Treaty* (European Institute of Public Administration, 2005).

I. Vörös, "Az EU-csatlakozás alkotmányjogi, jogdogmatikai és jogpolitikai aspektusai (2)" *Cég és Jog* (2002) évi 10. szám, 28.

CHAPTER 7

The Parliament of Austria: A "Normative" Tiger?

Barbara Blümel and Christine Neuhold

1 Introduction

The fact that the Austrian national Parliament should be able to have an important role when it comes to EU-affairs was a significant consideration during Austria's accession process to the EU. Accordingly, since Austria's accession in 1995, the foreign policy competences of the *Nationalrat* and especially those of its Main Committee were strengthened.[1]

The main driving forces behind this quest were the perceived democratic deficit of the European Union and the fear of being a 'toothless tiger' within the Austrian decision-making process regarding EU-affairs. This motivated MPs to ensure a rather strong role for Parliament. Furthermore, one has to stress that the then Federal Government was not supported by the two-thirds majority in Parliament necessary to pass the Constitutional Acts on Austria's accession to the EU. Two opposition parties – the Liberal Forum and the Greens – had to be convinced to vote in favour of the changes, and the provisions to strengthen the Parliament's position with regard to EU matters were part of the compromise.[2]

Several so-called Constitutional Acts played an important role on Austria's path to the EU. Finally, the Federal Constitutional Law on Austria's accession to the European Union was put before the Austrian people in a referendum in 1994.[3] By way of this law, the competent constitutional organs were empowered to conclude Austria's Accession Treaty to the EU.

The legal provisions that were enshrined in the Austrian constitution after accession empower the parliament with rather extensive competences. A number of authors even go as far as considering that the Austrian legal stipulations are some of the most far reaching in comparison to other Member States.[4] The EU Main Committee of the *Nationalrat* is the pivotal actor in the parliamentary decision-making process regarding EU affairs.[5] Therefore, this paper focuses on parliamentary control over European decision-making in Austria performed by the *Nationalrat* and its committees. The question at stake here is whether parliaments with relatively strong scrutiny systems such as the Austrian parliament actually make use of their *ex ante* controlling powers over Austrian ministers negotiating within the Council. This question will be embedded in a description of both the legal and institutional setting of parlia-

1 Neisser (1994) 336f.

2 Khol (1995) 275ff; Fitzmaurice (1996) 91; Wohnout (1999) 71f.

3 See EU-Beitritts-Bundesverfassungsgesetz, Federal Law Gazette No. 744/1994.

4 Morass (1996) 37; Falkner (1998) 231; Maurer/Kietz (2004) 13.

5 The *Nationalrat* (the second chamber) is directly elected. The primary task of the indirectly elected *Bundesrat* (first chamber) lies in advocating the interests of the provinces in the federal legislative process. The chamber has eight weeks to decide whether or not to raise a reasoned objection to the enactment of the *Nationalrat* but may do so only by objecting to the enactment as a whole. If the law does not directly concern the interests of the federal provinces, this veto has merely delaying power (a 'suspensive veto'). In such cases, the *Nationalrat* may reiterate its original decision in the presence of at least half of its members ('can override the veto'); the original *Nationalrat* enactment thus stands.

mentary scrutiny and then the functioning of the system will be evaluated. The paper will close not only with concluding remarks but also with an outlook on the possible evolution of the system before the background of the respective provisions of the Constitutional Treaty.

2 Norms Regulating the Flow of Information about EU Decision-making (with a Link to the Respective Provisions in the Constitutional Treaty)

It goes without saying that, in order to be able to use parliamentary controlling powers effectively, parliaments need to be informed not only about European legislative proposals but also about the state of affairs of the negotiations and the Austrian position.

The modus of parliamentary information concerning EU-matters was laid down in a constitutional amendment, which was passed by the *Nationalrat* on 15 December 1994.[6] This amendment established a system in which both chambers of the Austrian parliament are involved in EU affairs. Article 23e para. 1 of the Federal Constitution states:

> 'The competent member of the Federal Government –shall without any delay –inform the *Nationalrat* and the Bundesrat about all projects within the framework of the European Union and afford them opportunity to vent their opinion.'

The phrase 'projects within the framework of the European Union' is interpreted comprehensively: all EU-documents should be submitted to parliament – agendas, draft documents of any kind as well as white papers, green papers etc. This enables the Austrian Parliament to put any EU-document on the agenda of the competent committee.[7] This practice resembles the one that was established in the Treaty Establishing a Constitution for Europe (from now on: Constitutional Treaty) where the Commission, or where applicable other institutional actors such as the European Parliament or the Council, (*i.e. not* the respective national government) have to submit draft legislative acts to national parliaments.

Although the ratification process of the Constitutional Treaty is currently in a deadlock, it is noteworthy that the Austrian *Nationalrat* decided to amend its Rules of Procedure in order to strengthen the 'Europeanisation' of the parliamentary debate.[8]

Apart from novelties such as holding a plenary meeting of the *Nationalrat*, which is to exclusively deal with EU-matters[9] up to four times a year, having a

6 See Federal Law Gazette No. 1013/1994.

7 Neisser (2002) 138.

8 FLG I No. 29/2005.

9 Sect. 74b Rules of Procedure of the Austrian *Nationalrat*.

so-called general debate[10] at the beginning of each specialised Committee meeting (*i.e.* on EU-matters) and enshrining a new unit named 'EU coordination' within the administration of the Austrian parliament,[11] and setting up an office of the Austrian parliament[12] in the EP in Brussels in May 2005, the information rights of the parliament are to be strengthened as well.

In this context, it is interesting to note that the Federal Government has put itself under the obligation that each Federal Minister will submit a report on measures of the Commission's annual legislative and working programme when the issue falls into his or her respective sphere of competence.[13] Furthermore, these reports deal with specific EU-directives and EU-regulations by summarizing the aim of the respective proposal, the time-schedule and the Austrian position.[14] Several such reports have already been submitted to Parliament, where all of them are accessible via the Internet. These reports are then discussed in the specialized committees and in some cases can even be brought before the plenary of the *Nationalrat*.[15]

Furthermore it planned that introductory notes to EU-documents that are submitted to the Austrian Parliament should contain more information on the topic at stake: such as content, aims, status of the legislative procedure, the (possible) impact on the Austrian legislation, financial consequences and a statement on the question of subsidiarity. This procedure that is very much based on the ('frozen') provisions of the Constitutional Treaty could lead to a substantial improvement for the Austrian Parliament as regards to selecting those documents relevant for follow-up and as regards to the exercise of parliamentary scrutiny.

---

10 'Allgemeine Aussprache'.

11 This unit is designed to be the main link between the Federal Ministries and Parliament. It also provides information-dossiers to the topics debated at the EU-plenary.

12 This *Verbindungsbüro* is meant to be a link between the Austrian parliament and EU-institutions. Its functions are mainly those of gathering information, participation in joint parliamentary meetings and delivering information to the Austrian Parliament in order to facilitate the flow of information mainly during the Austrian Presidency during the first half of 2006. Bachmann (2005) 29-31.

13 See: Ministerratsbeschluss, 23. November 2004.

14 Newsletter. Die aktuelle Information für MandatarInnen, No. 2/2005, 28.9.2005, p. 2.

15 During the XXII Legislative term, 20 such reports have been submitted up to now (as of April 2006); *e.g.*: report by the Chancellery (III-125 d.B.), by the Federal Minister for Traffic, Innovation and Technology (III-128 d.B.), by the Federal Minister for Economy and Labour (III-129 d.B.), the Federal Minister on Foreign Affairs (III-135 d.B.) etc.; To see how such reports are discussed by the specialised committees, see *e.g.* Parlamentskorrespondenz No. 832/4.11.2005: Sozialausschuss: Bericht über EU-Vorhaben enderledigt. Opposition für mehr Aktualität in der Sozialdebatte.

3 Norms Regulating National Parliamentary Control of EU Decision-making and Institutional Setting of Parliamentary Scrutiny

3.1 Legal Provisions Regulating Parliamentary Participation

The modus of parliamentary involvement in EU matters was laid down in the aforementioned constitutional amendment.[16] The EU-Main Committee of the *Nationalrat* determines Austria's position, with the Federal Government, when it comes to the appointment of members of the Commission, Court of Auditors, Court of Justice, Court of First Instance and Board of Governors of the European Investment Bank. Furthermore, Article 23e para. 2 of the Federal Constitution states:

> 'Is the competent member of the Federal Government in possession of an opinion by the *Nationalrat* about a project within the framework of the European Union which shall be passed into Federal law or which bears upon the issue of a directly applicable juridical act concerning matters which would need to be settled by Federal legislation, then the member is bound by this opinion during European Union negotiations and voting. Deviation is only admissible for imperative foreign and integrative policy reasons.'

Ideally, the decision-making process should be as follows:
- decision-making by the Federal government;
- decision-making in Parliament;
- decision at the EU-level.

This ideal process does not occur in reality, as most of the time the Parliament does not know the Governments' stance on topics at the time the competent committee is debating the issue.[17] However, the Permanent Mission and the Austrian Federal Ministries provide reports on the results of Council Working Parties that often contain the Austrian position on debated topics. These reports are put in the EU-data base of the Austrian parliament. Each MP has the right to present draft binding opinions on issues falling not only into the first, but also within the second and the third Pillars.[18] The EU-Main Committee and the Standing Sub Committee on European Affairs can only pass a binding opinion with majority – draft binding opinions put before the committee by a member of one of the opposition parties have therefore only a minor chance to be passed.

---

[16] See Federal Law Gazette No. 1013/1994.

[17] Neisser (2002) 138.

[18] See Art. 23f of the Federal Constitution and sect. 31d para. 3 Rules of Procedure of the *Nationalrat*. Morass (1996) 38.

The legal character of the binding opinions is comparable to that of a resolution – however, an opinion contrary to a resolution is legally and politically binding.[19]

It is important to stress that if a member of the Federal Government wishes to deviate from a binding opinion the *Nationalrat* (and here the EU-Main Committee) must again be consulted. If EU legislation results in a change in federal constitutional legislation, such a deviation is not possible without the formal approval of the *Nationalrat* (EU-Main Committee). The obligation to report to Parliament is enshrined in the Rules of Procedure of the *Nationalrat*. This report would have to be distributed among all members of the *Nationalrat*, although it would not be public. Furthermore, the respective report could be put on the agenda of the EU-Main Committee, which would then be free to examine it.[20] So far, this possibility was resorted to merely once in connection with the very first binding opinion. As the respective legal provision in the Rules of Procedure of the *Nationalrat* were not in force at that time, the Government did in fact report back to Parliament, but no further action was taken.[21]

The Protocol on the Application of the Principles of Subsidiarity and Proportionality of the Constitutional Treaty aims to ensure that decisions are taken as closely as possible to the citizens of the Union. Any draft European legislative act should also contain a detailed statement making it possible to appraise compliance with the principles of subsidiarity and proportionality. This statement should include some assessment of the financial impact of the draft, and, in the case of a framework law, of the rules to be put in place by Member States (including where necessary the regional legislation). Furthermore, the reasons for concluding that a Union objective can be better achieved at Union level shall be substantiated by qualitative and, wherever possible, by quantitative indicators. How the Commission, as the 'motor of European integration', the main actor responsible for drawing up draft European legislative acts, with its limited financial and personal resources is to conduct this examination of draft legislative proposals remains unclear. The burden is only slightly taken off by involving other actors such as the EP. What is moreover noteworthy is that the protocol foresees that any national parliament or any chamber of a national parliament of a Member State may, within six weeks from the date of transmission of the Commission's legislative proposal, send to the Presidents of the EP, the Council of Ministers and the Commission a reasoned opinion stating why it considers that the proposal violates the principle of subsidiarity. The EU institutions shall take account of the reasoned opinions issued by the parliaments.

---

19 Neisser (1998) 339 + 349.

20 See Art. 23e para. 4 of the Federal Constitution; sect. 31d para. 1 subpara. 3 Rules of Procedure of the *Nationalrat*.

21 The Rules of Procedure of the *Nationalrat* contain provisions that specify the parliamentary scrutiny process, which is in practice ran by the EU-Main Committee and the Standing Sub-Committee on European Affairs. Sect. 31c, 31d, 31e of the Rules of Procedure of the (available in English at www.parlament.gv.at, menu: English; then: The Austrian Parliament – Find out more about the legislative process, and MPs); Walter (2004) 33-35; Zier (2004) 186.

Although this Protocol is not in force as the ratification process of the Constitutional Treaty has come to a halt, the Austrian Parliament initiated a Subsidiarity Conference 'Europe begins at home' in April 2006 in St. Pölten in Austria. The aim was to reach an inter-institutional agreement on a subsidiarity procedure of the national parliaments according to EU-law (esp. when it comes to art. 5 TEU and protocol 30 to the Amsterdam Treaty).[22] In his introductory note to a conference panel, the President of the *Nationalrat*, Andreas Khol, stated:

> 'European lawmaking should be based on principles so that national and regional parliaments have a greater say. (...) We have given this a lot of thought and our goal is the following: (...) First, concrete proposals as to a subsidiary test. (...) Furthermore, the Commission should go to work in order to introduce several ideas, and before a legal act is passed, parliaments should be informed about the intent of laws; the national parliaments should then be able to coordinate affairs at the level of COSAC.[23]

In his opinion, one does not need to wait for the ratification of the TEU but may refer to the respective protocols to the Amsterdam Treaty.[24]

3.2 The Institutional Setting of Parliamentary Scrutiny

The position of the EU Main Committee differs somewhat compared to other committees. Despite the fact that it can decide to bring matters before the plenary by drawing up a report, the place to discuss EU-matters is normally in the Committee itself. This is also the reason why meetings of the EU-Main Committee and the Sub-Committee on EU-affairs have been open to the public, and why summary minutes have been published since 1996.[25]

---

22 See: Parlamentskorrespondenz No. 1019/9 December 2005: NR-Präsident Khol zur parlamentarischen Agenda des EU-Vorsitzes. Neues Subsidiaritätsverfahren soll Entfremdung Bürger-EU überbrücken; critical: Gruber et al. 2006, p. 7.

23 http://www.eu2006.at/en/The_Council_Presidency/subsidiarity/documentation/index.html, 20.4.2006.

24 Parlamentskorrespondenz, No.329/18.4.2006.

25 See section 31c para. 6 of the Rules of Procedure of the *Nationalrat*. Previously, meetings of the EU-Main Committee had been confidential just like any other committee meeting. Accordingly, during the XX. Legislative Period for 26 out of 33 sittings of the EU-Main Committee, summary minutes were published. Since the beginning of the XXI. Legislative Period, summary minutes have been drawn up for every meeting. However, the manner of drawing up these minutes changed somewhat at the beginning of the XXII. Legislative Period, as the minutes are now prepared by the parliamentary press service and no longer by the parliamentary shorthand writers' service. Whereas the summary minutes during the XX. and the XXI. Legislative Period were more or less stenographic records in reported speech, now the minutes summarise the main arguments put forward in the respective meetings. When it comes to the content of the summary minutes, one must stress that now each motion for a binding opinion,

Figure 1: *The Process of Parliamentary Scrutiny in EC/EU Affairs in Austria*[26]

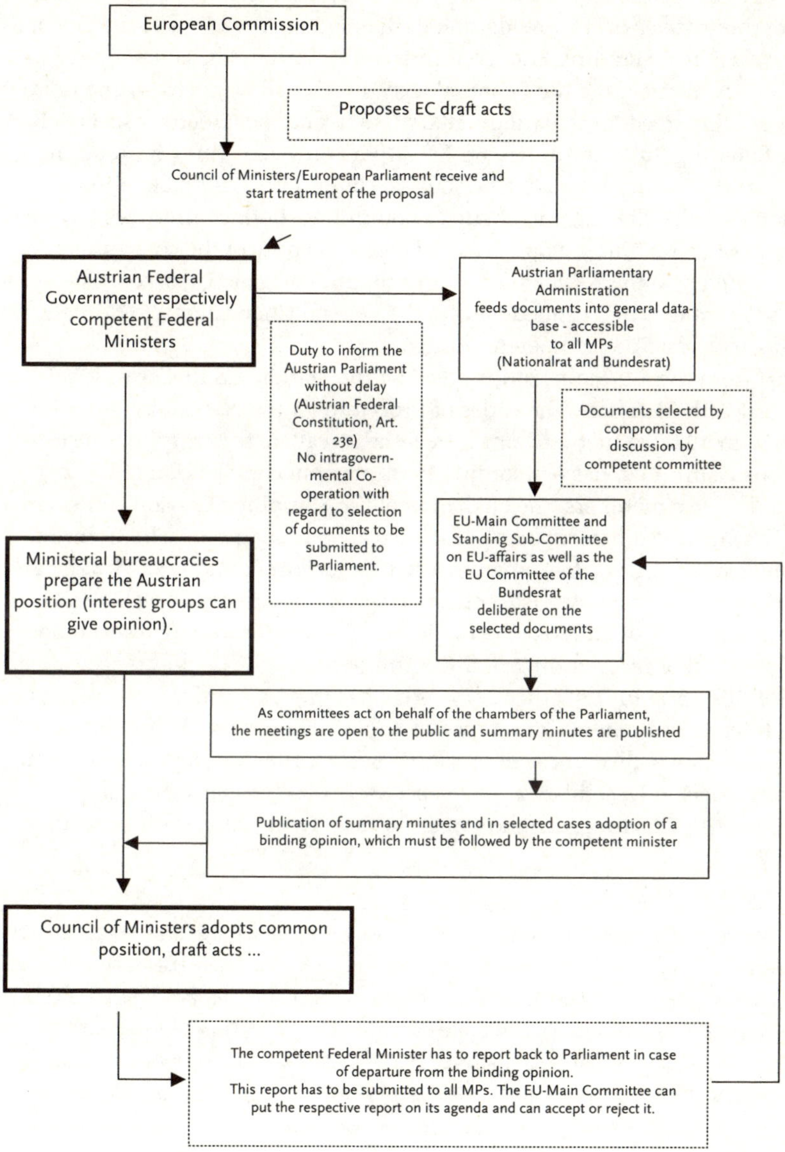

regardless whether it is to be adopted or not, shall be part of the summary minutes of the sittings of the EU-Main Committee and the Standing Sub-Committee.

[26] Source: Blümel/Neuhold (2001) 323.

During the XXII. Legislative Period, 32 MPs have a chair in the EU-Main Committee: 14 representatives of the People's Party, twelve Social Democrats, three representatives of the Freedomite Parliamentary Group[27] and the Greens respectively.[28] The Standing Sub-Committee on EU affairs has currently 13 members: six members of the People's Party, five Social Democrats, one representative of the Freedomite Parliamentary Group and the Greens respectively.

The Standing Sub-Committee on EU Affairs only came into existence in 1999, as in the former legislative periods no compromise could be found as to who should be the chairperson of such a committee. Both committees have the competence to pass binding opinions.[29] There is no duty of the committees to report separately to the *Nationalrat* when a binding opinion is passed. The opinion must be transmitted immediately to the Federal Chancellor, the Minister on Foreign Affairs and the competent minister.

Apart from the EU-Main Committee and the Standing Sub-Committee, which deal with EU-affairs the Rules of Procedure of the *Nationalrat* offer the possibility to install a further Committee, the so-called 'fire-brigade committee'.[30] This Committee has – according to the current composition of the *Nationalrat* – five members: the chairman of the Standing Sub-Committee on EU-affairs and one representative of each parliamentary group. The Committee is obliged to fulfil the task of a consultative body in Parliament with the aim of enabling the Austrian minister negotiating on the European level to reach a compromise at Council level[31] Formally this Committee must, however, not speak on behalf of the Standing Sub-Committee.[32]

Up to this point in time, this Committee has met to scrutinise the results of Nice Intergovernmental Conference in 2000.[33] Thereafter, the fire brigade committee was installed and 'put on alert' several times: on the occasion of the IGC in Brussels in December 2003, respectively to accompany the European Council meeting dealing with the Constitutional Treaty on 17/18 June 2004,[34]

27 At the beginning of 2005, the Freedom Party split up into two parties: the "old" Freedom Party (FPÖ) and the new "Bündnis Zukunft Österreich" (BZÖ) under the leadership of Jörg Haider. Since then, the BZÖ is the coalition partner of the People's Party in government. In Parliament, the "Freedomite Parliamentary Group" was formed compromising members of the FPÖ, the BZÖ and independent MPs.

28 The composition of the committees is regulated in the sections 30 and 32 of the Rules of Procedure of the *Nationalrat*. Following the system of D'Hondt, each parliamentary group gets the right to send a specific number of representatives to the committee. In smaller committees, the system according to Shapley is used.

29 See section 31d of the rules of procedure of the *Nationalrat*.

30 In German: *Feuerwehrkomitee*.

31 Neisser (1998) 351.

32 Wieser (1998) 81ff. This passage of the Rules of Procedure of the *Nationalrat* is considered to be soft law.

33 See Parlamentskorrespondenz, 1 December 2000, No. 719.

34 Posch (2004) 14. IV-10 der Beilagen zu den Stenographischen Protokollen des *Nationalrat*es (XXII. Legislative Period), p. 2.

the one in December 2004 dealing with the accession process of Turkey[35] and the European Council meeting dealing with the financial forecast 2007-2013 in December 2005.[36] Although the committee did not actually meet in Parliament, there was a vivid flow of information by telephone and e-mail, *e.g.* at the last occasion.

It has to be stressed that contrary to other national parliaments such as the Finnish parliament, it is not possible for the EU-Main Committee to transfer EU-documents to specialised committees. However, as around 70 percent of the laws dealing with economic matters are directly or indirectly influenced by EU-regulations, it will be necessary to strengthen the European perspective even in the work of the specialised Committees.[37] The EU-Main Committee may decide to bring certain matters before the *Nationalrat.*

4 Evaluation of Parliamentary Scrutiny in EU Affairs

4.1 The Scope of Parliamentary Scrutiny

In this section of the paper, we try to evaluate the system from two perspectives:

- the implementation of information rights: how are EU documents submitted and how many are actually discussed at committee level?
- the actual use of the tools of parliamentary control: how are binding opinions formulated in practice?

4.1.1 The Number of Documents Submitted to the Austrian Parliament

According to the constitutional provisions and the respective stipulations of the Rules of Procedure of the *Nationalrat,* all documents connected to the EU are submitted to the Parliament without any pre-selection or co-ordination by the competent government ministers. Normally, no explanatory abstracts are included, as there is no duty to submit additional information. The Government has agreed, however, to submit cover pages, which contain basic information concerning the respective document, but this has not led to a substantial change, as these papers are not very informative. Given the number of documents submitted to Parliament, one can easily imagine that this causes severe difficulties in selecting the material of relevance.[38] Some even argue that it is the 'idea of the bureaucracy to flood parliament with documents, until it is unable to breathe'.[39]

[35] IV-14 der Beilagen zu den Stenographischen Protokollen des *Nationalrates* (XXII. Legislative Period), p. 2.

[36] IV-18 der Beilagen zu den Stenographischen Protokollen des *Nationalrates* (XXII. Legislative Period), p. 3.

[37] Nowotny (1998) 10; Wohnout (1999) 79.

[38] Urbantschitsch (1998) 47-48; Wohnout (1999) 74 + 78.

[39] Falkner (1998) 232.

Table 1. Number of EU-documents submitted to the Austrian Parliament

XIX.	Legislative Period: 7.11.1994*-13.1.1996	17.968
XX.	Legislative Period: 14.1.1996-28.10.1999	75.875
XXI.	Legislative Period: 29.10.1999-19.12.2002	72.946
XXII.	Legislative Period: since 20.12.2002 (as of 10.1.2006)	65.769

* On 3 November 1995, the first EU-documents were submitted to the Austrian Parliament; Source: Austrian Parliamentary Administration – EU database.

One has to note, however, that in some cases, the Parliament receives the same document two or even three times, as for example different language versions are submitted and different ministries dealing with the same issue submit the same document.

Table 2. Categories of the incoming EU-documents

	XIX. Legislative Period*	XX. Legislative Period	XXI. Legislative Period	XXII. Legislative Period**
EU-reports and consultation results***	2.729	48.127	47.329	48.068
European Court of Justice	7	732	718	691
European Court of Audit	1	106	87	181
Draft documents concerning COREU	--	--	2.375	2.991
Draft directives	144	1.864	1.530	1.063
Draft regulations	270	3.180	2.281	2.093
Draft resolutions (Beschluss- und Entschließungsentwürfe)	--	--	3.511	3.446
Agendas	836	15.996	13.530	6.522
Others – not classified	487	5.870	1.584	714
Total	4.474	75.875	72.946	65.769

* During the XIX. Legislative Period the EU database was only built up. This is why not all incoming EU-document were classified. In total, 17.986 documents were submitted.

** data as of 10.1.2006

*** Within this category you will find various kinds of documents, such as Green and White Papers, reports of the Commission, reports from the various Council Working Parties and COREPER, reports of the Permanent Mission of Austria to the EU and reports of Austrian Federal Ministries as regards to the results of meetings of Council Working Parties.

Source: Austrian Parliamentary Administration

All incoming documents are inserted into a database, which is accessible for the parliamentary groups and employees of the Parliamentary Administration via Intranet. In 1999, the Austrian Parliament created a special e-mail address in order to speed up the submission of EU documents as well as to minimise the bureaucratic burden by not having to scan this substantial number of documents. On the whole, around 230.000 EU-documents were submitted to the Austrian Parliament from 1995 to December 2005.

4.1.2 The Number of EC/EU Documents Actually Considered by Parliament

The organisation of the Committee meetings is not the duty of a single Committee secretary but is divided between the parliamentary administration and the parliamentary groups. Subsequent to Austrian EU accession, a so-called preparatory group[40] (an MP of each parliamentary party as well as a *Klubsekretär*[41] respectively) decided by consensus as to which documents should be discussed during the meetings of the EU-Main Committee.[42] Now, it can be said that the *Klubsekretäre* fulfil this duty on their own. Interestingly, it is mostly the opposition parties that propose the EU-documents to be discussed during the EU-Main Committee meeting; only in a selected number of cases of Members of Parliament (MP's) of the government parties were active in this respect.[43] With regard to the topics selected to be discussed, matters were chosen which are regulated at the federal level and were seen as especially important for the Parliament's participation.[44]

40 In German: 'Vorbereitungskomitee'.

41 These are for the most part lawyers, working for one of the parliamentary groups, dealing with preparatory work.

42 Urbantschitsch (1998) 43.

43 See Fischer (1996) 167-178.

44 See Wohnout (1999) 75.

Table 3. EU-Affairs considered within the Austrian Nationalrat

	EU-Main Committee		Standing Sub-Committee on EU-Affairs	
	Number of EU-documents on the agenda	Number of binding opinions	Number of EU-documents on the agenda	Number of binding opinions
XIX. Legislative Period: 7.11.1994*-13.1.1996	92	18	--	--
XX. Legislative Period: 14.1.1996-28.10.1999	155	13	--	--
XXI. Legislative Period: 29.10.1999-19.12.2002	38	4	39	3
XXII. Legislative Period: since 20.12.2002 (as of 31.12.2005)	33	1	22	1

* On 3 November 1995, the first EU-documents were submitted to the Austrian Parliament.

Source: Agendas of the EU-Main Committee, the Sub-Committee on European Affairs and the respective summary minutes (all accessible via the Internet: www.parlament.gv.at; menu: Parlament und Europäische Union)

Combining the number of meetings of the EU-Main Committee and the EU-Sub Committee, one can say that 2005 was the busiest year since 1995. The reasons may be seen in the new regulations in force, a strengthened public discussion on European affairs following the negative referenda on the constitutional treaty in France and the Netherlands, and the Austrian EU-presidency in the first half year of 2006.

The topics of binding opinions vary from issues such as BSE, to animal protection, from employment policy to EMU, from biotechnological inventions, traffic issues to international relations. Security, agriculture, asylum and neutrality were also topics under consideration. The latest binding opinion of the EU-Main Committee dealt with the IGC 2003 and thus also with the EU-constitution. The Standing Sub-Committee has passed its latest binding opinion on agriculture and the problem of GMOs.

In March 2004, the EU-Main Committee passed a so-called *Ausschuss-Feststellung* (committee-statement) for the first time. These statements that generally contain additional explanations of acts passed by Parliament are not regulated in the Rules of Procedure of the *Nationalrat*. Nevertheless, committees make regular use of this instrument. During the last European Parliament election campaign, for example, the issue of MEP's salaries and expenses was put on the agenda by various actors, notably by Hans-Peter Martin. As a reaction, the EU-Main Committee issued a committee statement more or less addressed to the European Parliament requesting that the matter be regulated as soon as possible. As the addressee of this request was an EU-institution, a binding opinion was not possible so the committee statement was a way to state the Austrian Parliament's position on this issue.[45] Another committee statement was passed in March 2005 dealing with the relations between China and the European Union.[46] In June 2004, the Standing Sub-committee passed on the whole four committee statements dealing with budgetary matters[47], traffic and transit topics, agricultural policy and genetic engineering[48]; in November 2005, two committee statements, one dealing with internal security issues (Hague Program) and the other one dealing with targets of terrorism (esp. nuclear power stations)[49] were passed. These statements are all addressed to the Federal Government and not just the competent Federal Minister.

As one can see above, the number of binding opinions is decreasing while the use of committee statements is rising. Given the fact that the parliamentary majority doesn't want to bind the competent government minister, while nevertheless wanting to formulate a parliamentary opinion on certain issues, one may assume that the use of committee statements is a way to state the Parliament's opinion without binding the government. Consequently, MPs of the government parties put these statements before the committee.

Additionally, one has to stress that the Austrian *Nationalrat* issues politically, but not legally, binding resolutions. In October 2001, the plenary of the *Nationalrat* passed unanimously a resolution concerning the establishment of "a Convention" for the Post-Nice-Process to reform the EU-Treaties.[50] During the ratification process of the Constitutional Treaty, the *Nationalrat* passed two resolutions both dealing with the issue of European-wide referenda concerning questions of central common European interest.[51] Moreover, on 6 July 2005, the *Nationalrat* passed a resolution concerning the financial forecast of the EU and the Austrian position.[52] The wording of this resolution is very much equivalent to the wording used in binding opinions.

---

45 See IV-9 der Beilagen zu den Stenographischen Protokollen des *Nationalrates* (XXII. Legislative Period).

46 See IV-15 der Beilagen zu den Stenographischen Protokollen des *Nationalrates* (XXII. Legislative Period), p. 2 + 8 (text of committee statement).

47 See V-5 der Beilagen zu den Stenographischen Protokollen des *Nationalrates* (XXII. Legislative Period), p. 2, 8+9 (text of the committee statements respectively).

48 See V-6 der Beilagen zu den Stenographischen Protokollen des *Nationalrates* (XXII. Legislative Period), p. 2, 7 + 6, 10-12 (text of the committee statements respectively).

49 See V-12 der Beilagen zu den Stenographischen Protokollen des *Nationalrates* (XXII. Legislative Period), p. 4-5, 8-9 (text of the committee statements respectively).

50 99/E (XXI. Legislative Period)

51 99/E and 100/E (XXII. Legislative Period).

52 115/E (XXII. Legislative Period).

4.2 The Political Implications of Parliamentary Scrutiny

As a result of the aftermath of the first opinion concerning the directive on the conditions for the transport of animals, which led to a sub-optimal result, the binding opinions are formulated in a way so as to give the Government representative the chance to negotiate. In the notable case of the transport of animals, the Federal Minister for Agriculture had to comply with a binding opinion, which stated that he had to block any Community legislation that would lead to a lowering of Austrian standards. At the end of the day, the directive was not only adopted against the Austrian vote, but contained provisions, which were even less stringent than a proposed compromise solution at the European level. Although the Federal Minister tried to re-consult the EU-Main Committee in the quest to get it to review its opinion, he reportedly could only get in touch with the night-watch of the Parliament.[53] After this incident, soft formulations like 'the minister shall work towards' or 'make a strong effort' are used within binding opinions in order not to restrict the room for manoeuvre of the respective minister negotiating at the European level too much.

There are also positive examples, for instance the unanimous vote on a binding opinion concerning the Council Regulation No. 2092/91 on organic production of agricultural products and indications referring thereto on agricultural products and foodstuffs. This time a compromise was reached to clarify the Austrian position and to leave enough room for negotiating for the Federal Minister.[54] It became clear that the Austrian Parliament must not exercise its right to give binding opinions in such a way that government ministers are handcuffed.

5 Discussion

Building on constitutional provisions, the Austrian political system is based on the close co-operation between the executive and legislator: the Government needs the trust and assent of the *Nationalrat* and depends on the *Nationalrat* in so far as the latter has the possibility of a vote of no-confidence and, in daily business more importantly, has the power to pass laws, control the executive and approve the budget. It is Parliament that, by way of parliamentary resolutions, puts forward special guidelines for the activity of the administration. On the other hand, the activity of the Government affects the *Nationalrat* substantially, a fact that is not only reflected in the importance of governmental bills, but also in the dominance of the Government with regard to financial and personal resources. Members of government principally have the right to take

---

53 Urbantschitsch (1998) 54-56.

54 Schäffer (1996) 62; Parlamentskorrespondenz, 7.3.1995 and 16.5.1995.

part in the sessions of the *Nationalrat* and its committees and to take the floor under privileged circumstances.[55]

The important role of the executive in the decision-making process becomes even more salient when looking at the Austrian decision-making process with regard to European affairs: the Parliament is 'showered' with information by the government, but does not have the resources to respond within the very stringent time limits prevalent at European level and is not involved at the initial stages of the national decision-making process. Looking at the instrument of binding opinions, Heinz Fischer, then President of the *Nationalrat*, observed in 1996:

> 'The system works, if the positions formulated by the different countries indicate trends and priorities but do not lay down the negotiating positions until the last full-stop and comma.' [56]

There is a general recognition that a balance must be found between the need for ensuring a 'parliamentary imprint' and securing a reasonable degree of negotiating flexibility for ministers.[57] However, it is also important for the Parliament itself that its possibilities of participation are optimised. Margit Körner, then employee in the parliamentary Group of the People's Party argued:

> 'If this model can be implemented by way of agreement between the political parties and if one can agree on a strategy, whereby the Parliament is not paralysed, then the position of the Parliament also after Austria's accession to the EU would be protected to a great extent'.[58]

Evidently, the role of national parliaments in EU-matters and the possibility even to bind Federal Ministers is based on the principle of democratic legitimacy.[59] Accordingly, the involvement of the Austrian Parliament can also be considered to be strengthening the Austrian representative in the Council as he or she has the opinion of the Parliament to fall back on. However, some lawyers argue that a rigid mechanism used by the Parliament to bind the Austrian representative in the Council conflicts with EU-regulations.[60]

---

55 Fischer (1997) 116.

56 In German: 'Das System funktioniert dann, wenn die Positionen, die in den einzelnen Ländern formuliert werden, Tendenzen und Prioritäten angeben, aber nicht ein Anbinden der Verhandlungspositionen auf Punkt und Beistrich sind.' Fischer (1996) 177-178.

57 See J. Fitzmaurice (1996) 92.

58 In German: 'Kann dieses Modell einvernehmlich zwischen den Fraktionen im Parlament umgesetzt werden und kann man sich auf eine Vorgangsweise einigen, die das Parlament nicht lahmlegt, dann würde der Stellenwert des Parlaments auch nach dem EU-Beitritt größtmöglich gewahrt.' Körner (1995) 523.

59 Morass (1996) 39.

60 Öhlinger (1996) 70-71.

When examining the role of national parliaments within the European arena, one can conclude that despite the Austrian Parliament being a 'normative tiger', overall, it cannot be described as a real 'winner' of the European integration process. The fact that Austria was outvoted in the issue of animal transport made apparent that a number of aspects cannot be controlled by national parliaments as many decisions in the Council are taken by qualified majority, for example. Even if unanimity is required for certain issues and in theory the Parliament could succeed to impose its standpoint not only on the Government, but also push it through within the European arena, the sheer volume of documents transmitted to the Austrian Parliament prevent this in practice.

6 Concluding Remarks

On the other hand, the constitutional treaty, which contains a number of stipulations that aim to improve parliamentary involvement, seems to be a trigger for attempts to structurally change the Austrian scrutiny system. Through the provisions of the constitutional treaty, the task to furnish national parliaments with information is for the first time taken 'off the shoulders of national governments' and is transferred to EU institutions (mainly the European Commission). A plethora of draft legislative acts and consultation documents are in principle to be forwarded to national parliaments. This apparently is to help national parliaments in their quest of selecting the draft legislation where an opinion could possibly be issued. How the Commission with its limited personal and financial resources is to comply with these provisions is as yet unclear. The burden is only slightly taken off the Commission as, for example the EP is to be involved, but only to a very limited extent.

At the end of the day, this might imply that if national parliaments want to be effective players within the European system and make active use of the proposed constitutional rights, they would more than ever need the cooperation of their governments (as for example the detailed statements by the Commission only relate to the principle of subsidiarity and do not take national specificities into account.) On the Austrian level, one seems to anticipate these needs to enhance the parliamentary participation rights and thus a number of structural reforms have been implemented into the practical political process already at this stage, even though the constitutional treaty is currently not being implemented. One of the objectives of the Austrian Presidency, however, is to revive this legal document, that is, to reopen the debate.[61]

---

61 The Austrian Foreign Minister Ursula Plassnik called for a 'new step in the debate on the future of Europe' under the 'constitution process which has slowed down and which is now covered in a blanket of snow, waiting for Spring', *The Independent*, 9.1.2006.

References

Austrian Delegation: *Leitlinien zu den voraussichtlichen Themen der Regierungskonferenz 1996*, 30.5.1995.

Austrian Delegation: *Regierungskonferenz 1996. Österreichische Grundsatzpositionen*, 26.3.1996.

S. Bachmann, "Europa-Themen im Parlament. Neuerungen im Gefolge der EU-Verfassung", *Forum Parlament* 3:1 (2005) 29-31.

B. Blümel, C. Neuhold, "The Parliament of Austria: A large Potential with Little Implications", in: A. Maurer, W. Wessels (eds.), *National Parliaments on their Ways to Europe: Losers or Latecomers?* (Baden-Baden: Schriften des Zentrums für Europäische Integrationsforschung (ZEI), Nomos Verlagsgesellschaft, 2001) 313-334.

G. Falkner, "Österreichische Politiknetzwerke und EU-Mitgliedschaft: Ergebnisse und Trends", in: G. Falkner, W. Müller, C. Wolfgang (eds.), *Österreich im europäischen Mehrebenensystem. Konsequenzen der EU-Mitgliedschaft für Politiknetzwerke und Entscheidungsprozesse* (Vienna, 1998) 221-247.

G. Falkner, "How Pervasive are Euro-Politics? Effects of EU Membership on a New Member State", *Journal of Common Market Studies* 38:2 (2000) 223-50.

H. Fischer, "Die Demokratisierung der EU aus Sicht des österreichischen Parlaments", in: A. Leicht (ed.), *Regierungskonferenz 1996. Wohin steuert die EU?* (Vienna, 1996) 167-178.

H. Fischer, "Das Parlament", in: Dachs, Herbert et.al. (eds.), *Handbuch des politischen Systems Österreichs. Die zweite Republik* (Vienna: Manz, 1997) 99-121.

J. Fitzmaurice, "National Parliamentary Control of EU Policy in the Three New Member States", West *European Politics* 19:1 (1996) 88-96.

S. Gruber, K.A. Lang, A. Maurer, *Aufräumarbeiten und neue Impulse für Europa. Die Ratspräsidentschaft Österreichs*, SWP-Aktuell 2, Januar 2006.

http://www.parlament.gv.at; menu: Parlament und Europäische Union.

Informationsbüro des Europäischen Parlaments für Österreich: Das Europäische Parlament und Österreich, Vienna, 1999.

I. Kerle, C. Müller, *Das österreichische Parlament und die europäische Integration. Die Praxis des EU-Hauptausschusses und des EU-Ausschusses des Bundesrates seit dem Beitritt Österreichs zur EU* (Vienna, 1999).

A. Khol, "Demokratieabbau durch EU-Regierungsgesetzgebung?", in: Österreichische Parlamentarische Gesellschaft (ed.), *75 Jahre Bundesverfassung. Festschrift aus Anlaß des 75. Jahrestages der Beschlußfassung über das Bundes-Verfassungsgesetz* (Vienna, 1995) 273-288.

M. Körner, "Das EU-Begleit-Bundesverfassungsgesetz – die Mitwirkung der Parlamente von Bund und Ländern bei der Schaffung von neuem EU-Recht", in: A. Khol, G. Ofner et al. (eds.), *Österreichisches Jahrbuch für Politik 1994* (Vienna, 1995) 513-525.

C. Leitner, C. Neuhold, "The Intermediate Level of Government and Administration in Austria", in: T. Larsson, K. Nomden, F. Petiteville (eds.), *The Intermediate Level of Government in European States: Complexity versus Democracy?* (Maastricht, 1999) 291-314.

A. Lijphardt, *Patterns of Democracy* (Yale University Press, 1999).

A. Maurer, D. Kietz, *Die neuen Rechte der nationalen Parlamente. Umsetzungsprobleme und Empfehlungen*, SWP Berlin Diskussionspapier 2004/04, März 2004.

M. Morass, "Österreich im Entscheidungsprozeß der Europäischen Union", in: E. Tálos, G. Falkner (eds.), *EU-Mitglied Österreich. Gegenwart und Perspektiven: Eine Zwischenbilanz* (Vienna, 1996) 32-49.

H. Neisser, "Parlamentsreform und EU-Beitritt", in: P. Gerlich, H. Neiser (eds.), *Europa als Herausforderung. Wandlungsimpulse für das politische System Österreichs* (Vienna, 1994) 43-69.

H. Neisser, "Die Mitwirkungsbefugnisse des *Nationalrates* im Entscheidungsprozeß der Europäischen Union", in: H. Schäffer, W. Berka et al. (eds.), *Staat – Verfassung – Verwaltung. Festschrift anläßlich des 65. Geburtstages von Prof. DDr. DDr. h.c. Friedrich Koja* (Vienna, 1998) 335-355.

H. Neisser, "Die Funktionen des Parlaments im Wandel", in: H. Neisser, R. Puntscher, S. Riekman (eds.), *Europäisierung der österreichischen Politik. Konsequenzen der EU-Mitgliedschaft* (Vienna, 2002) 133-152.

E. Nowotny, "Europa und wir", in: *Wiener Journal* (September 1998) 10-11.

T. Öhlinger, "Die Mitwirkung des Bundesparlamentes sowie der Länder in Österreich an der Entstehung von Europäischem Recht", *Zeitschrift für Gesetzgebung* (996) 57-74.

Parlamentsdirektion (ed.), *Österreichisches Parlament und Europäische Union. The Austrian Parliament and the European Union. Le Parlement autrichien et l'Union Europèene* (Vienna, 2006).

Parlamentskorrespondenz (PK) – daily press service by the Austrian Parliamentary Administration.

J. Pollak, P. Slominski, "Influencing EU politics? The case of the Austrian Parliament", *Journal of Common market Studies* 41:4 (2002) 707-729.

G. Posch, "Europäische Angelegenheiten im österreichischen *Nationalrat*", *Forum Parlament* 2:1 (2004) 11-15.

H. Schäffer, "Österreichs Beteiligung an der Willensbildung in der Europäischen Union, insbesondere an der europäischen Rechtssetzung", *Zeitschrift für öffentliches Recht* (1996) 3-73.

G. Schefbeck, "Verhandlungsökonomie – EU-Mitwirkungsrecht – Ausschußöffentlichkeit. Zur Reform der *Nationalrats*geschäftsordnung", in: *Wiener Zeitung* – Beilage Parlament, Nr. 31 (October1996) 8-11.

G. Steiner, R. Trattnigg, "Sektorstudie Umweltpolitik", in: G. Falkner, W. Müller (eds.), *Österreich im europäischen Mehrebenensystem. Konsequenzen der EU-Mitgliedschaft für Politiknetzwerke und Entscheidungsprozesse* (Vienna, 1998) 139-173.

W. Urbantschitsch, *National parliaments in the European Union – the Austrian experience* (Graz, 1998) (Schriftenreihe des Forschungsinstitutes für Europarecht der Karl-Franzens-Universität Graz; 12).

T. Walter, "Der EU-Hauptausschuss des *Nationalrates*, *Forum Parlament* 2:1 (2004) 33-35.

B. Wieser, "Zur schwierigen Umsetzung der parlamentarischen Beteiligung an der innerstaatlichen Willensbildung in EU-Angelegenheiten: Das Komitee gem § 31 e Abs 3 GOGNR", Österreichische *Juristen-Zeitung* 3 (1998) 81-93.

H. Wohnout, "Die Mitwirkungsrechte des österreichischen Parlaments an der Willensbildung in der EU", *Die Union. Vierteljahresschrift für Integrationsfragen* 1 (1999) 69-80.

M. Zier, *Nationale Parlamente in der EU* (Göttingen: V&R unipress, 2005).

CHAPTER 8

The Dutch Parliament and the EU

A Constitutional Analysis

Olaf Tans

1 Introduction

The attitude of the Netherlands towards international co-operation has always been characterised by openness and pragmatism, an attitude that dates back to its early phases of development. In 1588, the Dutch state was first created in the form of a republic of seven united regions. This unification had strategic reasons in that the regions wanted to keep the Spanish army from concurring the Netherlands. It was also economically motivated in that the regions sought to coordinate their overseas trade. In the following decades, the republic proved to be both a military and commercial success. Nowadays it is considered to have laid the foundation of the so-called 'golden age' of the Netherlands.[1]

Openness and pragmatism also characterise the Dutch attitude towards European integration. Empirical research indicates that, compared to other Member States, the Netherlands and Luxembourg show the most stable and loyal attitude towards European integration.[2] This however does not entail that the Dutch have been strongly politically engaged. The fact that they are generally well disposed to the EU does not mean that they are very passionate about it. This is where pragmatism turns up. It seems like the Dutch have decided long ago that the EU, just like the republic of 1588, must somehow be profitable and then did not give it another thought.[3] The issue was entrusted to a specialised elite by which it was presented – if at all – as a technical and uncontroversial matter. Even during the sixties and the seventies, when the country went through a period of social change and polarising political climate, European integration was hardly put on the agenda. The Dutch were simply in favour and preferred to focus on domestic issues.

In this light, the negative outcome of the referendum on the European Constitution is remarkable, but it remains to be seen whether it represents a real change. On the one hand, it can be argued that the Dutch 'no' is the result of EU-scepticism that has been growing over the last decade, and that might well lead to a more reserved attitude to European integration all together. On the other hand, it can be argued that the Dutch 'no' is rather the result of a more general alienation of the electorate from the political establishment; a mistrust that was stirred up by the murdered politician Pim Fortuyn and that seemed to be kept alive by a severe economic recession.[4]

This contribution examines whether this attitude of openness and pragmatism is reflected in the organisation of parliamentary control of EU decision-making in the Netherlands. In accordance with the research-design that is unfolded in the first chapter of this book, though in a different order, this organisation will be analysed in three ways. Firstly, some general constitutional features of the Netherlands will be sketched. Secondly, the regime with regard

1 Israel (1995); Rowen & Lossky (1985); Price (1994); As referred to in: Van der Pot & Donner (2001) 107.

2 Janssen (2001) 135. As cited in: Hoetjes (2001) 337.

3 See: Hoetjes (1996).

4 For an analysis of the Dutch 'no' to the constitutional treaty: Tans (2006).

to parliamentary control of EU decision-making will be discussed on the basis of (a) constitutional norms governing the flow of information about EU decision-making to the parliament and (b) constitutional norms with regard to parliamentary competences to influence EU decision-making. Thirdly, a number of practices and habits affecting the controlling-power of the Dutch parliament will be discussed. Finally, we shall engage in a discussion about the main complications of the organisation of parliamentary control in the Netherlands.

2 Some General Constitutional Features

To understand the constitutional regime as it will be described in the following paragraphs, it is useful to have an idea of the political system at large. In this paragraph, a number of aspects that have bearing on parliamentary control will be discussed.

A parliamentary consensus democracy

It is no coincidence that the foundations of the actual political system of the Netherlands were laid in 1848, the year in which revolution spread over Europe. The threat of this movement, also affecting the stability of the Dutch state, forced King Willem II to accept a far reaching constitutional reform that strengthened the parliament's position vis-à-vis the government, notably by introducing full scale ministerial responsibility.[5] This 'silent revolution' paved the way for the development of a parliamentary democracy.

In the early years, the political life under the new constitution was characterised by tension between the parliament and various cabinets. On the one hand, the parliament started to gradually establish its role of a representative organ to which the government is always accountable and that can always force ministers to resign by carrying a vote of no confidence. On the other hand, the government was struggling to retain its dominance, for example by repeatedly making use of its constitutional right to dissolve the parliament. In short, the early years were marked by a relatively strong polarisation of the executive-legislative relationship, which was in accordance with the purpose of the new constitution that was inspired by the (liberal) idea of checks and balances.

In the course of time, however, the executive-legislative relationship has taken shape fitting the so called 'consensus democracy'.[6] This means that executive authority is no longer concentrated in the government, counterbalanced by an active parliament, but is rather diffused throughout the government and the coalition-parties. After the elections, a cabinet is formed on the basis of a coalition-agreement between a number of political parties to form a majority

5 In 1806, Napoleon had more or less forced Holland to accept his brother as King, thus turning the Dutch republic into a monarchy. When the Netherlands regained independence from the French in 1813, it was decided to keep this state form and to install Willem I – the only living son of the last stadtholder of the republic – as the new King.

6 Lijphart (1999).

and to support a certain government. Once the cabinet is installed, this agreement remains an influential factor in the executive-legislative relation. Members of the cabinet, for example, frequently consult the leaders of the government-parties in order to keep the coalition ranks closed.

This coalition-dominated political practice has a number of advantages, but it also has downsides that are increasingly acknowledged. The main problem is that, contrary to the intention of the 'framers' in 1848, the executive-legislative relation is now characterised by a strong unity of government and government-parties. Dutch scholars speak of a 'monistic' tendency, which may be good for the stability and strength of the government but at the same time hinders the intensity of political debate, at least in public.[7] In the following paragraphs, it will become clear that this tendency might also have a negative effect on the (future) role of the Dutch parliament in the European democracy.

An 'open' constitution

The openness to international influences can be further illustrated by the fact that the Dutch constitution contains an article stating that international law – as far as it contains provisions that bind anyone – is directly applicable in the national legal order, and an article stating that international law is superior to national law.[8]

This openness to international law generally weakens the controlling power of the Dutch parliament. If international law is directly applicable in the national legal order, this means that it does not have to be transformed by means of an act of the legislature. Parliamentary involvement will therefore always remain rather indirect, except when treaties have to be ratified.[9] In this respect, it may be worth mentioning that the Dutch constitution hardly contains ideological declarations – such as the principle of democracy or popular sovereignty – that could strengthen the parliament's position.

Moreover, the openness to international law entails a weakening of the authority of the national constitution, but strangely enough, the Dutch have always proudly accepted this consequence. When the constitutional reform of 1983 was discussed, for example, the parliament passed a motion stating that, in

---

7 Bovend'Eert & Kummeling (2004) 351-354.

8 More specifically, art. 93 of the Dutch constitution reads: 'Provisions of treaties and of resolutions by international institutions, which may be binding on all persons by virtue of their contents shall become binding after they have been published.' Art. 94 reads: 'Statutory regulations in force within the Kingdom shall not be applicable if such application is in conflict with provisions of treaties that are binding on all persons or of resolutions by international institutions.' Nowadays, these provisions seem to have lost relevance where it comes to the direct applicability of European law. Dutch legal doctrine generally accepts that this direct applicability is established by the *Costa v. Enel* and *Van Gend & Loos* decisions of the ECJ. Case 6/64, *Flaminco Costa v. Enel* [1964] ECR 585; Case 26/62, *Van Gend en Loos v. Nederlandse Administratie der Belastingen* [1963] ECR 1. The openness of the Dutch constitution is discussed in: Besselink (1996).

9 According to art. 91 of the Dutch constitution, treaties will only enter into force after prior parliamentary consent.

case of doubt, constitutional provisions must be interpreted in such a way that the process of European integration is not hampered.[10] The priority of supranational legal orders is further enhanced by the fact that the Dutch constitution prohibits constitutional review of acts of parliament (art. 120 Gw), whereas it commands the judicature not to apply these acts when they are in breach with directly applicable international rules.

A tradition of self determination and -regulation

Although it is difficult to describe a tradition in a few sentences, this section sketches some socio-cultural circumstances that may help to understand, or at least see the background of, the organisation of parliamentary control in the Netherlands. Two interrelated traditions will be discussed: self determination and self regulation.

Dutch society has a tradition of self determination in more than one way. Firstly, there is a tradition of local autonomy that goes back to the republic of seven united regions. Although the federal state-form has vanished over the years, decentralisation has remained an important constitutional principle in that municipalities are granted the power to regulate and administer their internal affairs. In fact, Dutch schools teach that the Netherlands are a 'decentralised unitary state'. Secondly, Dutch society is marked by a tradition of self-determination in the sense that various groups have struggled and succeeded to organise their way of life according to their own principles and ideas. This phenomenon is known as the 'pillarisation' of society (the development of separate lifestyles, social circles and institutions for Protestants, Catholics, Socialists, Liberals etc.) and is generally considered to have ended in the 1970s.

The essence is however that well-defined groups have always found ways to interact and establish an overall social cohesion through deliberation and participation in policy-making. In that sense, the pillarisation of Dutch society is all but over. In the 1990s, for example, Holland attracted some international attention because of its so-called 'polder-model': an informal mode of public decision-making involving the government, trade unions and organisations of employers. As Hoetjes remarks, this shows '...how the legacy and 'reflexes' of consociational democracy in the Netherlands are still very much alive – in virtually all fields of policy.'[11]

It may be useful to see the functioning of the Dutch parliament in this context. Rather than operating autonomously, members of parliament are caught up, first of all in the game of party-politics, but also in a complicated social network in which a variety of non-political actors manage to generate considerable power. This is another way of saying that Dutch politics is strongly influenced by informal mechanisms of interest articulation, negotiation and decision-making. Holzhacker seems to confirm this picture by stating that, compared to the practices of Germany and Denmark, the Dutch parliamentary

10 TK 1979-1980, 15049, nr. 16.

11 Hoetjes (2001).

practice is relatively unrestrained by formal rules.[12] Given the fact that Dutch politics nevertheless show a remarkable peace and stability, this must mean that self-regulating forces have a considerable impact.

3 Constitutional Norms with regard to Parliamentary Controlling Power

Judging from the Dutch constitution, the controlling power of the parliament with regard to EU decision-making depends almost entirely on the doctrine of ministerial responsibility that more generally governs the relation between government and representatives. The Dutch must rely on the fact that their ministers are the link between the national and the Communitarian order and that their national parliament can exert influence by holding them accountable. There is one exception: a remarkable attempt by the Dutch parliament to self-handedly increase its controlling-power. As we shall see, this attempt raises an interesting constitutional issue.

Formally speaking, the doctrine of ministerial responsibility can be based on Article 42, paragraph 2, of the Dutch constitution, which reads: 'The Ministers, and not the King, shall be responsible for acts of government.' It may come as no surprise that this brief statement has proven to give little or no guidance by itself and has only acquired a specific meaning through development of certain parliamentary practices in concert with development of doctrine in legal and political literature. This is to say that parliamentary controlling power does not follow primarily from clear-cut written rules, but is mainly the product of socially constructed normative commitments.

This paragraph describes the Dutch doctrine of ministerial responsibility and other constitutional norms, as far as they affect the power of the Dutch parliament to control EU decision-making. We shall make use of the theory set out in the introduction to this book, namely that (political) control has two basic elements: knowing about the object of control and being able to influence the object of control. On this basis, two types of constitutional norms with regard to parliamentary control of EU decision-making will be analysed: (1) constitutional norms governing the flow of information about EU decision-making to the Dutch parliament, and (2) constitutional norms governing the Dutch parliament's competence to influence EU decision-making.

3.1 Constitutional Norms Governing the Flow of Information about EU Decision-making

According to Article 68 of the Dutch constitution, the ministers and state secretaries give (both chambers of) the parliament all the information requested by one or more of its members, as long as this is not at variance with the interest of the state. Article 70, furthermore, gives both chambers the right

---

12 Holzhacker (2005).

to conduct a parliamentary investigation. These parliamentary prerogatives are specified in the regulations of both chambers and the *Wet op de Parlementaire Enquete* (Parliamentary Investigations Act), that roughly give members of parliament a right to interpellate, to ask written and oral questions, to get answers to those questions and to propose starting a parliamentary investigation.

The contribution of these written rules to parliamentary controlling-power is limited in that the duty to inform is only constituted in a passive sense: whenever information is requested it has to be given. In practice, however, the government takes on a much more active role in keeping the parliament up to date, both with national and with European affairs. This will be discussed in the third paragraph.

The question to be answered here is whether the Dutch constitution provides a basis for this more active role in informing the parliament. An affirmative answer to this question is conceivable in light of the following. Some authors defend that the constitutional foundation of the duty to inform the parliament lies not primarily in Article 68 of the Dutch constitution, but in Article 42, second paragraph, that expresses adherence to the principle of ministerial responsibility.[13] In their view, ministerial responsibility is inextricably linked to a duty to inform. To be politically accountable, so the argument goes, does not only mean being responsible for certain decisions or behaviours, but also to enable others to control these decisions or behaviours.[14]

The Dutch government, by the way, has theorised the duty to actively inform the parliament slightly differently. In a recent note, it was argued that this duty is an unwritten legal obligation related to the rule of confidence, which is generally considered to be an unwritten constitutional norm.[15] The government has also stated that this duty is not limited to the aforementioned types of communication (interpellation, questions, investigations), but that it applies to all sorts of contact between parliament and cabinet.[16] One way or the other, these opinions lead to the same conclusion, namely that, apart from a constitutional norm establishing a passive duty to inform the parliament, it can be argued that the Dutch constitutional order also contains a norm establishing a duty to actively inform the parliament. This only facilitates *ex post* control of EU decision-making, simply because the parliament is not given the right to be informed about communitarian decisions before they have been taken.

13 Broeksteeg (2004) 15-17. According to Elzinga, the process of giving account goes through three phases: (1) the phase of giving information; (2) the phase of debate; (3) the phase of sanction. Elzinga (1994) 42. See also: Bovens (1998) 86; Besselink (1991) 119.

14 This view is adopted in a report of an external commission on ministerial responsibility: "Steekhoudend ministerschap, Rapport van de externe commissie Ministeriële verantwoordelijkheid", Den Haag 1993, TK 1992-1993, 21427, no. 40-41, 8. The same view is held in: Bovend'Eert & Kummeling (2000) 215-217.

15 TK 2001-2002, 28362, no. 2, 3. Earlier, the government has also considered the duty to actively inform the parliament to be a consequence of democratic government. TK 1985-1986, 19014, no.5, 6. See also: Broeksteeg (2004) 14-15.

16 TK 1976-1977, 14225 (R1051), no.3, 4.

3.2 Constitutional Norms Governing the Power to Influence EU Decision-making

The power of the Dutch parliament to influence EU decision-making relies to a large extent on two related constitutional norms: the principle of ministerial responsibility (Article 42 Gw) and the rule of confidence. Starting with the former, we can say that the principle of ministerial responsibility enables the parliament to exert influence in basically two ways.[17] Firstly, it obliges ministers to give account, not only in the sense of giving information, but also in the sense of answering questions and engaging in debate. Ministers have to justify their conduct vis-à-vis the parliament. It is difficult to determine the precise measure of control that is established by this norm; this depends to a large extent on parliamentary practices that will be discussed later.

Of course, the Dutch constitution contains more specific rules shaping the way in which the parliament can influence EU decision-making in the course of its debate with the government. Apart from the parliamentary prerogatives that were mentioned earlier (the right to ask questions, to start an investigation etc.), one can think of the general right to establish the budget, the right to table a motion and the right to establish a special committee.

Secondly, the principle of ministerial responsibility increases parliamentary influence in that it prescribes that ministers can be held accountable. In the Dutch system, this accountability is assumed to be connected to the office of being minister, as opposed to the person that holds the office, which means that ministers can be held accountable for the conduct of their predecessors. Furthermore, ministerial responsibility is generally considered to apply either to individual ministers or to the cabinet as a whole. Again, we must say that the exact degree to which this adds to parliamentary controlling-power is largely determined in practice.

In the same way, the rule of confidence, according to which ministers must resign if a motion of no confidence is passed by the parliament, adds to parliamentary controlling power. This rule is often considered to be a part of the principle of ministerial responsibility, but Broeksteeg stresses that it has an independent function in the Dutch political system.[18] A minister can be asked to give account without the issue of confidence coming into play, and the issue of confidence can be raised even though a minister has sufficiently accounted for his or her office.[19] Nevertheless, we can say that the principle of ministerial responsibility and the rule of confidence are linked in that the latter provides the ultimate sanction to effectuate the former.[20]

As mentioned, these norms provide the Dutch parliament with a fairly unspecific controlling-power. The degree to which the parliament can affect

---

17 Broeksteeg (2004) 17-21.

18 Broeksteeg (2004) 24. See also: Bovend'Eert (2002) 33-34.

19 The parliament can lose confidence on the basis of, for example, private conduct.

20 Elzinga (1994) 47.

decision-making depends to a large extent on a complicated political process that is ultimately based on the premise that the government and the parliament are mutually dependent. In the case of EU decision-making, the Dutch parliament generally gains less control in this political process, due to the well known facts that (1) it is more difficult for the parliament to be properly informed about EU affairs, and (2) that it is more difficult for the parliament to control national ministers as these ministers in turn have less control over EU decision-making.[21]

The Dutch system shows one remarkable exception: a mechanism of *ex ante* control created by the parliament more or less self-handedly. When it was considering to approve the Treaty of Maastricht, the parliament felt that decision-making on the basis of the third pillar and the sixth title of the EC Treaty, dealing with justice and internal affairs, would suffer from lack of democratic legitimacy, as the European parliament was not given any controlling power in this respect. Baring in mind that decisions in these areas would have significant national implications, the parliament found the following solution.[22] In the approval act of the Treaty of Maastricht it created a right of approval with regard to decision-making on the basis of the third pillar and the sixth title of the EC Treaty.[23] A similar provision was included in the the approval act of the Treaty of Amsterdam.[24]

Although this arrangement may appear to be satisfactory from a democratic viewpoint, it raises some serious doubts. Del Grosso, for example, argues that the relation between government and parliament should be organised constitu-

---

[21] If, for example, a Dutch minister is overruled in the Council of Ministers, he can only be held accountable for the way he defended the national viewpoint, not for the decision in itself.

[22] Del Grosso (2000) 62-69.

[23] Art. 3, section 3 of the approval act (goedkeuringswet) concerning the Treaty of Maastricht states that before a representative of the Kingdom co-operates to establish a decision based on the sixth title, this must be approved by (both chambers of) the Dutch parliament. As far as the flow of information to the parliament is concerned, this approval act (goedkeuringswet) states (in Article 3, paragraph 1) that the parliament has to be informed about draft decisions on the basis of the title VI of the Treaty of Maastricht, as soon as the text of these draft decisions has been established. This legal arrangement was inspired by a procedure that was introduced when the Dutch parliament was considering to approve the Schengen-Treaty. As this treaty was going to have significant national implications, and given the fact that European parliamentary control was not arranged, the Dutch parliament requested some sort of control. The minister of foreign affairs proposed a procedure according to which the parliament would be informed as soon as the Executive Committee, as established in the Schengen-Treaty, started preparing self-executing or politically important decisions (HTK 1991-1992, 3152 and 3214). To scrutinize these draft decisions, the parliament would have to use its regular instruments. Del Grosso (2000) 63-65.

[24] In this (goedkeuringswet), the Dutch parliament claimed (by means of an amendment) a temporary right to approve decisions that were going from the third to the first pillar, based on the argument that it would take five years for the European parliament to start using its controlling-powers.

tionally.[25] In the political system of the Netherlands, this relation is characterised by independence – formally speaking – except in those cases in which the constitution forces the government and the parliament to co-operate. The right of approval with regard to decision-making in the third pillar, however, forces the government to co-operate with the parliament on the basis of an ordinary approval act. This means that the relation between government and parliament has been altered without any constitutional foundation. Not everyone, by the way, shares the opinion that this is a matter of great concern. Besselink and Kummeling argue that there are more laws limiting the exercise of executive powers without an explicit constitutional basis.[26] They admit that it is preferable that such a basis exists, but the authors stress that there is no rule of constitutional law according to which the relation between the government and parliament can only be regulated constitutionally.

4 Practices and Habits Affecting Parliamentary Controlling Power

The controlling power of the Dutch parliament over EU decision-making is significantly affected by parliamentary practices and habits that are not necessarily prescribed by constitutional norms. This paragraph discusses: (1) the general procedure(s) to control EU decision-making; (2) the parliamentary practice with regard to the right of approval, and (3) the way the Dutch parliament is realising its new role of guardian of the principles of subsidiarity and proportionality, as defined in the Treaty of Amsterdam (and in two protocols attached to the Treaty Establishing a Constitution for Europe). In describing these practices and habits, we shall focus on the same two aspects that were identified earlier, namely, the flow of information about EU decision making on the one hand and the means to influence this decision-making on the other.

4.1 General Procedures to Control EU Decision-making

This section focuses on the general scrutiny-procedures of the upper chamber.[27] As in most Member States, the Standing Committee on European Union Affairs (SCEU) is the pivotal actor.

---

[25] Del Grosso (2000) 68-69.

[26] Besselink, Kummeling, De Lange, Mendelts, Prechal (2002) 79.

[27] In the Netherlands, the upper chamber (called the second chamber) is the most political, directly elected section of the parliament, playing a dominant role in legislation and political control. It has a general standing committee for European affairs (Algemene Commissie voor Europese Zaken). The lower chamber (called the first chamber) plays a secondary role in that it reviews legislative proposals as a whole and can only decide to either pass or reject them. It also has a standing committee for European affairs (Commissie Europese Samenwerkingsorganisaties), which has a relatively modest attitude with regard to the input it gets from the second chamber. See: Del Grosso (2000) 253/254.

Control of the Council's decision-making

Since 1991, the parliament is informed about the European Commission's draft decisions in the form of so-called 'fiches', prepared by a committee composed of civil servants from various Ministries.[28] These fiches describe the content of draft decisions, their implications for the Netherlands, their relevance to Ministries, and recently also whether they are in accordance with the principle of subsidiarity. The SCEU monitors these fiches, selects those she finds especially important and sends them to specialised committees or individual MP's in charge with their subject matter. The SCEU also informs the parliament by means of a weekly newsletter and operates more generally as manager of the stream of EU related information.

Strangely enough, the fiches are not structurally discussed in the parliament, which means that a chance is missed to influence decision-making early in the process, and that the SCEU hardly has to account for its selection-policy. This reluctant behaviour can be explained in various ways. Firstly, it may be related to the fact that the fiches-procedure was originally not meant to facilitate parliamentary control, but to prepare the implementation of EU decisions. Secondly, it is conceivable that the Dutch parliament does not want to get in the way of the European parliament, that also plays an important role in controlling Commission proposals. Thirdly and finally, it may also be the case that the Dutch parliament is simply not overly interested in EU affairs.

It becomes slightly more active when draft decisions appear on the agenda's of Council meetings, which are translated and annotated by civil servants from various departments. For a long time, there has been dissatisfaction with the content and distribution of these annotated agendas, but a number of agreements have improved this situation.[29] More recently, the protocols concerning the role of national parliaments and the application of the principles of subsidiarity and proportionality have put the government under pressure to inform the parliament as soon as possible. A problem that remains, however, is that 'a'-points are often put only on the very last version of the agenda of Council meetings.[30]

---

[28] Werkgroep Beoordeling Nieuwe Commissie-voorstellen.

[29] The agenda's have long been considered to contain too little information regarding the viewpoints to be defended by ministers in Brussels. In 1990, a motion has been tabled to alter the situation (Kamerstuk 21109, nr. 24). After the elections in 1994, there has been a slight improvement: some ministers have started to indicate their standpoint, albeit briefly. Other agreements to improve the situation are: (1) Agenda's and reports of Council meetings are not only sent to the chairman of the second chamber but also to the relevant committee and the General Committee of European Affairs; (2) Agenda's must reach these committee's at least a week before the meeting, reports within two days afterwards; (3) Provisional agendas and plannings are also sent to the parliament; (4) The agenda's of the various Councils are standardised; (5) The government will only react to green and white papers after they have been sent to, and studied by, the upper chamber; (6) European legislative proposals are sent to the parliament.

[30] In most cases, agreement about these – mostly technical – issues has already been reached on the departmental level. Their treatment in the Council is considered to be a purely formal matter.

The agenda's are discussed in gatherings of the SCEA, one or more sectoral committees and the ministers that will take part in a Council meeting. Since 1996, these meetings take place in the context of the 'Europa-deliberation', a procedure to streamline and coordinate the parliamentary involvement, which boils down to scheduling the meetings on the same day. This was meant to have the advantage that dossiers can be linked, that committee members can attend each others meetings (thus reducing the pillarisation of parliamentary involvement with the EU) and that the agenda-deliberation would become a regular and visible part of the parliamentary activities.[31] A recent development is that Dutch members of the European Parliament have been given the rights to speak in these Committee meetings.

After Council meetings, national civil servants make a report. On the basis of this report, ministers give account in gatherings of the same parties that were also involved in discussing the agenda. A complicating factor has been that Council meetings are not public, so that the committees have to rely on the way ministers describe the proceedings. Ministers can be called to account in a plenary debate, but this will only involve tabling of a motion and happens rarely in European matters. This is to say that the principle of ministerial responsibility does not seem to have much impact when it comes to *ex post* control of the conduct of ministers in European institutions.

Control of the European Council's decision-making

In the last few decades, the Dutch parliament has increased its control over decision-making in the European Council, by means of (1) preliminary information and consultation of (committees of) the parliament, and (2) ministerial account afterwards.[32]

Starting with the former: in the week before a meeting of the European Council, the government sends the agenda and a brief explanation to the second chamber.[33] Since 1991, this agenda is discussed during a gathering of the Prime Minister, the Minister of Foreign Affairs, the standing committee of foreign affairs and the SCEA. Ever more often, sectoral committees take part if their subject plays an important role in the upcoming meeting of the European Council. Mostly, there is no time to have a plenary debate in the parliament, but there have been exceptions.[34]

---

31 According to Hoetjes, the results of this initiative vary in terms of attendance, duration, co-ordination and attention. According to Del Grosso, the pillarisation of parliamentary involvement with the EU has not been reduced. Hoetjes (2001) 337-358; Del Grosso (2000) 188.

32 Del Grosso (2000) 166-171.

33 Members of parliament have complained frequently about the content and timing of this briefing. The agendas of the European Council meetings tended to contain general policy-issues rather than viewpoints to be defended by Dutch ministers.

34 For example in 1987, after the so-called 'black monday' of the international stock exchange. Prior to the meeting of the European Council dealing with this monetary crisis, a Dutch member of the second chamber, by the name Kok, asked for a plenary debate. Although it was an unusual request, it had success. See: Kamerstuk 20322, nr. 1-3, HTK 1987-1988, p. 1354.

As for the latter: after the meeting of the European Council has taken place, the government generally provides the second chamber with a report. Since 1978, the Prime Minister personally accounts for this report and his conduct in the European Council in a plenary session in the second chamber.

Control through the annual budget debates

As in most Member States, the annual budget debates have developed into a climax of parliamentary scrutiny, in which the government reports and accounts for the overall expenses and policy. Naturally, European affairs have gradually become more important in these annual debates. Originally, this issue was only dealt with in the context of the report and debate on foreign affairs. In 1988, the parliament adopted a motion asking for a more coherent and detailed report about the impact of the establishment of the internal market on various national policy-areas, a wish that was met by the government in 1992.[35]

As of 1998, however, European affairs are discussed in a separate session, on the basis of a separate report covering roughly the financial and policy implications of the Dutch involvement in the EU, and the political intentions and budget for the year to come. Although this report is named 'The State of the European Union', it discusses European integration from the Dutch perspective.[36]

4.2 The Approval-procedure concerning Decision-making in the Third Pillar

As mentioned, the Dutch parliament created a remarkable exception to the system as described so far in the approval act of the Treaty of Maastricht: a right to approve of cooperation of Dutch representatives in decision-making under the third pillar.[37] Although this right has become less important as more policy-areas became subject to Communitarian decision-making, it may nevertheless be worth to mention a few aspects.

With regard to the flow of information to the parliament, we can more or less repeat the picture sketched in the previous paragraph: legislative proposals and annotated agenda's are sent to the chairmen of the two chambers and then further distributed to the standing committees for Justice and Internal Affairs. There have been many complaints about the content and timing of information, motions have been tabled, and the government has agreed and promised to improve the situation.

In this case, however, a deadline is set for the parliament to ask for explicit approval of legislative proposals. The parliament generally gets 15 days, or rather, the standing committees for Justice and Internal Affairs get 15 days, as they

35 Kamerstuk 20449, nr. 3.

36 The most recent version of 'The State of the European Union' can be found, also in English, on the website of the Ministry of Foreign Affairs: <http://www.minbuza.nl>.

37 See TK 2004-2005, 30025, nr. 3, 20 and further.

have the task to first decide whether explicit approval is needed. If not, they will simply let the deadline pass with the result that parliamentary approval is considered to have been given implicitly. If so, this will be proposed to both chambers of the parliament. If one of the chambers agrees, this automatically leads to a reserve with regard to the draft decision, which means that the relevant minister cannot participate in decision-making in the Council.[38]

If the parliament opts for the explicit approval-procedure, there will be a gathering of the standing committees of Justice and Internal Affairs, and the relevant ministers, to discuss the agenda on which the draft decision is scheduled. On the basis of this meeting, the standing committees decide whether the reserve should be cancelled, in which case the second chamber is asked to give its explicit approval. It is agreed that this decision must be taken early enough for the first chamber to be able to discuss the issue before the Council meeting takes place. This means that the opinions of both the first and the second chamber have to be formed and expressed in 15 days.

4.3 The Joint Committee on the Application of Subsidiarity

Formally, the development of a parliamentary subsidiarity and proportionality check has nothing to do with the Dutch constitution. It is a result of international regulation, in the treaty of Amsterdam and later in the Treaty Establishing a Constitution for Europe.[39] However, as this development is likely to significantly affect the future organisation of parliamentary control of EU decision-making in the Netherlands, it cannot be disregarded in this contribution.

The most interesting aspect is that the Dutch parliament introduced a novelty in reaction to this international regime, namely, a Joint Committee with the task to examine how the subsidiarity and proportionality check had to be organised.[40] After an extensive inquiry, this committee advised installing a Standing Committee on Subsidiarity, also consisting of members of both the first and the second chamber. There were two main reasons for this. Given the fact, firstly, that the international regime allows national parliaments a period of only six weeks to react to breaches of the principles of subsidiarity and proportionality, the old system (in which both chambers have to give their opinion) was considered to be too slow and inefficient.[41] Secondly, a Joint Committee would increase the chance of reaching unanimity between the two chambers, which is necessary to have a significant influence on European decision-making.

---

38 As the (JBZ-Raad) only takes unanimous decisions this means that decision-making is blocked.

39 See also: Peters (2005) 70-72.

40 More specifically, it was proposed to allow a seat in the committee to every party with more that 20 seats in the second chamber or 10 seats in the first chamber, and to every party represented in both chambers.

41 This is argued, for example in Van Baalen (2002-2003). In 2003, a motion was tabled in both chambers, asking the chairmen to establish a common committee with the task to propose a reform of parliamentary scrutiny of EU decision-making (28473, nr. 158g, 28473, nr. 13).

It was proposed, and accepted by both chambers in December 2004, that the Standing Committee on Subsidiarity would function as follows. Its general task is to determine whether proposals by the European Commission are in accordance with the principles of subsidiarity and proportionality. In order to make that judgement, the Committee distributes these proposals among sectoral committees with the request to give their opinion within three weeks. The Standing Committee gives its advice on the basis of these opinions and sends it to both chambers of the parliament, of which the members can decide to vote on them. As this procedure puts a lot of pressure on the members of parliament, the 'civil society' and the local governments, it was proposed that legislative proposals be published on a website, in the Government Gazette, and that stake holders are to be informed via e-mail. In sum, this procedure is meant to foster participation (of both the parliament and the civil society) and transparency.

It is not yet entirely clear how this works out in practice. In March 2005, COSAC launched an experiment in which national parliaments were asked to scrutinise a number of proposals by the Commission.[42] Following the aforementioned procedure, the (temporary) Joint Committee passed the proposals on to sectoral committees of both chambers of the parliament. It turned out that these sectoral committees scrutinised the proposals differently and that they came up with divergent opinions.[43] The Joint Committee decided to organise a combined meeting with the purpose to arrive at a consistent and unanimous advice, which took quite a bit of argument.

After the French and Dutch referenda on the European constitutional treaty, the Joint Committee suspended its activities in order to allow a 'period of reflection'. It appeared however that the Dutch and other parliaments were still committed to pulling the subsidiarity check through on the basis of the Treaty of Amsterdam. Therefore, it was suggested that COSAC should take the matter in hands and propose a uniform procedure for a subsidiarity and proportionality check by national parliaments in the EU. In October 2005, the UK Presidency of COSAC proposed such a procedure.[44] In December 2005, the temporary joint committee gave its final advice, basically stating that the Standing Committee on Subsidiarity should take over and organise its activities in accordance with the COSAC-line.[45] Although members of the second chamber expressed a few doubts about this advice in a plenary debate, it was decided that the Standing Committee on Subsidiarity would start to function in January 2006.[46]

---

42 Conférence des Organes Spécialisés en Affaires Communautaires. The proposals can be found in: E040148-E040152/COM(2004)140-144.

43 The standing committee of the first chamber gathered a few times, operating mostly as a team. In the second chamber, the process got more politicised: much work was done by separate political groups that also got in touch with their party-members in the European Parliament. It was remarkable that the standing committees of the first and the second chamber did not get in touch with each other.

44 See: <http://www.cosac.org/en/meetings/previous/London2005/oedinary/meetingdocuments>.

45 TK 2005-2006, 30389, nr. 1.

46 TK 15 December 2005.

5 Complications of the Dutch Scrutiny-system

5.1 The Fiction of Ministerial Responsibility

As mentioned, the Dutch constitutional regime is to a large extent based on the principle of ministerial responsibility, according to which ministers (1) must give account of everything that happens under their responsibility, and (2) can be held accountable afterwards. This construction has a number of problematic aspects, especially where it comes to responsibility for EU-related behaviour.

This can first be illustrated by looking at the national context.[47] Dutch political and legal literature expresses an increased awareness of the complication of the principle of ministerial responsibility in light of the fact that ministers can oversee nor control everything going on in their departments. Civil services, for example, tend to operate fairly independently. Some have argued that ministers cannot be held accountable for things they cannot influence and have proposed a doctrine of blameworthiness: only when a minister can have knowledge of wrongful action he can be held accountable. Others have argued that absence of blameworthiness does not diminish political accountability in itself, but can lead to a limitation of the sanction.[48]

Similar complications arise in the EU-context.[49] In principle, the Dutch parliament can hold ministers accountable for their EU related conduct and that of their subordinates. In at least two ways, however, a lack of control and insight makes it difficult to see this as more than mere fiction. Firstly, it is difficult to hold ministers accountable for their behaviour in the Council, as decision-making often takes place by qualified majority. They remain responsible for the way they defend the Dutch interests, but the fact that Council meetings are held behind closed doors, and more generally the inscrutable nature of the political process, hinders the effectuation of this responsibility.

Secondly, the preparation of EU decision-making can cause accountability-problems. Although decisions are formally taken by the Council, they are often informally prepared or even drafted lower in the hierarchy, sometimes with the aid of civil servants operating under national instructions, for example in COREPER. Apart from the fact that it is sometimes difficult to determine which minister is responsible for this preparatory work (the one in charge of the preparatory work itself or the one taking part in the final decision-making in the Council), it is not easy for the Dutch parliament to be properly informed, let alone to exert influence on the process. Even ex *post* control is quite complicated, as this preparatory work takes place in a relatively inaccessible political process involving European institutions and national departments. Other factors playing a role might be the close ties between government and coalition parties, or the

47 See: Bovens (1998) 85-89; Broeksteeg, "Political accountability in the Netherlands", forthcoming.

48 Broeksteeg (2004); Bovens (1995) 259.

49 See for example: Van Gerven (2005) 64-80. Del Grosso (2000) 58-62.

aforementioned reluctance to get in the way of the European parliament, or a more general conviction that the government should have a certain freedom to manoeuvre when it operates internationally.

In short, we can say that the principle of ministerial responsibility offers the parliament limited means to seriously control the Dutch contribution to EU decision-making, and that another constitutional concept seems to be needed to bring improvement. This is illustrated by the fact that Dutch ministers rarely get into political trouble because of their EU related behaviour.

5.2 Low Level of Parliamentary Involvement

Political control of EU decision-making is also weakened by the fact that the Dutch parliament does not show much enthusiasm for this subject matter. As in many other parliaments, EU affairs are often left to a small group of members specialising in it. Even a major issue such as the constitutional treaty did not lead to well attended plenary sessions, which is illustrated by the following. During the debate about the outcome of the Convention, a member of the Senate (Erik Jurgens of the Labour Party) remarked that the debate was held in the margin of a governmental address, whereas it would have been more appropriate to give centre stage to a major issue such as a draft treaty establishing a constitution for Europe. As Jurgens remarks, however, this is quite indicative of the parliament's attitude. 'It is typical...,' he adds, '...that as soon Europe is discussed the listeners leave the room.'[50]

This attitude can be explained in various ways. Firstly, it is – at least partly – a result of the fact that the Dutch parliamentary activity is based on a committee-system. Secondly, one can imagine that the feeling of hardly being able to influence European decision-making anyway, if only due to lack of insight, lead to a certain resignation among members of parliament. As if European regulation is a fact of life one can only learn to accept. Thirdly, members of parliaments may simply be more attracted to national issues because they draw more attention and therefore give better opportunities to score politically. As Hoetjes remarks: 'The motive for parliamentary involvement in European integration is the desire to control all national government representation in international organisations – basically, a national reflex rather than an intrinsic interest in EU-affairs'.[51]

Whatever the reason may be, the fact remains that a low level of parliamentary involvement indicates an impoverishment of the political process. If only a small section of the parliament is seriously engaged in European affairs, this means that Dutch political control of EU decision-making is determined by a limited representation of the Dutch people. In other words, it has a negative

---

[50] TK 2002-2003, 28473, 158e and 33, 11. According to Del Grosso, the Dutch parliament fails to make full use of its power to control decision-making in the Council of Ministers. She wonders whether this has to do with lack of genuine interest in European affairs. Del Grosso (2000) 177.

[51] Hoetjes (2001) 337-358.

effect on the role of this national parliament in legitimising EU decision-making democratically.

5.3 The Non-political Nature of Parliamentary Scrutiny

When the parliament *does* get involved in EU affairs, its scrutiny is negatively affected by another type of political passivity, namely a reluctance to engage in serious, fundamental, political debate. The parliamentary treatment of the constitutional treaty, for example, remained rather flat. Even in the final stages of the campaign, when the polls forecasted a massive 'no' by the Dutch voters, the government and the main parties produced little more than the unanimous message that it was important to say yes, mainly because that would not jeopardise the further development of the EU. No serious attempt was made to discuss why Holland would be in favour of this further development. As most EU-affairs it was treated as being uncontroversial, technical and practical.

This is probably related to the aforementioned consensus-oriented nature of the Dutch political practice that is often cherished for its stability, predictability and the ability to produce practical results. In sociological terms, one could say that the Dutch parliament relies heavily on self-organisation: unregulated mechanisms of interest articulation, deliberation and decision-making. The downside to this parliamentary behaviour, however, is that it leads to an absence of open political conflict. One may argue that this leads to another type of democratic impoverishment.

By engaging in conflict, namely, a parliament makes clear that there is something at stake and that differences of opinion are possible. If voters can relate to one of these opinions that will generate a sense of being represented; the impression of a political arena in which interests and preferences are played out.[52] In the national context, this absence of political debate is to a certain extent compensated by all sorts of informal mechanisms, but it seems to have caused an alienation of the Dutch people from the EU, which becomes clear by simply recalling the figures: 85% of the parliament supported a treaty that was rejected by over 61% of the voters. This means that although there was a considerable level of agreement in the Dutch parliament, this did not reflect the opinion of the electorate. It can be argued that the absence of political conflict that is typical for (former) consociational democracies plays a role in this gap between representatives and the people.

---

52 The issue of political representation with regard to the EU constitutional progress is discussed in: Crum (2005).

6 Conclusion

In this contribution the Dutch constitutional regime and political practice of parliamentary control of EU decision-making has been analysed. The constitutional regime is characterised by a remarkable absence of legal rules that specifically organise national parliamentary control of EU decision-making. In this respect, the Dutch parliament must rely on the, vague, rules that more generally regulate the way in which the parliament is informed and on the general principle of ministerial responsibility. There are two exceptions: an *ex ante* control-mechanism with regard to decision-making under the third pillar, laid down in the approval act of the Treaty of Maastricht, and the watchdog-role with regard to the principles of subsidiarity and proportionality, laid down in the Treaty of Amsterdam and the shelved constitutional treaty.

As for the political practice, it has become clear that the standing committees on European affairs play a crucial role in both informing the parliament and in trying to influence the Dutch government. An interesting new development is the establishment of a joint committee with the task to realise the subsidiarity and proportionality check on behalf of both chambers of the parliament.

An attempt is made to put this constitutional regime and parliamentary practice in the light of the Dutch political system at large, notably the fact that the Netherlands are a consensus-democracy, have a constitution that is open to international law and have a tradition of self regulation and -determination. The main complications of the Dutch scrutiny-systems are related to these features. Firstly, the concept of ministerial responsibility seems to offer the parliament too little specific means to influence the Dutch role in EU decision-making. Secondly, the parliament suffers from passivity vis-à-vis European affairs, both in the sense of low involvement and a low level of serious political debate and conflict about EU affairs.

References:

K. Aarts & H. van der Kolk, "Understanding the Dutch 'No': the Euro, the East, and the Elite", *Political Science and Politics* 39:2 (2006) 243-246.

H. van Balen, "Op tijd is te laat – Versterkte democratische controle en politieke invloed op Europese besluitvormingsprocessen; opties voor de Nederlandse volksvertegenwoordiging", parliamentary report, HTK 2002-2003, 28632, nr. 1.

L.F.M.Besselink, "Aard en grondslag der ministeriële verantwoordelijkheid", in: *De ministeriële verantwoordelijkheid* (Antwerpen: Interuniversitair centrum voor staatsrecht, 1991).

L.F.M. Besselink, "An open constitution and European integration: the kingdom of the Netherlands", *Deutsche Wissenschaftliche Gesellfschaft für Europarechte und Nomos Verlagsgesellschaft*, Baden-Baden. Berlin 9.-12 Oktober 1996, part I, 361-394.

L.F.M.Besselink, H.R.B.M.Kummeling, R.de Lange, P.Mendelts, S.Prechal, *De Nederlandse Grondwet en de Europese Unie* (Groningen: Europa Law Publishing, 2002).

M.A.P. Bovens, *The Quest for Responsibility* (Cambridge: Cambridge UP, 1998).

M.A.P. Bovens, "De ministeriele verantwoordelijkheid", in: J.Th.J. van den Berg, Th.L. Bellekom, H.-M.Th.D. ten Napel, E.M.Peeters (red.), *Inleiding Staatkunde* (Deventer: Kluwer 1995).

P.P.T. Bovend'Eert & H.R.B.M. Kummeling, *Het Nederlandse Parlement* (Deventer: Kluwer, 2004).

P.P.T. Bovend'Eert, *Ministeriele verantwoordelijkheid* (Nijmegen: Ars Aequi Libri, 2002).

J.L.W. Broeksteeg, "Political accountability in the Netherlands", forthcoming.

J.L.W.Broeksteeg, *Verantwoordelijkheid en aansprakelijkheid in het staatsrecht* (Groningen: Kluwer, 2004).

B. Crum, "The EU Constitutional Process: A Failure of Political Representation?", paper presented at the annual work conference of the Netherlands Institute for Government 2005, Nijmegen.

N.Y. Del Grosso, *Parlement en Europese integratie* (Deventer: Kluwer, 2000).

D.J. Elzinga (ed.), *Ministeriële verantwoordelijkheid in Nederland* (Zwolle: Tjeenk Willink, 1994).

W. van Gerven, *The European Union. A Polity of States and Peoples* (Oxford and Portland: Hart, 2005).

B.J.S. Hoetjes, "The Parliament of the Netherlands and the European Union: Early Starter, Slow Mover", in: A. Maurer & W. Wessels (eds.), *National Parliaments on their Ways to Europe: Losers or Latecomers?* (Baden-Baden: Nomos, 2001) 337-358.

B.J.S. Hoetjes, "The Netherlands", in: D. Rometsch & W. Wessels (eds.), *The European Union and Member States – towards institutional fusion?* (Manchester/New York: 1996) 155-184.

R. Holzhacker, "The Power of Opposition Parliamentary Groups in European Scrutiny, *The Journal of Legislative Studies* 11 (2005) 428-445.

J.I. Israel, *The Dutch republic. Its rise, greatness and fall* (Oxford: Clarendon, 1995).

J.J.H. Janssen, *Publieke steun voor de Europese Unie – analyse van de publieke opinie in 12 lidstaten 1952-1998* (Maastricht, 2001).

A. Lijphart, *Patterns of Democracy. Government Forms and Performance in Thirty-Six Countries* (New Haven/London: Yale UP, 1999).

J.A. Peters, "National Parliaments and Subsidiarity: Think Twice", *European Constitutional Law Review* 1:1 (2005) 68-72.

C.W. van der Pot & A.M. Donner, *Handboek van het nederlandse staatsrecht* (Deventer: Tjeenk Willink, 2001).

J.L. Price, *Holland and the Dutch republic in the seventeenth century. The politics of particularism* (Oxford, 1994).

H.H. Rowen & A. Lossky (eds.), *Political ideas and institutions in the Dutch republic* (1995).

M.P.C.M. van Schendelen, "The Netherlands: From Founding Father to Mounding Baby", in: Ph. Norton (ed.), *National Parliaments and the European Union* (London/New York 2004).

O.J. Tans, "The Dutch Parliament and the European Constitution: How Yes Led to No", in: Ph. Kiiver, ed., *National and Regional Parliaments in the European Constitutional Order* (Groningen: Europa Law Publishing, 2006) 79-95.

CHAPTER 9

National Parliamentary Control of EU Decision-making in Denmark

Peter Riis

1 Introduction: Denmark's Hesitant Approach to the EU[1]

How is national parliamentary control of EU decision-making organised in Denmark, and why have things been organised the way they have? These two interrelated questions form the main questions for this article. Before studying these questions in depth, I will first provide the reader with an introduction to the overall Danish approach to the European Union and its predecessor, the European Economic Cooperation. Furthermore, I will highlight a very decisive norm in Danish political culture – the established norm of consensus building – with unmistakable importance for the general approach to the EU.

Since Denmark became a member of the European Economic Cooperation (EEC) back in 1973, the Danish Parliament has had an important role in controlling and mandating the Government's EU-policy. Questions related to the EEC (today the EU) have through the years caused considerable political tensions among political parties, interest groups and the electorate. For good reasons, EU-policy has been very difficult to label: is it foreign policy or domestic policy? Maybe the former president of the European Commission, Jacques Delors, was very accurate when he once described the EU as a UPO (Unidentified Political Object).

Originally – back in the 70s – the Danish Government and a majority in the Danish Parliament basically considered the EU (at that time, the EEC) as a pragmatic foreign political cooperation in a rather limited economic area. Labelling it as foreign policy led to a strict governmental coordination to ensure a common and coherent Danish position in the Council. On the parliamentary level, a similar structure was established by the foundation of the Market Committee with the task to coordinate the position of the Parliament as a whole. The Market Committee replaced the so-called Market Negotiation Committee established in 1961, which purpose was to monitor the negotiations leading to Danish membership of the EEC. After the coming into force of the Maastricht Treaty in 1993, the Market Committee was renamed The European Affairs Committee indicating the emergence of a political union.

To fully understand the weight of the argument for a united Danish voice in the European institutions, however, one has to pay attention to the generally accepted historical ideal among the major political parties of internal cohesiveness. This is not just a coincidence. Social and national integration actually formed the basis of the policies of the Social Democrats and Social Liberals who governed Denmark from 1929 to 1940[2] – as a kind of alternative to military armament in this historical period. The minister of Foreign Affairs at that time was the social liberal P. Munch (1870-1948), who defined the foundations of the Government's foreign policy in three lectures delivered at *L'Institut Universitaire d'Hautes Etudes Internationales* in Geneva in 1931. The main topic was the moral

[1] This article represents the author's personal viewpoints and does not necessarily cover the official viewpoints of the EU-Secretariat or the European Affairs Committee of the Danish Parliament.

[2] Østergaard (2000) 169.

authority of the small nations (mainly the neutrals of World War I: Denmark, Norway, Sweden, the Netherlands and Switzerland), which was to be based on a high degree of cohesion within their national communities. The strategy was to keep totalitarian ideologies at arms length by means of a 'Nordic' welfare state.

An important step in implementing this strategy took place in January 1933 on the eve of Hitler's takeover in Germany. The Danish Social Democrats and Social Liberals pushed a major crisis agreement with the Conservatives and the Liberals through Parliament: the so-called 'Kanslergadeforlig', named after the street on which the Prime Minister Thorvald Stauning (S) lived. With this package of laws, the governing Social Democrats offered the Agrarians in Venstre (The Liberals) subsidies for the farmers and devaluation of the currency in exchange for public works programs and a social security bill, which primarily included higher unemployment compensation. But more importantly, the purpose of the agreement was to save the parliamentary system, to preserve social order and thereby national coherence.[3] In a long-term perspective, the strategy of strengthening internal cohesiveness in the Danish society has had a significant impact on Danish policy-making, consensus-building among parties, institutions and organisations and not least on the collective psychology of the Danes.

Even after more than 30 years of EU membership, the image of the Danish welfare-state as a unique, greatly superior way of organising the society still plays a dominant role in the public debate. Following this line of reasoning, the general Danish perception on the EEC/EU originally was considered to be a pragmatic, intergovernmental cooperation on specific areas of economic interest. This perception also has had and still has a major impact on the Danish institutional adaptations to the EEC/EU-membership.

However, over the last few decades – especially since the introduction of the Single European Act in 1986 – it has been generally acknowledged that the traditional understanding of EU policy as foreign policy is not valid anymore. Formally, it cannot be characterised as domestic policy, but it is obvious that EU-policies have more and more direct impact on national legislation in the Member States. This development has also been described as a move towards a 'normalisation' of EU-policies, which has put key institutions in Denmark under a constant pressure to adapt to a new political environment.[4]

It therefore becomes relevant to ask: to what extent has this development been reflected in the Danish institutional system dealing with EU-policies – on the governmental level as well as on the parliamentary level?

The rest of this chapter will address that question in the following way. Firstly, I will briefly present the Danish parliamentary system. The long tradition of minority governments and the institutionalised consensus-building in the Parliament – and in the society as such, including tripartite talks on the

---

3 Østergaard (2000) 170-171.

4 Mouritzen (1997); Riis & Zepernick (2001).

labour market – has been decisive for the institutionalised treatment of EU-policy in Denmark.

Secondly, I will go through the formal Danish EU-decision making procedure and present the relevant players/institutions within the Government and the Parliament. I will also briefly touch upon the Danish tradition for having referendums on EU-issues, which can be described as an element of direct democracy in Denmark's way of dealing with treaty amendments and other major EU-issues.

Thirdly, I will describe and discuss the parliamentary control as it takes place in the parliamentary committees including the European Affairs Committee as well as the sector committees. Also discussed will be issues important for a democratic treatment of EU-policies like an early involvement of the parliament, a high degree of openness and the mandating procedure in the European Affairs Committee.

Finally, I will discuss to what extent the institutionalisation of the treatment of EU-issues in the Danish Parliament reflects the widely recognized fact that EU-policies have a major impact on national legislation. Is there a move towards a "normalisation" of EU-issues – including a systematic involvement of the Parliament – and to what extent is the Parliament facing the European challenge with an offensive attitude?

2 Constitutional Background of the Danish Scrutiny System

2.1 The Danish Parliamentary System

The Danish Parliament (*Folketinget*) has since 1953 been a unicameral institution. It consists of 179 members and the electoral system is based on the following two main principles:

1) the election shall be by proportional representation to secure equal representation of different opinions in the electorate;
2) when determining the number of seats to be allotted to localities attention must be paid to the number of inhabitants, the number of electors and the population density.

The minimum percentage of votes required for representation is 2 per cent of the votes. In practice these norms allows a relatively high number access to the Parliament. Furthermore, the electoral system makes it hard for a single party to get a majority in the parliament. Therefore the Danish governments usually are coalitions between two or more parties – as a matter of fact, they are usually minority-coalitions. Since Denmark joined the EEC back in 1973, there has been only one majority coalition. It consisted of four parties (Social Democrats, Social Liberals, Centre Democrats and Christian Democrats). It lasted for only one year

(1993-1994) because the Christian Democrats did not get enough votes to secure its representation at the election in 1994.

2.2 The Danish Constitution on Foreign Policy, Referendums and Transfer of Sovereignty

The Danish Constitution does not lay down any specific parliamentary body or any detailed procedures as to how to deal with EU-affairs. When it comes to foreign policy – including the EU's Common Foreign and Security Policy – the Government is bound by the Constitution to consult the Foreign Policy Committee of the Parliament before making any decision of major importance to foreign policy. Paragraph 20 in the Constitution states:

> '1. Powers vested in the authorities of the Realm under this Constitutional Act may, to such extent as shall be provided by statute, be delegated to international authorities set up my mutual agreement with other states for the promotion of international rules of law and cooperation.
> 2. The enactment of a Bill dealing with the above, a majority of five-sixths of the members of the Folketing shall be required. If this majority is not obtained, whereas the majority required for the passing of ordinary Bills is obtained, and if the Government maintains it, the Bill shall be submitted to the electorate for approval or rejection in accordance with the rules for referenda laid down in section 42.'

The use of referenda on EU issues has either been based upon provisions in the Constitutional Act or upon political considerations, which has led to a law on a consultative referendum. To transfer sovereignty to supranational institutions, the Constitution requires either a majority of five-sixths in the Parliament or approval by the electorate in a referendum. But even though not all EU Treaty amendments have implied transfer of sovereignty (*e.g.* the Amsterdam Treaty) the Government has chosen (for political reasons) to call a referendum on the proposal for a treaty amendment.

2.3 The Legal Basis of the Mandate System

Ever since Denmark first considered joining the European Economic Community, there has been a political emphasis to ensure that the Danish Parliament has control over the Government's EU-policy. The institutionalisation of the parliamentary control dates back to 1961, when the Parliament appointed an ad hoc committee – the Market Negotiation Committee – to monitor the negotiations concerning Denmark's accession to the EEC. The Committee considered the Bill on Denmark's accession to the EEC, which was passed after a supportive referendum on 2 October 1972 leading to Danish membership of the EEC from the 1 January 1973.

As a result of the Danish Accession Act of 1972, a permanent parliamentary Market Committee was established. The Government became obliged to inform the Committee of EC decisions that would be directly applicable in Denmark or required the action of the Parliament (the Folketing). The Accession Act of 1972 (section 6 (subsection 2)) reads:

> 'The Government informs a Committee set up by the Folketing about proposals for Council decisions which become directly applicable in Denmark, or the fulfilling of which requires the approval of the Folketing.'

The decisive provisions which lays down the competence of the Committee is however to be found in the very first report of the EEC-Committee of 29 March 1973, which reads:

> 'The Government shall consult the Market Committee of the Folketing in questions relating to EC policy of a major importance so that the regard for the influence of the Folketing as well as the freedom to negotiate are respected.
>
> Prior to negotiations in the EC Council of Ministers on decisions of a wider scope, the Government submits an oral mandate for negotiation to the Market Committee. If there is no majority against the mandate, the Government negotiates on this basis.'

Thereby the Danish scrutiny model right from the start was a 'mandate system' providing the Market Committee with a competence to act on behalf of the Danish Parliament as a whole and to adopt negotiation proposals, which were politically binding on the Danish Government.[5] The wording of the report: "if there is no majority against" is based on the principle of negative parliamentarism – contrary to legislation in the plenary, where a bill requires a majority of the votes to pass. Basically, the most important competence of the Committee still rests upon the provisions in the first report dating back to 1973.

The formal framework for the sector committees involvement in EU-issues is laid down in the Standing order of the *Folketing* and in the regularly reports adopted by the European Affairs Committee. In the recently revised standing order of the *Folketing* – which came into effect on 1 January 2005 – it is now stated that EU issues are an integrated part of the sector committees' area of responsibility.[6] Thereby it is officially recognised that EU-policies to a still higher extent influence domestic policies.

5 In the Third bi-annual Report from the COSAC-Secretariat (May 2005), a distinction is made between Document based scrutiny systems and mandating systems.

6 *The Standing Orders Committee shall make decisions on the committee's areas of responsibility, including EU-issues.* (The Standing Order of the Folketing, Section 7, subsection 2, (1 January 2005)).

3 The Danish Decision-making Process with regard to European Affairs

3.1 The National Decision-making Process – In Brief

The mandate procedure in the European Affairs Committee (EAC) usually takes place at a rather late stage in the negotiation of a concrete proposal for EU-legislation. Before the Government presents a negotiation proposal in the EAC a long, very systematic, inter-ministerial coordination-process has taken place within the Government led by the Ministry of Foreign Affairs. In this section, I will give a brief introduction to the decision-making process in the Government before the European Affairs Committee is actively involved.

The first important step in the Danish decision-making procedure takes place in one of the EU-Special Committees (EU-*Specialudvalg*). The number of committees has risen significantly from 19 back in 1973 to 33 in 2005. The EU-Special Committees are chaired by a civil servant from the relevant ministerial department and their main task is to coordinate the viewpoints of the involved ministries concerning a single proposal or policy, for instance internal market, environment, agriculture etc. Also, representatives from regional and local authorities are usually represented in these committees as well as representatives from the relevant branch- and trade organisations, labour organisations and other interest groups.

In some of the larger EU-Special Committees like 'Environment' or 'Growth and Competition,' more than 50 members (including ministries, interest groups etc.) are represented while some of the smaller EU-Special Committees like 'Shipping' or 'Culture' have less than ten members. A representative from the Ministry of Foreign Affairs is represented in all the EU-Special Committees. Even though the work of the Committees originally was thought to be of a specific and technical nature, they also include strong political elements.[7] The presence of a high level of expertise provides the EU-Special Committees with a solid basis for the first important formulation of the Danish position. Usually it is the chairman and the secretariat in the relevant ministry who formulate the first draft of the Danish position and who coaches it through the process.

The next step in the process is the EU-Committee (*EU-Udvalget*). It consists of civil servants from the 10-12 ministries most engaged with EU-issues. Other ministries can be called on an ad-hoc basis. The EU-Committee is chaired by a higher civil servant from the Ministry of Foreign Affairs. The EU-Committee meets every Tuesday, and their main function is to coordinate the recommendations coming from the EU Special Committees to ensure there is a single, consistent Danish position on every EU-proposal before a decision has to be taken in the Council.

Questions requiring a political decision are forwarded to the Government's Foreign Political Committee who determines the Government's final nego-

7 Von Dosenrode (2000) 388.

tiation position. The committee exists in two different formations: The one formation consists of the Prime Minister, the Minister of Foreign Affairs and those ministers most engaged in EU-questions. It deals with issues related to the EC-treaty (pillar 1, including the single market, etc.). The second formation deals with the Common Foreign and Security Policy of the EU (pillar 2) and the police cooperation (pillar 3). Both of these formations are chaired by the Minister of Foreign Affairs.

Figure 1. *Graphic illustration of the Danish EU decision-making procedure*

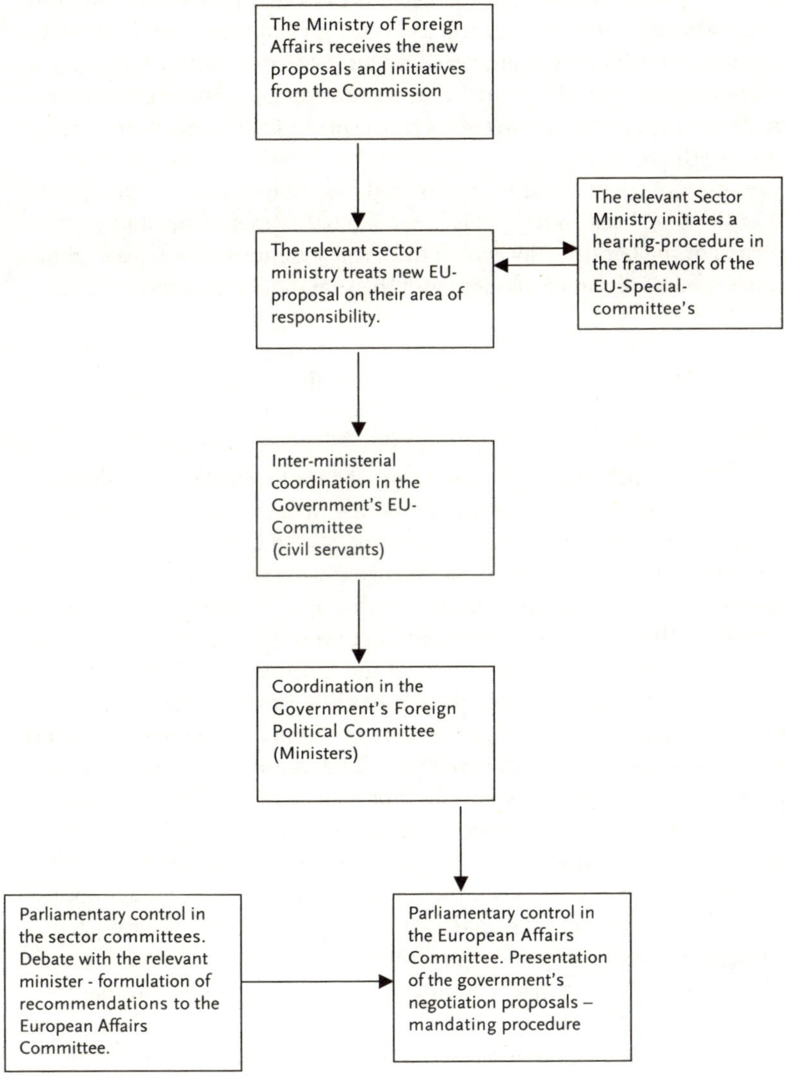

When the position of Danish Government has been confirmed in the Foreign Political Committee, the next step involves the EAC of the Parliament. At this level a long, time-consuming coordination process has taken place – formally without involving the parliamentary level.

On the one hand, it can be argued that this thoroughly inter-ministerial coordination process leaves the EAC with only a limited room of manoeuvre unless they are prepared to obstruct the negotiation position of the Government. On the other hand, one has to emphasise that the Government right from the beginning of the process is aware of the necessity of obtaining a mandate from the EAC. Thereby the Committee exerts a certain invisible, informal influence during the process without being involved directly. In some political sensitive cases, it is not unusual that the minister in an early stage in the process makes an informal call to the EU-spokespersons from some of the opposition parties to facilitate a smooth process.

As a passing remark, it could be mentioned that Denmark, since it became a member of the EEC back in 1973, has been one of the most rule-abiding Member States of the community, which to a large extent can be explained by the early involvement of the Parliament and the mandating procedure in the EAC.

3.2 How does the Government obtain a Mandate for Negotiation?

In practice the mandating procedure takes place as follows. When a minister – on behalf of the Government – presents a negotiation proposal at a meeting in the EAC, one or more rounds of questions (from the Committee-members) and answers (from the minister) take place. At the end of the discussions, no formal vote is held, but the chairman concludes whether there is a majority against the Government's negotiation proposal or not.

Politically the composition of members of the Committee reflects the composition of the Parliament. Since 1973, it has been common practice for the Chairman of the Committee to count the votes based upon the members political statements expressed during the meetings. The members of the individual parties carry a voting weight reflecting their party's number of seats in the Parliament. It is obvious that this procedure depends heavily on the strong tradition of "party-discipline" among parties in the Danish Parliament. If a party is not represented at a particular meeting, or if a member is present without taking part in the discussions, the chairman assumes that the relevant party supports the government's negotiation proposal.

The EAC rarely refuses to give a mandate, but this does not mean that the Committee has little influence on the government's EU-policy. Firstly, it is not uncommon for the government to change or modify its original negotiation proposal as a consequence of the discussions in the Committee. Secondly, the civil servants in the Government – who take part in the negotiations at an early stage in Brussels as well as in Copenhagen – continuously have to bear in mind that the negotiation result in the end needs approval by the EAC.

3.3 Referendums on EU-matters – Direct Democracy in Practice

It has been argued that Denmark has two political systems with regard to EU-matters. On the one hand, a representative, parliamentary democracy with respect to on-going legislation, on the other, a direct democracy in connection with EU-matters affecting Denmark's constitutional relations with the EU.[8] Today it seems unlikely that any Danish Government would refrain from calling a referendum on a new treaty amendment. Actually the present government had called for a referendum on the constitutional treaty to be held the 27 September 2005 – but the referendum was being postponed due to the No-votes in France and the Netherlands, which has been followed by the so called 'time for reflection' in the EU.

Experiences from the former referendums show that they on the one hand stimulate the debate on EU and thereby increase the knowledge on EU among the citizens. On the other hand, the debate very often tend to focus upon the basic question of whether people are in favour of Danish membership or not. That makes it almost impossible to give an exact interpretation of the results of the referendums – especially when the result turns out to be a 'no'.

When a majority of the electorate voted no to the Maastricht Treaty in 1992, it was up to the political parties to make the interpretation, which resulted in the Danish opt-outs in four areas. These concern the third phase of the EMU, defence policy, Justice and Home Affairs cooperation on the supra-national level and finally citizenship of the Union. The Danish electorate has been given the promise by every Government since 1993 that the opt-outs form a part of the Danish EU-policy and that they can only be removed as a result of a referendum. In 2000, a majority of the electorate voted against the removal of the opt-out concerning Denmark's participation in the third phase of the EMU even though an overwhelming majority in the Parliament supported a Yes to full Danish participation in the EMU.

While some support the direct involvement of the electorate in referendums on major EU-issues, it can also be argued that the referendums basically suspend the representative democracy, which usually is being considered as the basic democratic foundation in most European political systems. Furthermore, the referendums on EU-issues to a certain extent have contributed to the unfortunate perception of EU-policy as something distinct from domestic policy – a perception which runs counter to the efforts made in the Parliament to integrate EU-policies into the daily political work.

---

8 Laursen (2001) 8.

Table no. 1. *Danish Referenda on EC/EU questions*

Topic of Referendum	Date	Participation%	Yes votes%	No votes%
Danish EC-membership	2 Oct 1972	90.1	63.4	36.6
The Single European Act	17 Feb 1986	75.4	56.2	43.8
The Maastricht Treaty	2 June 1992	83.1	49.3	50.7
The Edinburgh Agreement	18 May 1993	86.5	56.7	43.3
The Amsterdam Treaty	28 May 1998	76.2	55.1	44.9
Adherence to the Euro	28 Sept 2000	87.6	46.8	53.2

Source: EU-Information Centre of the Danish Parliament, www.euo.dk.

4 The Parliament's Treatment of EU-issues

4.1 Early Treatment of EU-issues in the EAC and in the Sector Committees

A thorough parliamentary treatment of EU-issues presupposes a close, continuous cooperation between the EAC and the sector committees. Although a systematic involvement of the sector committees is not formally required, the overwhelming majority of the more than twenty sector committees in Parliament today deal with EU issues in one way or another.

The most important task for the sector committees is to carry out the first reading of the main legislative proposals of the Commission. Thereby the parliamentary scrutiny process benefits from the technical and professional expertise being present in the sector committees. To foster early treatment, the EAC – supported by the EU-Secretariat in the Parliament – goes through the Commission's yearly working program and picks out some of the most important new future proposals, and as soon as they have been made public, the proposals are distributed to the relevant sector committees for early treatment. After having discussed the new proposals from the Commission, the sector committees in some cases draw up a report or a written recommendation and send it to the EAC. These recommendations serve as useful guidelines for the EAC before the mandating procedure takes place at a later stage in the EAC.

Furthermore, most of the sector committees tend to consult ministers in the week before Council meetings. This may lead to a written recommendation from the relevant sector committee to the European Affairs Committee, which is very useful, notably in cases where the Government asks for a negotiation mandate. However, the fundamental problem remains: treating EU-issues at this stage does not give the opportunity to exercise any significant influence on the proposals from the Commission. Therefore, the sector committees need to systematically carry out substantial and political treatment of new proposals from the Commission as early as possible – at the latest, immediately after the proposals have been made public.

The need for early involvement of sector committees is even more pressing due to the fact that a growing number of EU proposals are passed already after the first reading in the European Parliament.[9] The Folketing and other national parliaments are thereby put under considerable pressure. The second circumstance is related to the presently unknown destiny of the Constitutional Treaty. The new treaty introduces a procedure for the subsidiarity check in the national parliaments as described in the following.

4.2 The Subsidiarity Check

While the EAC coordinates the monitoring of the principle of subsidiarity, it is the task of the sector committees to make the first evaluation of whether a proposal conflicts with the principle of subsidiarity. All important new proposals are immediately sent to the relevant sector committee by the EAC. The recently adopted report from the EAC proposes a detailed procedure with strict dead-lines to facilitate a quick parliamentary treatment of the most important new proposals. This procedure was agreed upon in late 2004 and was (see Appendix 1) made to comply with the Protocol on the application of the principle of subsidiarity and proportionality annexed to the constitutional treaty.[10]

The present uncertain future of the constitutional treaty has not diminished the need for the sector committees to discuss new proposals and their compliance with the principle of subsidiarity. In practice, the standstill of the ratification process has resulted in a more pragmatic implementation of the detailed procedure adopted by the EAC on the treatment of the principle of the subsidiarity – especially when it comes to the very short deadlines. Anyhow it should be emphasised that the relevant provisions in the constitutional treaty have had a significant effect on the still more substantial and political involvement of the sector committees in EU-matters. The still more systematic involvement of the sector committees seems relatively unaffected by the uncertain destiny of the constitutional treaty. It could be said that the EAC has used the draft constitutional treaty as a stepping stone to a further strengthening of the parliamentary control on EU-matters in the negotiations with the government.

---

9 In a report on reforming the Folketing's treatment of EU issues, it is estimated that up to 30-40 per cent of all proposals are passed at this early stage.

10 The protocol states: "Any national Parliament or any chamber of a national Parliament of a Member State may, within six week from the date of transmission of the Commission's legislative proposal, send to the Presidents of the European Parliament, the Council of Ministers and the Commission a reasoned opinion stating why it considers the proposal in question does not comply with the principle of subsidiarity."

4.3 Systematic Treatment of Green and White Papers

Green and White Papers and other hearing documents from the Commission (Communications, reports, etc.) are being dealt with by the EAC and the relevant sector committees in cooperation. Shortly after the Commission has published a hearing document, it is being put on the agenda at a meeting in the EAC. At the meeting committee, members discuss whether the document should be handled by the EAC, or whether it should be sent to the relevant sector committee(s) with a request that it should be handled there. When the answer from the sector committee(s) becomes available, the matter is again put on the agenda at a meeting in the EAC for the purpose of making a final decision as to whether a statement on the issues submitted for consultation should be issued, and how the matter should be treated in advance of this – *e.g.* sent for a hearing or a conference, a consultation with the minister responsible, a debate with questions or other treatment.

This procedure results usually in a parliamentary reply from the Danish Parliament – coordinated by EAC – to the European Commission on the hearing documents. In some cases, these replies contain a minority statement due to political divergences within the committees. The involvement of the parliamentary committees in the treatment of hearing documents implies that the Commission very often receives two official hearing replies from Denmark: one from the government and one from the Danish parliament.

4.4 Openness in the European Affairs Committee

Over the years, the question of openness in the treatment of EU issues in the *Folketing* has drawn a great deal of attention, also from the EAC itself. In its report of 10 December 2004, the committee stated: 'It is, and always has been, the wish of the European Affairs Committee to ensure the greatest possible degree of openness regarding its work. In general, a high degree of openness helps to improve the opportunities for control on the part of the public and the press, at the same time as it increases the public's general insight into EU issues. Openness is also a decisive precondition for a broader democratic debate, which will give EU issues a more prominent place on the political agenda in the social debate in Denmark'.

At the same time, the EAC recognises that the special nature of EU issues necessitates a certain degree of confidence in relation to the government. It is not in the interests of the EAC to limit the government's opportunities to achieve the best result for Denmark at the negotiations in the Council of Ministers. In this sense, the following in the first report of the EAC (1973) still applies: 'The Government shall consult the EAC of the Folketing on questions relating to the EU-policy of a major importance so that the regard for the influence of the Folketing as well as the freedom to negotiate are respected'.

The ordinary meetings in the EAC were originally closed for the public but since 1 October 2006 meetings as a starting point have been open for the public. It was a decision taken in common by the Committee and the government in June 2006 to further strengthen the openness and transparency of the work of the Committee.[11] It should be emphasised though that meetings can be closed in specific cases when detailed questions on, for instance, the government's negotiation positions and other confidential issues are being discussed. The decision to close a meeting has to be taken in common by the Committee and the Government. Practice has until now shown that meetings have been closed in only very few cases. Minutes of the open part of the Committee meetings are distributed to the members of the Committee and furthermore made public on the internet.

It is still too early to evaluate the consequences of the relatively new decision to make meetings open for the public. The openness and transparency of the Committee will be further increased in 2007, when the technical facilities necessary for television broadcasting has been set up.

Efforts to enhance openness and transparency in the Danish EU decision-making process cannot solely depend upon procedures and working methods related to the EAC. The need for openness must be assessed on an ongoing basis, not least in the light of the dynamic of European developments, which have to a great extent erased the distinction between foreign and domestic policy. Important steps towards broadening the EU-debate in the public sphere have been taken by a more frequent and systematic involvement of the Folketing's sector committees. This can be seen as a way of normalising EU-policy, and thereby slowly changing the widespread perception of EU-policy as a very complicated, purely technical area.[12]

4.5 Cooperation with Members of the European Parliament

Until 2004, cooperation between the EAC and Danish members of the European Parliament remained limited to individual joint meetings and other ad hoc activities. But since the spring 2005, the cooperation between representatives from the two different parliaments has been organised in a more systematic framework. The purpose of the joint meetings – held approximately once a month – is to give the Danish MEPs a good impression of viewpoints in the national Danish debate on specific topics and, at the same time, provide the members of the EAC with a valuable insight in the work and the decision making process in the European Parliament.

---

11 Report of the European Affairs Committe, 23 June 2006.

12 In a report on the Folketing's treatment of EU-issues (Dec. 2004) the EAC stresses the need for more parliamentary debate. Every six months there will be a debate with questions on the current Presidency programme and once a year there will be a debate on the Commission's legislative and working programme and on the Council's multi-annual strategic programme.

5 Conclusion and Future Perspectives

Member States have encountered the EU differently. In 'External Danger and Democracy' (1997) Hans Mouritzen distinguishes two diametrically opposite national strategies: a defensive strategy and an offensive one.[13] The defensive strategy stresses the necessity of mobilizing self-control in the face of the EU challenge to national autonomy. National subunits – including governmental agencies, regional/local authorities, interest groups etc. – consult each other with the purpose of ending up with one common national position before the Government takes part in the negotiations

in the Council. The process is characterised by a high level of secrecy and a lack of public debate and parliamentary involvement. But this democratic deficit is considered to be a price worth paying in the name of national compromise.

By contrast, the offensive strategy is based on the assumption that national self-control has been undermined by the EU, making it pointless to spend time and resources to do something about it. As a matter of fact, national sub-interests are so divergent that compromises often look like the lowest common denominator. Trying to speak with one voice could even hamper initiative. Instead, time and resources should be used to exploit the low EU self-control.

In scheme: Table no.2. *Two national strategies towards europeanisation*[14]

The Defensive strategy	The Offensive strategy
1) Denmark shall speak with one, unambiguous voice in the EU (the Council)	1) The reality consists of many different – at times contradictory – interests
2) Interdepartmental coordination – consultations take place between national and local authorities, interest groups, trade organisations, experts, etc.	2) Coordination is waste of time and resources. Open conflicts and management of interests are preferable.
3) Confidentiality among Danish players to protect and/or strengthen the Danish negotiation position	3) Open confrontations means a high level of transparency.
4) The relevant arena: Denmark	4) The relevant arena: Europe.
5) Characterised by a relatively strong Ministry of Foreign Affairs on the administrative level	5) Characterised by relatively strong sector ministries on the administrative level
6) and a relatively strong European Affairs Committee on the political-parliamentary level.	6) and by relatively strong sector committees on the political-parliamentary level.

13 Mouritzen (1997) 101. The distinction between the defensive and the offensive strategies in this chapter is based upon Mouritzens *External Danger and Democracy* (1997).

14 *Europeanisation* (def.): 'The incremental process of reorienting the shape of politics to the degree that EU political and economic dynamics become integral parts of the organisational logic of national politics and policy-making'. Maurer (2001) 36.

When Denmark joined back in 1973, the EEC was basically considered as a pragmatic, intergovernmental cooperation. As a consequence, the general Danish attitude towards the EU has been based upon the values and assumptions formed by the defensive strategy. Today EU-policies are much more far reaching and cover a greater variety of policy-issues than back in the early 70s. As in most Member States, this development has led to the institutionalisation of certain procedures in the Danish Parliament. Let me just briefly emphasise the involvement of the sector committees on EU-matters, more open debates in Parliament on major EU-issues and action programmes and lately a stronger, well organised cooperation between the members of the EAC and the Danish members of the European Parliament.

However, the institutional adaptations have been very pragmatic and have not fundamentally challenged the defensive approach towards the EU. The defensive strategy has only to a certain extent been replaced by a more offensive strategy based upon values well known from the domestic arena. Today, the Danish Government still spends a lot of resources on coordination among players on the domestic arena to secure that Denmark speaks with one, united and coherent voice in the Council. Even though the sector specific policies on a day to day basis are managed by the sector ministries, the institutional structure of the decision-making procedure still provides the Ministry of Foreign Affairs with the overall coordinating function. On the parliamentary level, it is still the European Affairs Committee who provides the Government with the necessary negotiating mandates before the decisive meetings in the Council.

In this article, it has been demonstrated that EU-policies today are being treated by a great number of players within the governmental bodies and within Parliament. In Parliament the sector committees today play an active role in the parliamentary control of the Government's EU-policy, but it is still the EAC who coordinates and provides the Government with the relevant negotiation mandates on behalf of the Parliament as such. With an eye on the offensive line of thought, there still seems to be some way to go before EU-policies will become a fully integrated part of the domestically arena in Denmark. A complete integration of EU-matters into domestic policies would include a further strengthening of the role of the sector committees.

Following the offensive strategy, the EAC would ultimately have to hand over its mandating power to the sector committees. However, this development is not very likely within the foreseeable future even though it would give the sector committees a very strong incentive to become more involved with EU-matters. But one has to recognise the fact that a great majority of the political parties supports the present system where the mandating procedure takes place in the EAC. A strong argument for not providing the sector committees with the mandating power is that it would mean the loss of an overall parliamentary control and coordination. Providing the sector committees with the mandating power would probably lead to a loss of a coordinated, coherent parliamentary viewpoint, but it could possibly be counterbalanced by a faster, more influential, less time-consuming and more open decision-making process.

But then, what would be left for the EAC? The Committee would obviously be less involved in day-to-day businesses than as today. One could argue that the EAC should concentrate on the major institutional issues, like treaty amendments, rounds of enlargements and other major cross-sectoral issues. Secondly, the Committee could have a mediating, coordinating function within the Danish Parliament concerning certain inter-disciplinary issues (for instance, Trans European Networks, Galileo, a future European Energy Policy, the financial framework, etc.) involving two or more sector committees.

Finally, the EAC could – at least in a transitional period, on a more general level – monitor the stream of information from the Government to the parliamentary committees to make sure it live up to the common agreements made between the Government and the EAC. The overall purpose of course would be to ensure the best possible parliamentary control and to ensure a high level of democratic legitimacy in the national EU decision making process.

References

H. Branner and M. Kelstrup (eds.), *Denmark's policy towards Europe after 1945 – History, Theory and Options* (Odense: Odense UP, 2000).

S.Z. von Dosenrode, "Danish EU-Policy Making", in Branner & Kelstrup (2000) 381-402.

H. Jensen, *Europaudvalget – Et udvalg i Folketinget* (Aarhus: Universitetsforlag, 2003).

F. Laursen, *The European Affairs Committee of the Danish Folketing – "Mini-Parliamentarism" in Operation*, Working Paper No 1/2001, Centre for European Studies, University of Southern Denmark.

A. Maurer, W. Wessels (eds.), *National Parliaments on their Ways to Europe: Losers or Latecomers?* (Baden-Baden: Nomos Verlagsgesellschaft, 2001).

H. Mouritzen, *External Danger and Democracy – Old Nordic Lessons and New European Challenges* (Dartmouth: 1997).

P. Riis & D. Zepernick, "EU: En udfordring til dansk politik", *politica, tidsskrift for politisk videnskab* 3 (2001) 287-309.

U. Østergaard, "Danish National Identity: Between Multinational Heritage and Small State Nationalism", in Branner & Kelstrup (2000) 139-184.

Reports and other Documents

Danmarks Grundlov (The Constitutional Act of Denmark) rev. 1953

http://www.ft.dk (choose between Danish or English language-versions)

Forretningsorden for Folketinget (Standing Orders of the Folketing), rev. February 2005

http://www.ft.dk (choose between Danish or English language-versions)

Report on reforming the Folketings's treatment of EU issues (- the inclusion of sector committees, – controlling the principle of subsidiarity, – a better basis for decisions, – openness), Report issued by the European Affairs Committee, 10 December 2004

http://www.euo.dk (choose between Danish or English language-versions)

Collection of Reports issued by the Market Committee and the European Affairs Committee in the period 1973 – 2001, The Danish Parliament Folketinget.

http://www.euo.dk (choose between Danish or English language-versions)

Developments in the European Union – Procedures and Practices Relevant to Parliamentary Scrutiny (third bi-annual Report), 2005, the COSAC-Secretariat, Bruxelles.

http://www.cosac.org (choose between English or French language-versions)

Appendix 1. *Model for treating the principle of subsidiarity in the sector committees and in the European Affairs Committee*

Step	Procedure	
(1)	The Commission introduces a proposal for a legislative act.	
(2)	No later than two weeks after the proposal has been forwarded	The Government prepares and forwards a preliminary subsidiarity memorandum within two weeks to the European Affairs Committee and the relevant sector committee(s). The EU Secretariat sends the subsidiarity memorandum and the accompanying proposal for an electronic hearing on the EU information website. The European Affairs Committee considers the proposal and sends relevant suggestions for a hearing in the sector committee(s) in question. The relevant sector committee(s) are informed of any issues submitted for consultation electronically.
(3)	No later than four weeks after the introduction of the proposal	The Government has forwarded a basic memorandum to the sector committees and to the European Affairs Committee. The Government's assessment of the degree to which the principle of subsidiarity has been complied with is incorporated into the basic memorandum. The sector committees have considered the proposal and possibly prepared and forwarded a statement to the European Affairs Committee. COSAC[1] is informed if the sector committees feel that there are problems in relation to the principle of subsidiarity.
(4)	No later than six weeks after the introduction of the proposal	The European Affairs Committee assesses the compliance of the proposal with the principle of subsidiarity on the basis of the statement from the sector committees, the Government's basic memorandum, including the subsidiarity memorandum, any statements on issues submitted for consultation electronically, and any remarks from other Parliaments and /or COSAC. A joint meeting will be convened in cases of discrepancies between the statement from the sector committees and the attitude of the European Affairs Committee. The European Affairs Committee's recommendation is signed by the chairperson of the European Affairs Committees and/or countersigned by the Speaker of the Folketing. The recommendation is sent to the Government, the Commission, the Council, and the European Parliament, as well as to the other national parliaments in the EU (COSAC).

1 COSAC (The Conference of Community and European Affairs Committees of Parliament of the European Union) is a interparliamentary cooperation between committees of the national parliaments dealing with European affairs and representatives from the European Parliament.

CHAPTER 10

Parliamentary Control of EU Decision-making in the Czech Republic

Lenka Pítrová and Martina Coxová

1 Introduction[1]

It is clear that the increasingly complex institutional and procedural labyrinth of the EU is less and less comprehensible to ordinary citizens. Transparency, democracy, solidarity and subsidiarity should be the pillars of the bridge spanning the gap between the EU and its citizens and thus enhance its legitimacy. Strengthening the influence of national parliaments in the formulation of Member State governments' positions – a trend which can already be observed in the EU[2] – is just one of the means of developing the democratic dimension of the EU. It is in the interest of both the Government and the Parliament to maximize their cooperation as a means of achieving a political consensus.

The aim of this contribution is to present the development of the Czech model of parliamentary control of European affairs, the constitutional and legal basis for this model, as well as to illustrate the issues and difficulties that have been encountered in practice. Although the Czech Republic's relatively short experience to date with EU membership does not allow an entirely objective assessment of the functioning of this model, this new form of parliamentary control is trans-national in scope. A comparative advantage of the Czech model of parliamentary control of European affairs is that the Czech Republic was able to draw on the experiences of the other parliaments in Member States and this contribution refers to certain such aspects.

2 The General Idea of the Czech Scrutiny System

During the deliberations of the 'Euro-amendments' of the rules of procedure of the Chamber of Deputies and of the Senate, political and expert debates were held on the character and nature of this control mechanism. The prolonged deliberation of both legislative proposals in Parliament demonstrates how difficult it was to achieve a relationship between the Government and the Parliament with respect to European affairs. In general, the controlling powers of the Czech parliament are mostly concentrated in the Chamber of Deputies. With regard to European scrutiny, however, it was decided that the corresponding competences belong to both chambers of Parliament. The underlying logic is that both chambers participate in the legislative process and the subsequent transposition of legislative acts adopted at the EU level into national law.

---

1 Excerpts of this contribution have previously appeared in the publication "Parliamentary Scrutiny of EU Affairs in the Chamber of Deputies of the Czech Parliament," published by the Office of the Chamber of Deputies of the Parliament of the Czech Republic.

2 The increasing efforts to actively involve national parliaments in the scrutiny of the legislative procedure at the EU level may also be seen in the establishment of minimum standards of parliamentary scrutiny as provided for in the Copenhagen parliamentary directives that were adopted at a meeting of the Conference of European Affairs Committees (COSAC).

Nevertheless, this controlling power varies and has different consequences in both chambers. While in the case of the Chamber of Deputies, the Government is obligated to take into account its positions and to reflect these in its negotiations in EU bodies and thus, *de lege ferenda*, this relationship may be perceived as an imperative mandate, this is not the case in the Senate. The stronger control function of the Chamber of Deputies may also be illustrated by the obligation of the members of Government and the Prime Minister to attend the meetings of the relevant Committee of the Chamber of Deputies on its request, which also often occurs in practice. In contrast, the Senate Rules of Procedure only provide for the attendance of '*representatives*' of the members of Government and not the actual members of the Government themselves.[3]

If a joint European affairs committee were to be established as provided for under Article 10b of the Constitution, then it would effectively lead to a further strengthening of the Senate's position with respect to the Government and a weakening of the Chamber of Deputies' position. This is also one of the reasons why it will be difficult to find the necessary political support for such a measure. Given the different political composition of both chambers and the fact that deputies are elected on the basis of proportional representation whereas senators are elected on the basis of majority vote, the question remains as to how it would be possible to reflect and combine the different composition of both chambers in such a joint committee.

3 Constitutional Norms Governing Parliamentary Control

3.1 The 'Euro-amendment' to the Czech Constitution

In the Czech Republic, the model of parliamentary control is based on the following: constitutional norms, statutory regulations in the form of the rules of procedures of both chambers of Parliament, Government resolutions and parliamentary practice and usage. In late autumn 2001, the Czech Parliament approved a 'Euro-amendment' to the Czech Constitution that came into effect on 1 June 2002.[4] This constitutional amendment made the legislative changes necessary in order for the Czech Republic to comply with the obligations and exercise the rights of membership in the European Union. Moreover, it provided for the future ratification of the fundamental treaties upon which the European Union is built. In addition, it incorporated the principles of the relationship between Czech law and the distinctive system of European law, the relationship between national and Community 'constitutional' bodies in the

---

3 Article 119f (1) SRP.

4 Constitutional Act No. 395/2001 Coll., of 18 October 2001, amending the Constitutional Act of the Czech National Council No. 1/1993 Coll., (the Constitution of the Czech Republic), as amended. The draft constitutional law was adopted by the Chamber of Deputies on 3 July 2001, by the Senate on 19 October 2001 and it was signed by the President on 30 October 2001.

Czech constitutional legal order and finally, last but not least, the parliamentary control of EU affairs.

The newly formulated Article 10b of the Constitution reflects a political will for the greater involvement of the national Parliament in Community lawmaking and in EU affairs following accession. This provision is clearly inspired by the Protocol on the Role of the National Parliaments in the European Union that forms a part of the Amsterdam Treaty:

> '1) The Government shall inform the Parliament regularly and in advance of issues related to obligations arising from the Czech Republic's membership in an international organisation or institution provided for in Article 10a.
> 2) The chambers of Parliament shall express their views on the decisions in preparation of such international organisations or institutions in accordance with their rules of procedure.
> 3) An act governing the principles of dealings and relations between both chambers as well as externally may entrust the exercise of the chambers' competence pursuant to paragraph 2 to a joint body of both chambers.'

The mechanism of exerting parliamentary influence and scrutiny is based upon the duly and timely supply of information and documents. Even though the wording is quite general and refers to the Czech Republic's membership in any international organization or institution to which certain sovereign powers of the Czech Republic have been delegated pursuant to Article 10a of the Constitution, the legislator had intended to create a special method of providing information regarding the EU. As a result, the Government has a special duty to inform, which coexists with those general duties to inform commonly found in relations between the Government and the Parliament in all parliamentary democracies.

The general formulation of this provision also allows the Parliament (provided there is sufficient political will) to exert control and influence in the 'virgin territory' under the second and third EU pillars in which parliamentary involvement is mainly restricted to consultations and *ex post* information.[5] This provision may be compared with the form of parliamentary control provided for under Article 88-4 of the French Constitution. It does not, however, go so far as to give the Parliament the power to mandate ministers (as is the case in Denmark). Nevertheless, this does not mean that the role of the national parliament could not be subsequently further strengthened in the provisions of the rules of procedure or in the act on the principles of dealings and relations between both chambers, which is provided for under the Constitution.

The possibility of establishing a joint body of both chambers that would deal specifically with European affairs has been left open which, in theory, could be in the form of a joint CEA. It should be noted that the existence of such committees is relatively rare in bicameral systems (*e.g.* Spain and Ireland), and the question remains as to whom such a body would be accountable. From a theoretical

[5] Craig & Harlow (1998) 209 et seq.

constitutional law perspective, this solution is controversial as the establishment of such a body would affect the different positions of both chambers in the parliamentary political system. Although both chambers are entrusted with legislative powers, the Chamber of Deputies' position is nevertheless stronger, given that it may override vetoes or amendments made by the Senate. Moreover, with respect to the executive branch, the Government is only accountable to the Chamber of Deputies. In addition, the realization of this model is contingent upon the adoption of the act governing the dealings and relations between both chambers of Parliament, which is unlikely to happen at the moment. This provision therefore remains in practice unfulfilled. As a result, parliamentary control of European affairs is currently carried out independently by both chambers on the basis of the statutory procedural provisions provided for in their respective rules of procedure.

3.2 The 'Euro-amendments' to the Rules of Procedure of the Czech Parliament

The role of national parliaments is not a new theme, but one that has reoccurred repeatedly in discussions on the democratic deficit of the decision-making procedure and the predominance of the executive branch in the creation of EU legislative acts and documents.[6] In the Czech Republic, this discussion took place at two levels – first in relation to the drafting of the Euro-amendment of the rules of procedure of both chambers of the Czech Parliament, and secondly with respect to the drafting and deliberation of the Treaty Establishing a Constitution for Europe (hereafter 'constitutional treaty').

3.2.1 The Euro-amendment of the Rules of Procedure of the Chamber of Deputies

The amendment of the Rules of Procedure of the Chamber of Deputies came into effect on 7 May 2004. It governs the procedure for deliberating EU affairs and included the European agenda, in light of its importance, as one of the Chamber of Deputies' expressly enumerated roles.[7] The amendment was a joint initiative of deputies encompassing the broad political spectrum of parliamentary political parties.[8] At the same time, it was the result of several years of ongoing discussions in the Committee for European Integration of

6 Pítrová (2002); Georgiev (2002); Kysela (2000); Kysela (2001).

7 *Zákon č. 90/1995 Sb., o jednacím řádu Poslanecké sněmovny* (Act No. 90/1995 Coll., on the Rules of Procedure of the Chamber of Deputies, as subsequently amended, hereinafter "CDRP"). One of the powers of the Chamber of Deputies is to '*pass resolutions on the position to be taken regarding legislative proposals and documents of the European Communities and the European Union.*' (Art. 50(1) CDRP).

8 The draft amendment was initiated by Pavel Svoboda, Chairman of the Committee for European Integration, together with deputies Vladimír Laštůvka, Libor Rouček and Jaroslav Lobkowicz (Chamber of Deputies Document No. 337, IVth Election Period).

the Chamber of Deputies as to what the form of parliamentary control and the model of government-parliament relations in exercising this control should be, particularly with respect to the drafting of European legislation. These discussions were based largely on the experiences of the parliaments of existing Member States, which had shown that effective parliamentary control requires methodology, proper timing and attention to detail.[9]

The amendment to the Rules of Procedure turns the Committee for European Integration into a key player in the system of parliamentary control. At the same time, the Committee, which remains an obligatory standing committee of the Chamber of Deputies, was renamed as the 'Committee for European Affairs' (from here on: CEA).[10] The procedure introduced by the amendment covers the following three main areas:

1) the deliberation of European legislative proposals and documents submitted by the Government on the basis of its preliminary position;
2) the scrutiny of the Government prior to negotiations in the Council;
3) the deliberation of important nominations.

Deliberation of European legislative proposals and documents submitted by the Government on the basis of its preliminary position

Taking into account the experiences of other national parliaments, the common institutional model was selected. The Government fulfils its obligation to inform Parliament, as provided for under Article 10b of the Constitution and Article 109a(1) CDRP, by submitting European legislative proposals and documents to the Chamber of Deputies via the CEA. This procedure should enable the effective monitoring of the EU legislative procedure as well as the timely and continuous informing of the Chamber of Deputies and its bodies, particularly the respective committees.

In general, the principle applies that the CEA deliberates European legislative proposals and other documents without undue delay on the basis of the Government's preliminary position, which is usually in the form of a framework position. The Committee may at any time reopen discussion of a given matter based on developments in deliberations in EU institutions. Moreover, the Rules of Procedure also provide for the involvement of the other relevant standing committees. The CEA, as the guarantor of the monitoring and assessment of all European legislative proposals sent by the Government, may transmit such proposals to other standing committees and may at the same time set a time period for their deliberation. Setting a time period for deliberation is of importance as it aims to ensure that the committees take a position on the proposal prior to its final approval in EU institutions and so that they may influence the

[9] With respect to parliamentary scrutiny of the Government in the pre-accession phase, see: Zralá (2004).

[10] Article 32(1) CDRP. The Committee is comprised of 21 deputies proportionally representing all the political parties elected to the Chamber of Deputies. The Committee convenes regularly and its meetings are generally open to the public. The Committee has a subcommittee for regional and cross-border cooperation.

Government's position in its negotiations on a given proposal. The CEA or the respective standing committees takes its position on the proposal in the form of a resolution.

Given the extensive number of legislative proposals and documents presented each year, mostly by the European Commission (of which over 400 are legislative proposals), it may be expected that only with regard to politically important legislative proposals or documents will a given matter be included on the agenda of the plenary session. Otherwise the parliament would be overloaded and its control function paralysed. This is confirmed by the fact that plenary scrutiny happened only twice during the first year of the Czech Republic's membership in the EU.

To enable the CEA to do its job on behalf of the rest of the parliament, the Rules of Procedure provide for a 'legal fiction': a resolution of the Committee is deemed to represent the position of the Chamber of Deputies if the Committee resolution is not included on the agenda of the plenary session as outlined above or in accordance with Article 46(4)(c) CDRP or if the Chamber of Deputies did not decide on its inclusion on the agenda in accordance with Article 54(4) to (6) CDRP. Resolutions of the Committee or the Chamber of Deputies are sent to the Government, which must 'take them into account' when formulating its position for negotiations in the institutions of the European Communities and the European Union.[11]

Scrutiny of the Government prior to negotiations in the Council

An important power granted to the CEA is that it can request that members of Government who will be present at the Council negotiations appear before the Committee (the Prime Minister before the European Council). Article 109b (1) of the Rules of Procedure states that 'a member of Government shall attend the meeting of the CEA if so requested by the Committee and shall provide information regarding the position that the Czech Republic will take in Council negotiations with respect to a particular matter.' This phase of deliberation in the Committee should relate to the final form of the legislative proposal or document, which will frequently undergo numerous changes in negotiations at the European level, and should also result in the deliberation of the final mandate of the Government as well as the final position of the Committee.

The Government shall send, without undue delay, a report on the results of negations in the Council as well as the position taken by the Government to the CEA following its approval or consideration by the Government.

Article 109b(3) CDRP provides for the classic mechanism of parliamentary control commonly referred to as 'scrutiny reserve'.[12] The aim of this mechanism is not to prevent the Government from adopting a final position, but rather to

[11] Article 109a (5) CDRP.

[12] This term refers to the time period during which a legislative proposal or document is being deliberated in the Chamber of Deputies as outlined above and during which the Government may not adopt a final position in Council deliberations. In practice, Member State governments raise objections during

ensure that its position is formulated by means of consensus so as to reflect the interests of the Czech Republic and to obtain Parliament's support for the position the Government plans to adopt in the Council. The Protocol on the Role of the National Parliaments in the European Union, which forms an integral part of the founding Treaties, also allows for scrutiny reserve in so far as it is not possible to include a legislative proposal on the Council agenda before the elapse of six weeks from its transmission to the Council and the Member State governments. The provisions of the Rules of Procedure governing scrutiny reserve also provide for an important exception to its application that is aimed at ensuring that in urgent cases Council deliberations are not blocked and which relates to proposals or other documents of exceptional urgency. It is not, however, at the Government's discretion to determine which proposals will be deemed to be of exceptional urgency as these are to be interpreted as such within the meaning of the Protocol on the Role of the National Parliaments in the European Union.

Deliberation of important nominations

A provision on the deliberation of important European nominations was included through an amendment. Pursuant to Article 109c CDRP, the Government must submit to the CEA for deliberation nominations of the Czech Republic to the posts of European Commissioner, judges of the European Court of Justice and members of the governing bodies of the EIB and EBRD. The Committee then deliberates these nominations before the Government adopts a final decision. It is also possible to include the deliberation of such nominations on the agenda of the plenary session of the Chamber of Deputies.

3.2.2 The Euro-amendment of the Rules of Procedure of the Senate

At the same time that the Euro-amendment to the Rules of Procedure of the Chamber of Deputies was being deliberated, discussions were also being held on the amendment of the Senate's Rules of Procedure.[13] The proposed amendment contained a section that expressly provided for the deliberation of European affairs.[14]

Drafting and deliberation

The draft bill of the amendment was the result of the work of the Senate Commission for the Constitution of the Czech Republic and for Parliamentary Procedure. As was the case with the amendment of the Rules of Procedure of the Chamber of Deputies, the Government's first reaction was negative. During the discussion of the Senate proposal in the Chamber of Deputies, the section

---

Council deliberations in the form of scrutiny reserve by referring to ongoing discussions in national parliaments.

13 Kysela (2004); Palatová (2004).

14 Chamber of Deputies, Document No. 387, IVth Election Period.

dealing with the deliberation of European affairs was deleted by the Chamber of Deputies' Constitutional Committee with the explanation that a constitutional relationship of accountability only exists between the Government and the Chamber of Deputies and not between the Government and the Senate. Only after political negotiations was it possible to persuade the Government and the Chamber of Deputies that the Senate proposal would not exceed the scope of the constitutionally delimited accountability of the Government and that it does not attempt to impose an imperative mandate (*i.e.* a binding instruction on the Government) on what actions it should take in EU bodies. Furthermore, concerns were appeased that the draft proposal exceeded the constitutional framework by obligating members of Government to attend deliberations of European proposals in the Senate bodies.[15]

In the end, the procedure that was adopted in the Senate was the result of a compromise. The position of the Senate with respect to the Government in European affairs is, as compared to that of the Chamber of Deputies, weaker and as such reflects the constitutional principle that the Government is only accountable to the Chamber of Deputies. At the same time, however, it reflects the position of the Senate as an actor in the legislative process. These provisions delimit the Senate's constitutionally guaranteed right to be duly and timely informed and its right to express its opinion and to be heard.

Contents of the Euro-amendment

Part Twelve of the amended Senate Rules of Procedure outlines the scope of control and the Government's duty to inform in that it defines what documents and information should be submitted by the Government to the Senate with regards to European affairs and it outlines the conditions and time periods for their deliberation.[16] Moreover, it delegates the responsibility of discussing European affairs to the Senate committees. These provisions are more detailed than those of the Rules of Procedure of the Chamber of Deputies. The provisions aim to regulate in detail the internal procedures for deliberating the different types of legislative acts and documents in the Senate bodies. They even set out specific obligations for certain Senate bodies; for example, they provide for the obligation to maintain records of European documents.[17] The Senate attempted to strengthen its position in relation to the Government by expressly setting a time period for the scrutiny reserve for the deliberation of legislative proposals.

Article 119a of the Senate Rules of Procedure specifies in greater detail the Government's duty to inform that is only provided for in general terms in Article 10b of the Constitution. It establishes, by means of a demonstrative list,

---

15 Unlike the Rules of Procedure of the Chamber of Deputies, the Senate Rules of Procedure provide for the attendance of "*representatives*" of the Government and not the actual members of Government.

16 *Zákon č. 107/1999 Sb., o jednacím řádu Senátu* (Act on the Rules of Procedure of the Senate), as subsequently amended (hereinafter "SRP").

17 It would probably be more appropriate to include this in the Senate's internal organizational rules as in the case of the Chamber of Deputies.

the obligation to regularly submit reports on developments in the EU and the assumption of obligations ensuing from membership in the EU into the legal order. Moreover, it establishes the Government's duty to inform about the schedule and results of the European Council and on the commencement and the course of negotiations regarding the amendment of the founding Treaties. The most important aspect of this is the informing of legislative proposals and the Government's preliminary position on them.

Unlike the Rules of Procedure of the Chamber of Deputies, which by law established the CEA as an obligatory body of the Chamber of Deputies, the 'delegated committee' is not specifically mentioned in the Senate Rules of Procedure. The Senate changed the name of the former Committee for European Integration into 'Committee for EU Affairs' and assigned to it the task of deliberating legislative proposals and EU policy documents as well as the corresponding Government positions. The Committee was also given the power to request of the relevant Senate committees their position on a given matter. The review of matters falling within the Common Foreign and Security Policy (the second pillar) and the Justice and Home Affairs (the third pillar) was delegated by Senate resolution to the Committee for Foreign Affairs, Defence and Security.[18]

In contrast to the flexible solution adopted by the Chamber of Deputies, the Senate Rules of Procedure provide that the Senate's position is that which is adopted by the plenary.[19] The plenary deliberates a legislative proposal or a proposal for a decision on the initiative of a committee after which it may then adopt its position based on these deliberations. Although the main responsibility for the deliberation of European affairs is borne by the two delegated Committees, the Rules of Procedure provide for a certain backup mechanism. Under this mechanism, a minimum of 17 senators may propose to the Chairman of the Senate that a given matter be deliberated in plenary session. Therefore, deliberation by the plenary is not only limited to the initiative of the delegated committees.

There are various procedures for deliberating different types of documents – whilst a limited scrutiny reserve applies to the deliberation of legislative proposals (for a period of 35 days from when the document is delivered to the Senate), proposals for binding measures in the second and third pillars are not subject to such a scrutiny reserve. The discussion of EU policy documents is not specifically provided for in this section of the Rules of Procedure and therefore is governed by its general provisions.

Given that the deliberation of the vast majority of legislative proposals in the European Council and the European Parliament generally takes much longer than the six week time period provided for under primary EU law, Committee deliberations are not in practice limited to a period of 35 days. As long as deliberations are concluded before the Council adopts a decision or before the end of the European Commission's consultation period, they may take longer.

[18] See Senate Resolution No. 428 of 29 April 2004, XVth Plenary Session.

[19] Article 119g SRP.

However, the Rules of Procedure also provide for a fast track procedure for deliberating legislative proposals that are deemed urgent.[20] As with the Rules of Procedure in the Chamber of Deputies, the interpretation of this rule should be based on the wording of the Protocol of the Role of National Parliament according to which the EU-institutions decide whether issues are urgent.

3.3 The Government Directive on Transmission of Draft European Legislative Proposals to the Parliament

On the basis of the aforementioned Euro-amendments of the rules of procedure of both chambers that implement Article 10b of the Constitution, the Government adopted by resolution in April 2005 a directive that provides in greater detail for the procedures to be undertaken by the Government and the various ministries in their relations with both chambers of Parliament.[21] Under these provisions, the Government's position on all European legislative proposals must be submitted automatically, whereas measures falling within the CFPS are only submitted at the Government's initiative or at the request of one of the chambers. As a result, it appears that the Government has accepted a scope of parliamentary control, which is not only limited to legislative proposals, but also covers the area of the Common Foreign and Security Policy.

The Directive also provides for the responsibility of the ministries for timely preparation of the Government's position on proposals so that these may be duly and timely deliberated in Parliament. Subsequent Government resolutions provide for the functioning of the inter-institutional electronic databases that contain draft legislative proposals and documents and the corresponding Government positions, which are accessible not only to the executive branch but also to both chambers of Parliament.

4 Assessment of the Enacted Amendments

4.1 The Chamber of Deputies

The model of parliamentary control introduced by the amendment may be assessed in terms of the scope of scrutiny, the timing and its results and effects. From a material perspective, it was possible to formulate the wording of the amendment broadly enough to achieve the necessary scope of scrutiny. It may be applied not only to legislative proposals, but also to documents of a consultative and policy nature and may, and in practice often does, include matters relating to the Common Foreign and Security Policy.

---

20 Article 119g SRP.

21 Directive of the Government on the procedure for transmitting EC/EU draft legislative acts and European Commission documents to the Chamber of Deputies and the Senate of the Czech Republic, adopted as an Annex to Government Resolution No. 415 of 13 April 2005.

From a timing perspective, the procedure is correctly set as being preliminary and thus precedes the deliberation of a legislative proposal or document in the Council. The scrutiny process begins in the initial phase of the legislative and decision-making procedure in order to provide a sufficient timeframe for the Chamber of Deputies to become familiar with it and to enable them to influence the Government's actions. It is likely that the role of monitoring the progress of the legislative and decision-making procedures in the EU will be concentrated primarily with the CEA given the work cycle of Chamber of Deputies and EU institutions. The other standing committees should gradually become more involved in scrutinising important legislative proposals. In contrast, matters involving key institutional or political changes should be submitted to the plenary session for deliberation, as was the case with the discussion of the draft Constitutional Treaty.

With regard to results or the influence of parliaments on decision-making in the Council, it is possible to differentiate between those parliaments that have a strong influence and which may use a veto and change the position of their governments during the decision-making procedure (*e.g.* Denmark, Austria and Finland), those parliaments with a lesser degree of influence that may impact the position of their governments, and finally, those parliaments with only slight influence that may neither influence, nor block the position of the executive branch.[22] The procedure introduced by the amendment may be assessed as a medium strength position of Parliament in that the Government must 'take into account' the Chamber of Deputies' position in its negotiations in EU institutions. If the political will is sufficient, the position of the Chamber of Deputies could be strengthened to a binding mandate by simply altering the wording of the provision.

Different forms of parliamentary involvement are to be found in those Member States which, like the Czech Republic, have a parliamentary form of government. Their constitutions are generally based on the exclusive legislative power of parliament (unless they are based on the principle of parliamentary sovereignty as in the United Kingdom). One of the parliamentary scrutiny systems most similar to that of the Czech Republic is the one used in Austria, which provides for the control of government in European affairs as follows: '*if the National Council has submitted to the respective member of the federal government a position on a given EU matter, which must be implemented by means of a federal law* [...] *then this member is bound by this position during deliberation and voting in the EU. The member may deviate from it only in case of imperative reasons of foreign and integration policies.*'[23]

---

[22] See also: Zralá & Pecháček (2002).

[23] Art. 23e of the Austrian Constitution. See also the Austrian contribution to this book.

4.2 The Senate

As with the Chamber of Deputies, the model of parliamentary scrutiny of European affairs introduced by the amendment in the Senate may also be assessed in terms of the scope of the control, timing and, finally, its effects and results.

From the wording of the amendment, it is clear that the scrutiny is not limited merely to legislative proposals, but that it is also aimed at involving the Senate in the deliberation of CFSP affairs and of documents of a more general strategic nature. The demonstrative list of deliberated proposals and documents provides a sufficient degree of flexibility for the subject-matter being deliberated.

Considering the timing of parliamentary control, it is evident that the Senate model is primarily a form of *ex ante* control, of which the functioning may be hampered by the fact that the chamber's position is formed by the plenary instead of delegated committees. Given the frequency of the plenary sessions, this may hinder the effectiveness of the Senate model.

With respect to the effects of the scrutiny of European affairs carried out by the Senate, it is necessary to note the different position of the Senate in the political system, which predestines its control functions in this area. Although the Government is not bound by the Senate's position, and although it is not obliged to take it into account (contrary to the Chamber of Deputies), it must nevertheless await the Senate's position, as both chambers' right to be heard is expressly guaranteed by the Constitution.

Given these characteristics, it is clear that the Senate should focus its attention more on documents of a fundamental and conceptual nature for which there is sufficient time for discussion. Moreover, it should define legislative priorities in a long-term perspective. The fact that the Senate's position requires a plenary resolution would thus be maximised. In addition, this would remove the duplicate deliberation of European affairs in both chambers of Parliament, which, in our opinion, is an excessive luxury given the size of the Czech Republic.

5 Experiences with the New Model of Parliamentary Control

5.1 The Chamber of Deputies

During the first year of the Czech Republic's membership in the EU, the Government fulfilled its obligation to inform Parliament by connecting the Chamber of Deputies to the Council's Extranet. The implementation of the information system was initially plagued with technical and conceptual problems. Moreover, not even a year after the Czech Republic's accession, all key documents of a legislative nature have been translated into Czech, which inevitably hampers the process of parliamentary control. This is in violation of the founding Treaties and, in its full application, the Parliament could theoretically insist that the six-week period during which a document may not be included on the Council agenda under the Protocol on the Role of National Parliaments shall begin only after the document is sent in Czech (as it is an official language of the EU). The CEA has repeatedly drawn attention to this matter in its resolutions.

The Chamber of Deputies had to create its own system for sorting the immense number of documents in the system to be able to immediately identify, in particular, all original legislative proposals and legislative acts submitted by the Commission in the form of COM final documents. The Senate and the ministries and centralized government agencies, which also receive documents in this manner, were in the same position.

When the CEA – which meets more frequently than the other committees – is not convening, the documents that have been selected are provided to the members of the Committee in electronic format with hypertext links. Based on the recommendations of the Chairman, the Committee then decides by vote which of the documents submitted by the Government will be deliberated at its next meeting and at the same time appoints a rapporteur. Thereafter, the draft act is deliberated based on the Government's preliminary position submitted by the relevant ministry and the rapporteur's report. The proposal is scrutinised on its legal basis, its compliance with international agreements and the subsidiarity principle, and on its economic and legal effects. The result of the deliberations is a Committee resolution. Legislative proposals and documents discussed in the Chamber of Deputies, as well as their resolutions on these documents are accessible to the public in a separate database of 'European documents'.[24] Through this database, the Chamber of Deputies seeks to make European affairs more transparent and accessible to the public.

In terms of the quantity of deliberated proposals and documents, it may be noted that during the first year of the Czech Republic's membership in the EU, the CEA deliberated 461 documents of which 60 documents were discussed in detail, 342 documents were taken into account, 29 documents were approved and 30 documents were still in the process of being deliberated.

EU documents deliberated by the Committee for European Affairs from 1 May 2004 to 1 May 2005

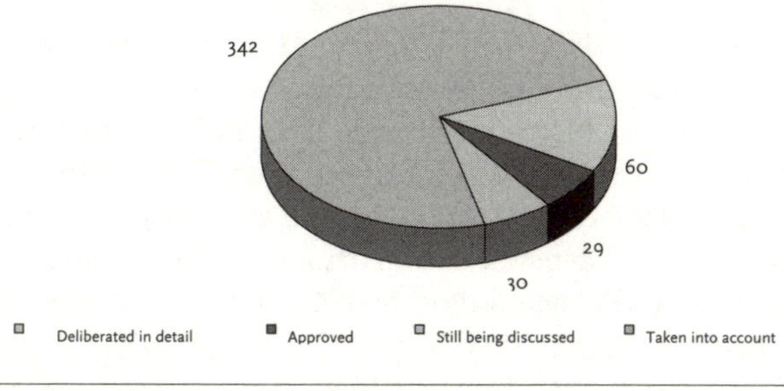

[24] Accessible at: < http://www.psp.cz/sqw/eulist.sqw>.

Although the Rules of Procedure provide enough leeway for the involvement of the other standing committees, this procedure was not employed during the first year of the Czech Republic's membership in the EU as often as may be expected in the future. This is due primarily to the fact that not all draft legislative acts submitted to the Chamber of Deputies were available in official Czech translations. As a result, documents were transmitted only for information purposes to the other standing committees, and only those key proposals available in the Czech language were submitted for deliberation.

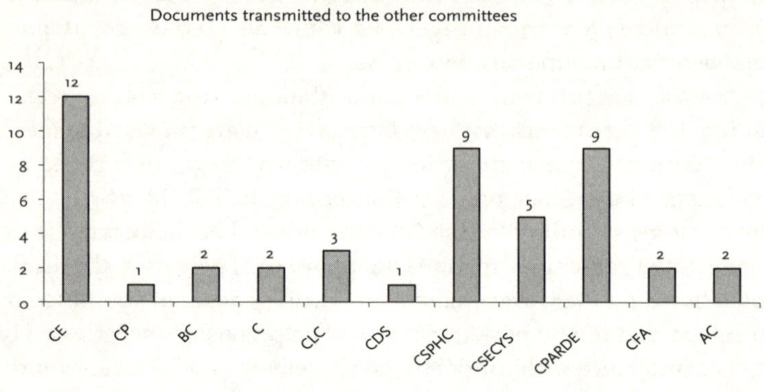

CE – Committee for Economics; CP – Committee for Petitions; BC – Budget Committee; C – Commissions CLC – Constitutional and Legal Committee; CDS – Committee for Defence and Security; CSPHC – Committee for Social Policy and Health Care; CSECYS – Committee for Science, Education, Culture, Youth and Sport; CPARDE – Committee for Public Administration, Regional Development and Environment; CFA – Committee for Foreign Affairs; AC – Agriculture Committee

It is clear from recent experiences that the prerequisite for effective control is the continuous processing of information and documents provided by the Government and EU institutions as well as sufficient expertise and qualified personnel for this difficult task. The Parliamentary Institute serves this purpose for the Chamber of Deputies.

5.2 The Senate

As with regards to the Chamber of Deputies, the Government fulfils its duty to inform the Senate of the obligations arising from the Czech Republic's membership in the EU and to provide it with EU documents primarily by means of the EU-extranet system. In the Senate, the sorting of these documents is carried out by the 'ParlSortEU' system and, on a personnel level, by the Office of the Senate's Independent Department for European Affairs.

A regular component of the meetings of both Committees is deciding which of the documents submitted shall be reviewed in more detail. The basis for making such a decision is, apart from the brief summary prepared by the abovementioned Senate Department, also the Government's preliminary position. The Rules of Procedure provide for the submission of the Government's preliminary position on legislative proposals, which should provide senators with information on how important a given proposal is to the Czech Republic, and why, and how long deliberation in the Council is expected to last. Given the time constraints of the scrutiny reserve, knowledge of the estimated time frame for deliberation is crucial in order to select the appropriate procedure for its discussion. This decision should ideally be preceded by discussions in the political parties.

If the Committee begins deliberation of a certain proposal, it will request additional information from the Government. Apart from an analysis on the effects of the proposal on the Czech Republic's legislation, budget and economics, etc., the information must contain in particular an outline of the position the Government intends to take in the Council. The Committee then deliberates the proposal in a meeting which is attended by a representative of the relevant ministry (usually a deputy minister accompanied by experts from the ministry). The intended position and the course of negotiations are discussed. If all questions are answered and the concerns and comments of the senators are resolved to the extent that the Committee has no objections to the Government's position, then the Committee will only take the proposal 'into account' and finalise its deliberation. Otherwise, the Committee shall prepare a draft position that must be approved by the plenary by a resolution (as noted above, in contrast to the Chamber of Deputies, the Committee's position may not replace that of the Senate plenary). If it involves a policy document by which the Commission is submitting for consultation for its long-term plans in a given field (for example a green paper), then there is the possibility of hearing experts, nongovernmental organizations or other stakeholders. Thus, it is possible to provide for a wider public response corresponding to the Senate's position and to submit it to the Government and the Commission.

Given the specific nature of matters falling under the second pillar, it is not viable for the Committee for Foreign Affairs, Defence and Security to attempt to become actively involved in the decision-making process on foreign or political-security questions.[25] It does, however, have the ability to concentrate on a number of specific priority areas and to undertake in these areas discussions regarding the development of EU policies or to analyze the Government's position on a given matter. As such, it may serve as a forum for the discussion of questions relating to common foreign and security policies. Not all documents within this pillar are automatically delivered through the EU-extranet system (for example, classified documents), but the Committee may request them from the Government.

---

[25] Within the scope of intergovernmental cooperation, there are operative measures, such as common actions and positions, which are often adopted in the span of a few days or even hours.

Number of documents sorted for the CEUA and the CFADS during the period 26 April 2004 - 24 April 2005

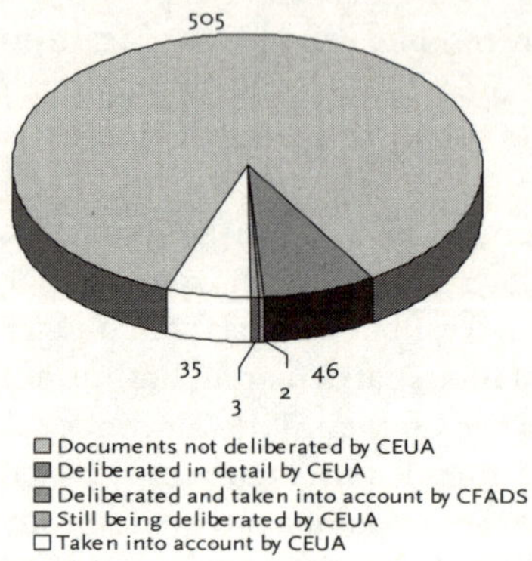

During the first year of the Czech Republic's membership in the EU (from 26 April 2004 to 24 April 2005), there were 591 documents selected for the Committee and the Committee for Foreign Affairs, Defence and Security, of which 505 documents were legislative proposals and documents that were not reviewed in greater detail by either committee. The Committee for EU Affairs took into account 35 documents and 8 of the 46 documents that it deliberated were sent to the plenary for deliberation. The Committee for Foreign Affairs, Defence and Security deliberated 2 documents, which it took into account. On a number of occasions, the Committee for EU Affairs requested the position of other committees, which occurred with 19 documents.

Positions requested from other Senate committees

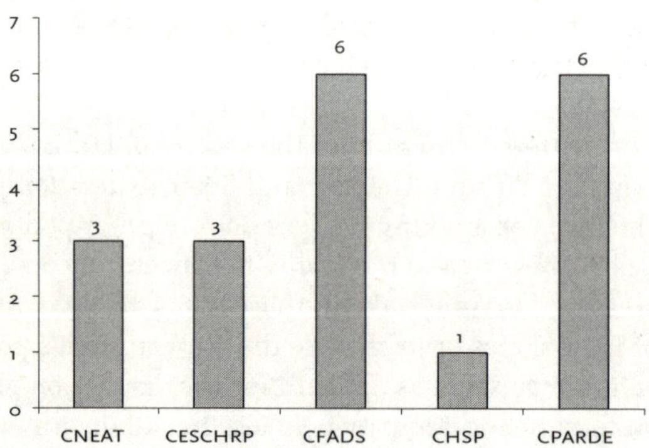

CNEAT – Committee for the National Economy, Agriculture and Transport; CESCHRP – Committee for Education, Science, Culture, Human Rights and Petitions; CFADS – Committee for Foreign Affairs, Defence and Security; CHSP – Committee for Health and Social Policy; CPARDE – Committee for Public Administration, Regional Development and the Environment

Source: *Working statistics obtained from the Office of the Senate's Independent Department for European Affairs*

6 Some Comments on a Future and Better Organisation of National Parliamentary Control of EU Decision-Making

Only after more than a year of the Czech Republic's membership in the EU is it possible to assess, given its day-to-day experiences, the parliamentary dimensions of the EU. Based on Parliamentary practice, the following general statements can be made:

a) It is necessary to activate the Parliament in questions relating to European affairs and to involve the political parties. A high degree of knowledge of European affairs is a prerequisite of the necessary political will to achieve this. It is necessary that deputies and senators realize that nearly 50 per cent of national legislation is derived from European legislation. If it is not possible to express and put forward the national will as early as in the preparatory phase of legislative proposals at the EU level, then Czech legislators shall become mere copiers of European legislation in their transposition.

b) A necessary condition for effective parliamentary control is the duly and timely provision of information about European policies and legislative acts in preparation and the existence of sufficient expertise and qualified personnel for the work of the respective parliamentary bodies. The information process is burdened by the large quantity of legislative acts and documents that are issued by the Commission and the fact that initial proposals are often substantially changed in the course of their deliberation in EU bodies.

c) It appears imperative that there is close cooperation with the Government, which would enable effective use of the scrutiny reserve and the Parliament's position during the negotiations of the Government in the Council. The Government is not only bound to take in to account and reflect the position of the Chamber of Deputies in Council negotiations, but it may also make use of the scrutiny reserve mechanism. It is positive that the Government does so in practice. Therefore, it is important not only to duly formulate the position, but also to timely transmit it to the Government prior to Council meetings. With respect to the Chamber of Deputies, this communication is facilitated by the possibility of requesting the attendance of a relevant minister at a CEA meeting prior to Council meetings (and that of the Prime Minister prior to European Council meetings). The necessity of being able to respond quickly and flexibly in practice has confirmed the optimal solution adopted by the 'Euro-amendment' of the Rules of Procedure of the Chamber of Deputies, which enables the CEA to react promptly.

d) It is necessary to strive for closer cooperation between all national parliaments of the Member States, particularly within the scope of the mechanisms being gradually developed by COSAC. The pilot project of the control of subsidiarity carried out by COSAC on the example of the Third Railway Package and the two subsequent projects concerning the Regulation (EC) No. 2201/2003 with regard to jurisdiction and introducing rules concerning applicable law in matrimonial matters and the Postal Directive demonstrated that such cooperation is in fact possible.[26] However, it also demonstrated how short the 6-week time period for the deliberation of a legislative proposal by the national parliaments is from the perspective of parliamentary practice, particularly in the case of more complex legislative proposals. Joint Parliamentary meetings and joint committee meetings are also a useful means for inter-parliamentary cooperation.

e) A key aspect of parliamentary scrutiny is the control of subsidiarity. If this control were effective, it would not only be a democratic element, but also an effective barrier to overregulation by the EU. Without increasing the quality and reducing the quantity of European legislation, it is hard to imagine a rationalisation of the legal environment at the national level. If the parliamentary control of the principle of subsidiarity could be carried out in a dual track – both in terms of the national government, as well as EU institutions, as provided for by the Protocol on the application of the principle of subsidiarity and proportionally annexed to the Constitutional Treaty, then this parliamentary control could be more effective. At present, the control of subsidiarity may be carried out by the national parliaments regardless of what the fate of the Treaty will be. It must however be stressed that without sufficient political will, knowledge and the proactiveness of all key actors, this control may remain a mere virtual reality and an exhaustive merry-go-round of documents.

7 Conclusion

In conclusion, both the Chamber of Deputies and the Senate play a role in the parliamentary control of EU decision-making in the Czech Republic on the basis of the provisions of the Euro-amendments to their rules of procedure. However, although both chambers currently in practice exercise parliamentary control, the basis for such control differs according to their differing constitutional and political functions, namely, in light of the fact that the Government is responsible only to the Chamber of Deputies. Nevertheless, it must be noted that the Euro-amendment of the Constitution and the Rules of Procedure of the Chamber of Deputies and the Senate are an *ianua reserata* – an open gateway. It allows for the effective application and further development of national parliamentary involvement in the drafting and formulation of European legislation and policies. However, whether or not this open gate will be fully utilized depends largely on political will and not only on formal legal provisions.

---

26 See: <http://www.cosac.eu/en/info/earlywarning/>.

References

P. Craig & C. Harlow, *Lawmaking in the European Union* (London: Kluwer, 1998).

J. Georgiev , "Národní parlamenty a Evropská unie: Současný stav a možnosti dalšího vývoje," in: *Parlamentní zpravodaj* 7-8 (2002) 28-32.

J. Kysela, "Právní a institucionální rámec působení Parlamentu v podmínkách členství ČR v Evropské unii," in: *Časopis pro právní vědu a praxi* 2 (2004) 83-96.

J. Kysela, "Aktuálně k roli druhých komor v procesu evropské integrace," in: *Senát* 2 (2001) 24-26.

J. Kysela, "Glosa k součinnosti Parlamentu a vlády ve věcech Evropské unie," in: *Evropské a mezinárodní právo* 4-5 (2000) 73-76.

E. Palatová E., "Tzv. Evropská novela jednacího řádu Senátu – první měsíce v praxi," in: *Časopis Senát* No. 3/2004.

L. Pítrová et al., "Úloha národních parlamentů v legislativním procesu v Evropské unii," in: *Právník* 10 (2002) 1013-1070.

M. Zralá, Š. Pecháček, "Projednávání evropských záležitostí Parlamentem po vstupu České republiky do Evropské unie," in: *Politologický časopis* 4 (2002) 464-477.

M. Zralá, "Kontrola vlády Poslaneckou sněmovnou v procesu integrace České republiky do Evropské unie," in: *Právník* 7 (2004) 633-649.

CHAPTER II

Conclusion: National Parliaments and the European Union

Coping with the Limits of Democracy

Olaf Tans

1 Introduction

The purpose of this book is to search for a common ground, a binding factor, in the organisation of parliamentary control of EU decision-making in a number of Member States. This undertaking is premised on the fact that national parliaments are widely regarded to be essential in reducing the EU's democratic deficit. Although their actual influence is often critically assessed, and although there is a European Parliament, the national parliaments are nevertheless generally considered to be indispensable in legitimising and controlling European integration. This is illustrated by the fact that their role has been an important issue in the attempt to establish a European constitution, resulting in the attachment of two protocols to the constitutional treaty.[1] Hence, also at the highest political level, national parliaments are treated as a vital part of the European representative democracy.

At the same time, it remains unclear what their role should be and how their function should be organised. The two protocols aim to bring uniformity by establishing a Union-wide early warning system and by turning the national parliaments into guardians of the principle of subsidiarity. Apart from the fact that these protocols may not come into force, they leave the most significant aspects of national parliamentary control of EU decision-making untouched. How are the national parliaments to arrive at their judgements as to whether legislative proposals conform to the principle of subsidiarity? How are they to deal with all their other potential objections? In the last few decades, Member States have been developing their own specific norms and practices. This book seeks to contribute to a more uniform regime for the role of national parliaments in the EU.

As set out in the introduction, this book adheres to a specific theory regarding the way such a uniform regime should be found. Rather than designing a normative framework on the basis of abstract theories about representative democracy, legitimacy or accountability, we primarily seek to draw from the Member States' constitutions and political cultures, as they exist today. This has been characterised as a 'bottom-up' approach to European constitutionalism, in which the Member States' political systems are considered to be the prime source of inspiration, the main input, to the process of establishing suprana-

[1] Two significant protocols have been annexed to the Treaty Establishing a Constitution for Europe: the Protocol on the role of national Parliaments in the European Union, and the Protocol on the application of the principles of subsidiarity and proportionality. They stipulate that the Commission must forward all draft European legislative acts, and all instruments of legislative planning, to national parliaments. Furthermore, they provide for a period of six weeks to elapse between a legislative proposal is made available to national parliaments and the date when it is placed on a Council agenda for decision. Chambers of national parliaments are given the right to give a reasoned opinion stating why a proposal would violate the principle of subsidiarity. If more than one third of the national parliaments were to give this 'yellow card', the European Commission would then be obliged to reconsider its proposal. A similar regime was already established in the Treaty of Amsterdam (1997).

tional norms. Behind this bottom-up approach lies the conviction that the debate about the EU's institutional design must be accompanied by reflections on the level of political and social philosophy.[2] These reflections help find the normative justification and empirical orientation that are needed to make institutional designs fruitful.

This final chapter consists of two parts. Firstly, it presents an analysis of the foregoing studies of national constitutional regimes, directed at exploring their common ground. What fundamental rules, principles or ideas underlie the organisation of national parliamentary control in the Member States that have been discussed, and what do these standards have in common? Secondly, this chapter discusses this common ground in the light of the further development of European democracy. Should we take it as a starting point for future constitutional ambitions, thus pulling through with our bottom-up approach, or might there be significant competing considerations? An attempt will be made to connect the analysis to contemporary debates about multilevel governance, legitimacy and accountability.

2 National Constitutions and European Scrutiny: Exploring Common Ground

Although the various scrutiny systems that have been discussed show differences, a number of commonalities can be identified. Most fundamentally, the role of all national parliaments in the EU is based on the principle of democracy. There are many ways to describe the principle of democracy, but here it may suffice to state that it prescribes that the will of the people be expressed, albeit by the interplay of elected representatives, in the way it is governed and subjected to legislation.[3] Although it is not always made explicit, all the scrutiny systems that are described in this volume ultimately depend on this starting point: because the Member States observe the principle of democracy, and given the fact that the European Parliament is widely regarded as generating too little democratic input, national parliaments have a role in the EU, namely, to redress the democratic deficit.[4]

Starting from that premise, this paragraph reveals a number of commonalities in the organisation of national parliamentary control of EU decision-making. First and foremost, it will be argued that all the scrutiny systems are governed by the constitutional principle of ministerial responsibility. This may sound like a rather trivial observation, but, in the course of this chapter,

[2] See for example: Curtin (1997); Verhoeven (2002).

[3] Andersen & Eliassen (1995) 5.

[4] This 'step back' to national democracy is often based on the argument that the framework of the nation-state provides the social cohesion, the *demos*, that is necessary for majoritarian rule to be experienced as legitimate. Because the minority feels part of a larger national collective, a *demos*, it can accept being overruled by the majority. See for example: Kiiver (2006) 171-172.

it will become clear that if we want to analyse and discuss the role of national parliaments in the European Union, the principle of ministerial responsibility is crucial and a cause for much debate. Secondly, this paragraph sketches the contours of a common practice that seems to be evolving among the Member States' national parliaments. Thirdly, this paragraph addresses the issue of how the various scrutiny systems are embedded in their political and social context, and whether these national circumstances add up to a supranational essence: a shared political culture that may be relevant to the future development of European democracy.

2.1 The Pivotal Role of Ministerial Responsibility

All the scrutiny systems that have been analysed in this volume depend, in one way or another, on the constitutional principle of ministerial responsibility, often in combination with the rule of confidence. There is a great variety of methods, procedures, provisions etc., but at the end of the day national parliamentary control of EU decision-making is to a considerable degree governed by: (1) the principle that ministers can be called to account and be held responsible for their conduct (and of their subordinates); (2) the rule that ministers must resign when a vote of no confidence is passed in the parliament. More generally, one can say that national parliamentary control of EU decision-making is based on the idea that governments depend on parliamentary support (the idea of parliamentary supremacy) and must therefore explain and justify their actions. Traditionally, this accountability is activated through ministers.[5]

A revealing insight in this constitutional construction is provided by 'agency theory', which analyses situations in which one party (an agent) acts on behalf of another (the principal) for mostly practical reasons.[6] In terms of agency theory, the fact that governments depend on parliamentary support means that the latter is the principal in the executive-legislative relation: the holder of original authority. Furthermore, the cabinet is conceived of as an agent to which this original authority is (partly) delegated. Consequentially, the cabinet becomes accountable to parliament. In order to make sure that delegated powers are used to serve the interests of the principal, namely, there must be control-mechanisms to keep the agent in line. According to agency theory, an agent is account-

---

5 Further reading: Bovens (1998); Besselink, (1991).

6 See for example: Strøm (2000) 261-289. The practical reasons may be, for example, that the agent has certain knowledge or skills, or more time, or is able to perform a certain task at lower costs. The principle-agent approach is used to analyse the relation between the EU and its Member States in: Bergman & Damgaard (2000).

able to his principle if (1) he is obliged to act on the latter's behalf, and (2) the latter is empowered to reward or punish him for his performance.[7]

All the national regimes that have been discussed in the previous chapters seem to comprise this ideal-typical *ex post* accountability of ministers to parliament, (mostly) enforced by the possibility of a vote of no confidence. With regard to some Member States, this is about all there is to say about the constitutional norms regulating national parliamentary control of EU decision-making. The scrutiny systems of Belgium and the Netherlands, for example, are almost entirely based on the principle of ministerial responsibility.

The majority of Member States have enacted (constitutional, statutory or procedural) rules that regulate the matter more specifically, in most cases to establish a certain degree of *ex ante* parliamentary control of EU decision-making. On the one hand, this is achieved by granting parliaments more detailed and far reaching information rights. Article 23e of the Austrian Federal Constitution, for example, states that the government has to provide both chambers of the Austrian parliament with information about all EU related projects. On the other hand, a certain degree of *ex ante* control is facilitated by giving parliaments the right to influence their governments prior to decision-making in the Council. Article 23 of the German constitution, for example, gives the Bundestag the right to state its position before the Federal government participates in legislative acts of the European Union. Similar rights, though expressed in various terms, have been created in the UK, Denmark, Finland, Hungary, Austria and the Czech Republic.

As for the new Member States, we may add that the eight former communist countries tend to opt for a mandate model. Interestingly, the contribution by Szalay and Juhász-Tóth argues that this is due to historic reasons:

> 'The notion of 'mandate' implies clear and strict power structures: there is the one possessing power and rights (Parliament) who assigns part of this power to someone else (the executive), but only to the extent defined in the mandate. The expression 'mandate' inherently includes the unquestionable right of control and control, for historic reasons, is a very dominant issue in these relatively new democracies'.[8]

This confirms the guiding role of the constitutional principle of ministerial responsibility in present day national parliamentary control of EU decision-making. In terms of agency theory, the various *ex ante* mechanisms only add

---

7 Fearon (1999) 55-97. As cited in: Strøm (2000) 267. According to agency theory, this relation between parliament and ministers is part of a longer 'chain of delegation' from the voters to those who govern. The original authority is transferred from (1) voters to their representatives in parliament; (2) from the representatives to the cabinet (3) from the cabinet to the heads of executive departments, (4) from the heads of departments to civil servants. This chain of delegation is mirrored by a corresponding chain of accountability running in reverse direction.

8 See the contribution by Szalay and Juhász-Tóth to this book, in the fifth paragraph. And: Szalay (2005); Olson & Norton (1996).

a third characteristic to the principle-agent relation between parliaments and their ministers, namely, that the former can condition the latter's conduct. This may take the shape of a binding mandate, a right to be consulted, a right to 'finish scrutiny', information rights, etc., but these constructions only make sense in the context of the fact that ministers are considered to be 'agents' in the first place, responsible to – and susceptible to sanction by – the parliament, their principal. If, for example, a government should happen to ignore a binding mandate, this would trigger the applicability of the principle that ministers must justify their actions vis-à-vis the parliament. If this justification is not found satisfactory, this in turn triggers the applicability of the rule that ministers must resign if the parliament passes a vote of no confidence. In other words, the *ex ante* control mechanisms fall back on the *ex post* control mechanisms of the traditional conception of ministerial responsibility. Following Cygan, we might also label this 'improved ministerial accountability'.[9]

2.2 The Contours of a Common Practice

Apart from the fact that the principle of ministerial responsibility seems to be the constitutional norm underlying most scrutiny systems, one can observe a certain commonality in the sphere of practices and habits. We shall leave in the middle to what extent these practices and habits are formalised in national constitutional, statutory or procedural rules, as the respective scrutiny systems show quite a variety in this respect. Furthermore, we shall *not* leave in the middle that the tendency towards uniformity is accompanied by attempts to establish union-wide regulation, notably by means of the protocols annexed to the treaty establishing a constitution for Europe and the procedure agreed upon within COSAC.[10] This is to say that the contours of a common practice are at least partly a result of active human design (and not a spontaneous development).

This common practice originates largely in the fact that national parliaments of the EU operate in a committee system in which standing European affairs committees have the task to organise the scrutiny process on behalf of the parliament. These committees generally play a leading role in both the information- and the influence-aspect of parliamentary control.[11] As for the information-aspect, they may be involved in selecting and distributing EU-legislative proposals to be scrutinised by the parliament, in preparing them for parliamentary treatment, in controlling whether the government provides sufficient infor-

---

9 See Cygan's contribution to this book.

10 Conférence des Organes Spécialisés dans les Affaires Communautaires et Européennes des Parlements de l'Union européenne/Conference of Community and European Affairs Committees of Parliaments of the European Union.

11 Apart from the country reports in this volume, detailed information about the functioning of European Affairs Committees can be found in: Travers, Coppolecchia, Tomlins (2003). See also: Kiiver (2006) 47-54.

mation, in organising hearings with cabinet members, etc. At any rate, one can observe a tendency to inform parliaments as early and completely as possible, driven by a growing belief that if national parliaments want to get rid of their label 'losers of European integration', the first priority is that they make up for their information arrears.

The impact of scrutiny is significantly affected by the extent to which the parliament is not only informed about the content of legislative proposals but also about the negotiating positions their governments intend to adopt. Raunio goes even further by stating that, in order to assess seriously a legislative proposal, a national parliament must be informed about the preferences and strategies of its own government, of the Commission, of the European parliament and of the other Member States.[12] The contributions to this book show that some Member States are trying to meet some of these requirements. The Hungarian scrutiny system, for example, prescribes that the government must inform the parliament about the position it intends to adopt and about the objectives to be achieved in the EU decision-making process. Moreover, the Hungarian parliament has the competence to request an extended version of the intended government position.[13] In this respect, some other parliaments depend more on verbal and sometimes informal exchanges.

Despite these attempts to bridge the information gap, however, one must conclude that national parliaments still suffer from a lack of oversight. Factors that still play a significant role are: the complexity, the remoteness and the intransparency of EU decision-making, limited expertise and interest among MPs, and also the increasing number of EU related documents to be processed by national parliaments.

As for the influence-aspect, the foregoing chapters show that the national parliaments of the EU have developed a variety of control mechanisms, in which the European affairs committees generally have a leading role. To get grip on this variety, let us first make use of a simple and useful categorisation provided by Kiiver, who states that the EU's national parliaments can be divided into three groups.[14] The first group consists of the 'mandate-givers' (covering the parliaments of Austria, the Czech Republic, Denmark, Finland, Hungary), that put the emphasis on controlling ministers prior to Council meetings by adopting a more or less binding mandate. The second group consists of 'systematic scrutinisers' (covering the parliaments of the UK and Germany) that focus primarily on sifting all incoming EU documents and on passing resolutions with regard to these documents. The third group consist of the 'informal influencers' (covering the parliaments of Belgium, the Netherlands and Spain), that focus on establishing an informal dialogue with the government with regard to European affairs they consider to be important.

12 Raunio (2004) 13. See also: Kiiver (2006) 101.

13 See the contribution by Szalay and Juhász Tóth to this book.

14 Kiiver (2006) 54.

These three methods have in common that European affairs committees play a leading role in them. As Riis describes, for example, the binding mandates of the Danish parliament come about in meetings of the European Affairs Committee.[15] The systematic, document-based scrutiny system of the UK parliament is to a large extent realised by the European affairs committees of the upper and lower chamber. The same goes for the rather informal influence that is exerted in the parliament of, for example, the Netherlands. Furthermore, European Affairs committees also tend to take the lead where it comes to calling the government to account after decision-making has taken place, if only because they primarily monitor the EU decision-making process and have special expertise.

It would be a mistake, however, to assume that the European affairs committees monopolise the entire scrutiny process. In general, they decentralise the treatment of legislative proposals to sectoral committees, which report their opinions back.[16] In fact, this combination of centralised scrutiny in European affairs committees and decentralised scrutiny in sectoral committees is an important feature of the uniform procedure that was proposed within COSAC. The previous chapters have shown that the sectoral input to the scrutiny process comes about in various (more and less formalised) ways.

In terms of agency theory, it can be argued that this committee system adds another link to the chain of delegation running from the voters to EU decision-making. This analysis undeniably holds true for parliaments that have provided their European affairs committees with the power to take decisions in name of the entire assembly: the German *Bundestag*, the Hungarian National Assembly and the Czech Chamber of Deputies. Other parliaments have not delegated their controlling power in such absolute and formal terms, but we may still say that their European affairs committees are pretty much acting as agents. At the end of the day, it does not seem to make much difference whether European affairs committees are formally entitled to act in name of the parliament or not. In both cases, we witness these committees carefully coordinating their positions with other committees, sometimes on the basis of procedural rules that explicitly demand such a process (as in the German case), sometimes as a result of a consensus-oriented political culture.

To conclude, it may be worth pointing out an interesting development, namely, that a number of Member States with bicameral systems have established joint European affairs committees, or are considering to do so, for a number of reasons and in a variety of ways. In the UK, the creation of a Grant Joint Committee for Europe has been proposed, mainly to share information

[15] This committee is composed in accordance with the composition of the parliament and the votes of the committee members have a weight reflecting their parties' number of seats (the Committee of European Affairs in the Czech parliament is entitled to request that cabinet members appear before the committee before they take part in meetings of the Council of Ministers). See Riis' contribution to this book.

[16] The Austrian system deviates from this picture: The EU Main Committee of the *Nationalrat* cannot transfer EU documents to specialised committees.

and to somehow stimulate the engagement of MPs with the European legislative process. In Spain, a similar joint committee has been established with the task to control the government in its use of the competence to adopt directly (without parliamentary consent) legislation needed to meet the demands of Community law. In the Netherlands, finally, a joint committee has been established to realise the subsidiarity and proportionality check.

2.3 A Common Political Culture?

Apart from tracing commonalities in the spheres of constitutional norms and parliamentary practices, the foregoing chapters have also tried to gain understanding of scrutiny systems in relation to their social context. This perspective can explain why and how Member States have organised things the way they have. It can help, in other words, to get a grip on the driving forces behind the various scrutiny systems.

More specifically, we wonder whether the Member States' political cultures have something in common, whether we can see traces of a shared political culture. Might there be, in Weiler's terms, a European *ethos* with regard to national parliamentary control of EU decision-making?[17] The relevance of this question lies in the fact that future attempts to establish a union-wide regime are likely to be more successful if they somehow respect or even reflect this ethos. This will lift the level of social support to these future constitutional ambitions. In other words, we subscribe to Baun's statement that '...unless a constitution reflects the predominant values of a society, its prospects for stable and successful operation – and the prospects for constitutionalism – are poor.'[18]

However, the fact that a certain cultural unity would be useful does not mean it actually exists. Let us first acknowledge that one can obviously find a lot of diversity among the Member States' political cultures. To name just a few dimensions: It seems to make a difference whether scrutiny occurs in the context of a federal or a unitary state. In the former case, the political culture tends to be characterised by an ongoing struggle to retain regional autonomy, which can go as far as regional parliaments conducting a full scale scrutiny of EU decision-making. Furthermore, the political cultures of Member States vary on the basis of their historical, political and ethnic background. For instance, it makes quite a difference whether a Member State has been a constitutional democracy, and EU member, for many decades or whether these are recent developments.[19] Finally, one may think of differences in beliefs with regard to the concepts of sovereignty and international integration. Cygan, for example, argues that the scrutiny system of the UK is driven by the desire to uphold

---

17 Weiler (1999) 336-343.

18 Baun (1995) 79. See also the second paragraph of the introductory chapter.

19 For an analysis of the scrutiny systems of the new Member States, see: Szalay (2005); Olson & Norton (1996).

parliamentary sovereignty.[20] National parliamentary control of EU decision-making is thus conceived of as a counterbalance to the legislative competences that have been transferred to the EU level. Other countries, such as Belgium and the Netherlands, have never cherished their (parliamentary) sovereignty to that extent, which seems to be reflected by their relatively weak scrutiny systems.

Despite all these differences, it may still be possible to discern a certain common ground in the political cultures of the Member States, namely, a political culture which is coloured by parliamentary democracy.[21] This basically means that the executive-legislative relation in these countries tends to be characterised by a mutual dependency in which parliaments are, in principle, dominant. Primarily, governments depend on parliamentary confidence, are subjected to parliamentary scrutiny and can be sent away by means of a vote of no confidence. As Van Gerven remarks, however, parliamentarism no longer exists in its purest form: parliaments conversely depend on governments, for example, because the executive often shares in legislative competence and because resignation of the cabinet will generally trigger the end of the parliament's term as well.[22]

This mutual dependence is most clearly visible in consensus democracies.[23] One of the main characteristics of this type of democracy is that executive authority is not concentrated in the government, counterbalanced by an active parliament, but is rather diffused throughout the government and a broad coalition in parliament. This co-operation is often formalised in a coalition agreement that remains an influential factor in the executive-legislative relation.[24] The cultural dimension becomes clear when taken into account that consensus democracy tends to originate in – historically – deeply divided societies in which various (religious, ideological, linguistic, regional) groups have found ways to work together despite their differences. Belgium provides probably the most typical example of this 'consociationalism', but it is also manifest in Denmark, Finland, Germany, the Netherlands and Austria. Furthermore, it can be argued

---

20 See Cygan's contribution, and: Cygan (2001).

21 Finland is generally considered a semi-presidential system. In his contribution about the Finnish scrutiny system, however, Raunio argues that recent constitutional reform has parliamentarised the executive-legislative relation.

22 Van Gerven (2005) 324. In pure parliamentarism, the executive is prevented from governing when a parliament is unwilling to give backing. This form lost its appeal with the third and fourth French Republics (1870-1958) and the German Weimar Republic (1918-1933).

23 Lijphart (1999) 31-48.

24 This does not necessarily imply a weakening of parliamentary influence. Whereas the Belgian contribution points out that the consensus oriented nature of Belgian democracy is one of the reasons for governmental dominance and parliamentary weakness in that country, the Finnish contribution rather suggests that the consensus oriented political culture in that country has contributed to the strength of European scrutiny, in that it entails a vivid dialogue between the government and the parliament, thus strengthening the accountability of the former to the latter. See the Belgian contribution by Vos, Staelraeve, Devos, Orbie, Van Liefferinge and Schrijvers, and Raunio's contribution about Finland.

that the EU itself fits the consensus model rather well. According to Lijphart, this makes perfect sense, for the consensus model is suited for typical plural societies such as the EU.[25]

At the risk of being over-speculative, one could thus argue that the dominant political culture within the EU is characterised by 'coping with diversity', which has resulted in a consultative style of political decision-making, also where it comes to parliaments controlling governments. In consensus-oriented political cultures decisions tend to be a result of ongoing deliberations and negotiations, partly on the basis of formalised procedures directed at these processes, partly on the basis of informal contacts and behaviours. In terms of agency theory, this means that the relation between the principal (the parliament) and the agent (the government) has become symbiotic; characterised by an intense mutual dependence that basically blurs the distinction between one and the other. In the next paragraph, it will be argued that this may work well in the national context, but it appears to have downsides when national parliaments seek to play a role in EU decision-making. Here, we first have to stress that there are clear exceptions to the analysis above. According to Lijphart, democracy in the UK is to be conceived of as 'majoritarian'. One of the main characteristics of this type of democracy is that executive power is concentrated in one party and bare majority cabinets.[26] Furthermore, it is doubtful whether the political cultures of the Czech Republic, Hungary and Spain fit the picture sketched above.[27]

2.4 Conclusion

The commonground of the organisation of present day national parliamentary control of EU decision-making seems to comprise the following. First and foremost, this organisation adheres to the idea that national parliaments must have a role in strengthening the EU's democratic legitimacy. This means that present day European scrutiny is primarily based on the principle of democracy, according to which – roughly speaking – the will of the people must be expressed in the way a political community is governed and subjected to legislation. Secondly, it has been argued that national parliaments primarily rely on ministerial responsibility, increasingly improved by *ex ante* mechanisms, in order to realise such an imprint of popular will on EU decision-making. By

---

[25] Lijphart (1999) 42-47. See also: Harlow (2002) 101-102.

[26] Lijphart (1999) 10-21.

[27] The fact remains, however, that these are all parliamentary democracies in which cabinets depend on parliamentary confidence. Furthermore, we may note that the executive-legislative relation in the UK may not be very different, at least where European scrutiny is concerned, from the one that has been developing in consensus-democracies. The dominant party in the House of Commons and the cabinet, namely, form a unity resembling the unity of coalition cabinets and -parties. Within this unity, executive power seems to be shared and controlled pretty much similar to the ways of the consensus democracy: through informal processes of consultation and negotiation, generally resulting in broadly supported compromises, that make the job for opposition-parties very difficult.

holding ministers accountable for EU-related conduct, these parliaments can try to exert influence. Thirdly, it has been argued that the parliamentary practice in which this all happens is to a large extent dominated by European affairs committees and by a political culture that is characterised by co-operation between governments on the one hand and parliamentary majorities on the other.

3 The Future Role of National Parliaments in the EU – Issues for Debate

This final paragraph presents a number of perspectives to reflect on the actual organisation of national parliamentary control of EU decision-making, and on the future development of European democracy. This reflection consists of two parts. The first part (3.1 and 3.2) discusses a number of complications related to the pivotal role of the principle of ministerial responsibility and the attempt to strengthen parliamentary controlling power by means of *ex ante* mechanisms. The second part (3.3 – 3.5) discusses a number of ways in which the role of national parliaments – and thereby democracy – in the EU might improve.

3.1 The Limits of Ministerial Responsibility

Having concluded, in the first paragraph, that the principle of ministerial responsibility is a normative cornerstone of national parliamentary control of EU decision-making as it exists today, we now have to deal with the question of whether this is a satisfying institutional arrangement. In order to do so, we shall first focus on the complications of the construction of ministerial responsibility in a national context. Then it will be argued that these complications also arise in the supranational, EU-context.

According to Van Bijsterveld, the principle of ministerial responsibility is widely regarded as functioning unsatisfactorily in Western constitutional systems, for a number of reasons.[28] Firstly, ministerial responsibility is often activated through incidents, in retrospect, with long delays, without using clear and previously applied standards. This means that it does not yield a structural parliamentary check on government, but rather functions as a medium for political communication.

Secondly, the functioning of the principle of ministerial responsibility is frustrated by narrowing its applicability, for example, by allowing blameworthiness to play a role in its application. In principle, personal blameworthiness is not an element of ministerial responsibility, but in practice ministers tend to escape sanction by stressing the fact that they cannot be blamed. In the same vein, the principle of ministerial responsibility loses force in light of the fact that it becomes increasingly difficult for ministers to oversee and control everything

[28] Van Bijsterveld (2002) 95. See also: Bovens (1998) 74-92.

going on in their departments. This lack of actual influence (for example, on civil servants) is often accepted as a reason not to hold ministers fully accountable, or to be more easy on them in the sanctioning-phase. This means that ministerial responsibility is no longer a purely functional mechanism enabling parliaments to control and sanction any wrongful conduct by the executive power.

Thirdly and finally, the sanction itself is considered to be of little use. The no-confidence rule stipulates that ministers must resign when they loose parliamentary support, but this sanction is so drastic that it is only appropriate as a reaction to scandals. The application of the no-confidence rule is also seriously hampered by party-politics: coalitions protecting their ministers *en bloque*. In sum, this rule does not play an important role in everyday parliamentary practice, which basically means that it does not add much to parliamentary controlling-power.

As the foregoing chapters have illustrated, these complications aggravate in national parliamentary control of EU decision-making. *Ex post* control of EU decision-making by calling ministers to account remains fragmentary and mild, for a number of possible reasons. Firstly, national parliaments simply suffer from a lack of information and oversight, even though in the last few decades the information-rights have improved. Secondly, national parliaments seem reluctant to hold ministers fully accountable for (their contribution to) such a remote and autonomous decision-making process, if only because it often involves qualified majority voting. Thirdly, a significant number of authors in this book report a remarkable disinterest of MPs in European affairs. The Belgian contribution, for example, states: 'There are no indications that members of parliament are asking for a structure which allows for a systematic follow-up of EU politics. Existing mechanisms are scarcely used and the parliament generally takes an indifferent attitude vis-à-vis Europe.'[29] This type of attitude probably plays a role in the fact that, generally speaking, ministers rarely get in serious trouble over European issues. Here, the no-confidence rule is applied even more rarely than with regard to domestic issues.

The most crucial factor however is that the Communitarian lawmaking and implementation process is significantly intermediated by a mostly invisible and unaccountable European bureaucracy.[30] The COREPER, for example, is formally responsible for 'preparing' the legislative and policymaking tasks of the Council of Ministers.[31] In practice, this means that consensus with regard to legislative decisions is often already reached, in a diplomatic process in and around the COREPER, before decision-making formally takes place in the Council.[32] If

29 See the third paragraph of the Belgian contribution to this book.

30 See: Harlow (2002) 25-52; Damgaard (2000) 168.

31 Committee of Permanent Representatives of the Member States. According to Article 207 (1) EC, this committee '...shall be responsible for preparing the work of the Council and for carrying out the tasks assigned to it by the Council'.

32 See: Van Gerven (2005) 20; Harlow (2002) 34; Van Schendelen (1996) 37; Wessels (1991) 140.

national parliaments want to hold ministers accountable for (their contribution to) such decisions, they run up against the fact that these ministers can only point at a bureaucratic machinery that somehow produced a certain (draft) decision. In principle, national parliaments can still hold these ministers accountable for their eventual voting behaviour, or for the way they sought to influence the consensus-building process, but in practice they tend to accept that ministers have limited control and can only be held accountable as far as they had a fair chance to exert influence.

The point is that the principle of ministerial responsibility is an unconvincing mechanism of national parliamentary control of EU decision-making. In theory, this control is supposed to be realised by parliaments calling their ministers to account for their contribution to EU decision-making, thus forcing these ministers to operate as their 'agents', but, in practice, this is hardly more than a myth. In terms of agency theory, the chain of delegation running from national parliaments, through ministers, to the EU, suffers from so much agency loss that we can hardly speak of a principle-agent relation. This raises the question of whether ministerial responsibility is a satisfactory normative cornerstone of European scrutiny by national parliaments. If it appears that these parliaments can hardly exert influence through their ministers, and find it difficult to hold them accountable for a decision-making process in which they only play a small and indecisive role, it may be necessary to search for new constitutional constructions; new ways for national parliaments to realise a democratic imprint on EU decision-making.

3.2 Vices and Virtues of *Ex Ante* Mechanisms

First, we need to discuss the attempt to strengthen the position of national parliaments by granting them the right to be informed about and exert influence on EU decision-making beforehand. Internationally, an early warning system has been designed in which national parliaments are supposed to function as watchdog of the principles of subsidiarity and proportionality.[33] Nationally, various Member States have equipped their parliaments with a variety of rights to influence their governments' positions prior to EU decision-making. The question is to what extent these *ex ante* control regimes solve the problems related to *ex post* control based on the principle of ministerial responsibility.

First and foremost, it must be noted that *ex ante* control mechanisms probably add to the strength of national parliamentary control of EU decision-making. Theoretically, this assumption can be supported by the simple reasoning that early intervention will generally lead to a more profound impact on the outcome of processes. In this way, it has been argued, for example, that control over the agenda of decision-making processes is an important element of having influence. Empirically, the assumption that *ex ante* control mechanisms contribute to

[33] See the introduction of this chapter.

the strength of national parliamentary control can be supported by a number of studies. Maurer and Wessels, for instance, consider the timing and management of scrutiny to be a factor affecting its strength.[34]

The contributions to this study, however, give an incentive to go beyond this 'strength-debate' and to evaluate *ex ante* control regimes in additional perspectives. Firstly, they bring a practical complication to the fore, namely, that *ex ante* control regimes can lead to an overload of work due to the sheer volume of European documents to be processed – under time pressure – by national parliaments. Pítrová and Coxová, for example, describe how the brand new Czech (moderate) mandate system has forced the Committee of European Affairs, being the guarantor of the monitoring and assessment of European legislative proposals, to develop quite a machinery for timely monitoring and distributing all the European documents.[35] The Czech parliament is supported by a relatively large parliamentary institute, but national parliaments remain relatively small organisations that were designed and equipped to monitor and scrutinise domestic matters, not the enormous domain of European affairs. In this respect Norton even remarks that: '...the existing workload of some parliaments means that it will be difficult for them to be more involved in EU affairs'.[36]

Secondly, this practical issue entails a more fundamental problem. No matter how strongly *ex ante* regimes entitle national parliaments to be informed and bind their governments with regard to their EU related conduct, their contribution to the democratic legitimacy of EU decision-making remains limited due to the fact that these *ex ante* mechanisms are employed selectively. From the totality of EU documents, European Affairs Committees must sift through a limited number of dossiers to be seriously scrutinised, of which an even smaller portion can be dealt with in plenary parliamentary sessions. This means that *ex ante* mechanisms cannot erase the fragmentary nature of national parliamentary control of EU decision-making, as it was earlier identified in relation to the *ex post* mechanism of ministerial responsibility. Thym goes even further by suggesting that an *ex ante* regime might even bring national parliaments into a worse position. The German government's wide-ranging constitutional obligations have resulted in such an overwhelming flow of information that it threatens to paralyse the parliamentary control functions. In this respect, Thym speaks of the danger of 'irrelevance through overload'.[37]

---

34 Maurer & Wessels (2001). Apart from timing, various studies indicate a number of other factors determining strength of controlling power. The degree to which national parliamentary opinions or instructions are binding on the government is obviously indicative. Given the fact, furthermore, that European Affairs Committees dominate the parliamentary practice, it is not surprising that Raunio and Wiberg stress the relevance of the strength of these committees, for example as indicated by the frequency of their meetings and the involvement of sectoral committees. Raunio & Wiberg (2000)146-168; Maurer & Wessels (2001).

35 See the Czech contribution to this book.

36 Norton (1996) 32.

37 See the contribution about Germany in this book.

Thirdly, it may be interesting to highlight an observation in the contribution by Neuhold and Blümel. After Austria joined the European Union in 1995, its parliaments have been empowered with extensive competences as to both the information and the influence aspect of European scrutiny.[38] Interestingly, the authors observe that, in the course of time, the number of binding opinions has decreased while the use of EU related Committee Statements has intensified. Furthermore, they observe that, as a result of the aftermath of the very first instance, binding opinions tend to be phrased in soft formulations such as 'the minister shall work towards' and 'make a strong effort'.[39] A majority in the Austrian parliament is apparently reluctant to bind ministers in spite of its right to do so. This is a significant observation, in that it indicates that (theoretically) strong scrutiny systems can turn out significantly weaker in the dynamics of everyday political life. It can even be doubted whether a binding opinion that a minister 'shall work towards' a certain goal has more impact than the non-binding version.

Fourthly and finally, it is necessary to reflect on the effect of *ex ante* control regimes from the viewpoint of the EU. Vos argues that although mandate systems may satisfy national needs to control ministers and thereby the EU decision-making process, this process itself may suffer from negative effects.[40] Decision-making in the EU (where various cultures and interests have to be reconciled) asks for negotiation and compromise. Package deals are often necessary to overcome deadlocks. This type of decision-making requires a limited number of participants having a considerable freedom to manoeuvre. If a significant number of participants would operate on the basis of specific mandates, this would hamper the dynamic of the negotiations. Vos puts it this way:

> 'The idea of giving national ministers of parliaments an exact and well-defined mandate seems very tempting and is easy to implement (treaty modifications are not required for this), but it has a perverse effect. At first sight this measure seems very sound from a democratic point of view, but doing this would endanger the integration dynamics'.[41]

---

[38] According to Article 23e of the Austrian Federal Constitution, both chambers of the parliament must be informed about all EU projects without any delay. Both chambers have the right to give binding opinions to ministers prior to decision-making in the Council of Ministers.

[39] See the Austrian contribution. The first binding opinion was phrased in absolute terms, which appeared to have a counter productive effect: the minister was unable to steer EU decision-making in the direction that was given by the parliament.

[40] Vos (SWP-paper).

[41] Vos (SWP-paper) 15.

3.3 More Direct Involvement of National Parliaments in EU Decision-making?

The foregoing leads to the conclusion that the attempt to give national parliaments influence on the basis of the principle of ministerial responsibility, with or without the help of *ex ante* mechanisms, is frustrated to the extent that one may rightly wonder whether this is an appropriate way to contribute to the democratic legitimacy of EU decision-making. In contemporary legal and political science, a similar observation has led to a call for more direct input by national parliaments. It has been proposed, for example, to turn the European Parliament into a bicameral institution, one of which would be composed of members of national parliaments.[42] A less drastic variant is to introduce a so-called 'chamber of subsidiarity' with the task of checking EU decision-making on the principle of subsidiarity. In the same vein, it has also been suggested to create a permanent conference of national parliaments, with the task of realising a subsidiarity check and to discuss the state of the Union more generally. Evidently, all these proposals aim to increase the democratic legitimacy of the EU by giving national parliaments more direct input – not intermediated by ministers – in the Communitarian decision-making process.

From a straightforward democratic viewpoint, this more direct input of national parliaments in European decision-making deserves support. Furthermore, it is in line with a spontaneous development over recent years, namely, that some national parliaments are already trying to get closer connections with Brussels, for example, by interacting with MEPs or by establishing offices in the Belgian capital.[43] There are however also ways to criticise this tendency. If national parliaments get a formalised role in Brussels, the European decision-making process will also be influenced by representatives that have been elected in national elections. Given the fact that European issues generally play a subordinate role in national elections, these representatives do not operate on the basis of an EU-related electoral mandate, which means that their influence on EU decision-making does not lead to more democracy. Apart from this theoretical point, it must be noted that the involvement of two types of parliaments – that are likely to develop forms of co-operation and consultation – will make the European political process more complicated and less transparent. The European citizens may well pay the price, in that it will become even more difficult for them to understand how and why decisions are taken – and controlled – within the EU.

---

[42] See for example: Maurer & Wessels (2000) 466-467. According to these authors, the second chamber would either be composed of directly elected senator MEPs or of delegated senator MEPs with weighted voting rights (The *Budesrat*-model).

[43] For example, the UK has its permanent parliamentary office in Brussels, Austria its *Verbindungsbüro* and the Hungarian National Assembly its delegated official working in the European Parliament. In addition, MEPs are more frequently given speaking rights in national parliaments. COSAC represents another attempt to connect national parliaments more directly with the EU decision-making process.

Moreover, the direct involvement of national parliaments in the European decision-making process is likely to run up against the same practical problems that complicate their indirect influence through ministers. This more direct involvement, namely, will have to come about by sending representatives to Brussels to act on behalf of their assembly. As Harlow remarks, there is no reason to believe why it would be easier for national parliaments to brief, or mandate, these representatives than the ministers that are sent to the Council.[44] In other words, this construction will probably suffer from the same type of agency loss that has been described in relation to the functioning of ministerial responsibility.

In sum, these proposals to involve national parliaments more directly in EU decision-making are in principle appealing, but they seem to be informed by a rather simplistic application and reading of the principle of democracy. They rely on the idea that the EU's democratic deficit is to be solved by organising more direct input from national parliaments in the European decision-making process, but they seem to disregard significant breaches occurring elsewhere in the chain of delegation running – ideally – from voters, via parliaments, to those who determine policies.

In this respect, it seems wise to establish a subsidiarity and proportionality check on the national level, as it was first formalised in the Treaty of Amsterdam and later in two protocols annexed to the Treaty Establishing a Constitution for Europe. This arrangement gives national parliaments direct influence in that they can force the European legislator to reconsider legislative proposals that violate the principles of subsidiarity or proportionality, while keeping the national and supranational parliamentary functions apart. However, although this arrangement has found wide support, it can be doubted whether it will have a significant positive effect on the democratic legitimacy of EU decision-making. As Besselink argues, the subsidiarity check may well turn out to endanger the much broader role national parliaments could play:

> 'In fact, it may force parliaments further into the 'levels' approach: once a matter is considered an EU matter, that is the end of a role for national parliaments, and only in the opposite case (a matter not being suitable for EU decision-making) is there a role for national parliaments.'[45]

3.4 Going Beyond the Input-legitimising Role of National Parliaments

It seems that we have to come to terms with the fact that our ambition to serve the principle of democracy is not always realistic in light of the complexity of political reality. In principle, we would like to see national parliaments redressing the EU's democratic deficit by influencing the content of Communitarian decisions, but it seems unlikely that this input-legitimising

44 Harlow (2002) 103/104.

45 Besselink (2006) 130. See also: Peters (2005) 70-72.

role can be realised in practice. The question is what to do with this insight. To finalise our discussion, let us address two possible approaches: an idealist and a pragmatic approach.

In the idealist approach, we simply cling to the ideal conception of democracy, in which popular will is imprinted on governance and legislation through the interplay of representative bodies. We repeat the observation that the functioning of the European Parliament does not bring about a satisfying articulation of popular will in European decision-making, and, therefore, plea for a role of national parliaments in redressing this deficit, even though it is unlikely that this will be fruitful.

At first sight, this appears to be a senseless approach, for it is like holding on to a dream. In its defence, however, we may point at the fact that constitutional ambitions are generally drenched in idealism, and that there is no reason why European constitutionalism would have to be an exception.[46] When the American founding fathers wrote that 'We, the people...' etc, they obviously used a rather unrealistic proposition to legitimise their constitutional ambitions, but this has not prevented this proposition from becoming an important expression of American constitutionalism. Many contemporary constitutions protect human rights in a rather unrealistic manner (prescribing, for example, equality and liberty) but this is generally not considered to be an obstacle to their importance and meaning to political life. In other words, the fact that European democratic ambitions are unrealistic does not in itself have to lead to the conclusion that these ambitions do not deserve our support.

To drive this point home, we may bear in mind that 'democracy' is an extremely unrealistic constitutional ambition in the first place, that is, also in the context of national political communities. Numerous writers have stressed the unrealistic character of democratic theory of governance. Empirical research indicates, for example, that there is a low degree of congruence between the political opinions of MP's and the preferences of the voters they are supposed to represent.[47] A similar observation inspired Dahl to argue that (representative) democracy is an unattainable political system.[48] In a post-modern style, democratic theory has more recently been debunked by calling it a 'myth' or a 'dominant narrative' or even a 'metaphysical booby-trap'.[49] As it stands, however, these and other de-mystification attempts do not stand in the way of a widely shared commitment to democratic theory in organising Western societies. Political communities seem happy to worship ideal constitutional concepts, so why would we force the EU to realism?

In a more pragmatic approach, the answer could be that national parliaments can be useful to the EU and its Member States in other ways than giving

---

46 I have analysed the unrealistic nature of constitutional ambitions in: Tans (2002).

47 Eulau (1987).

48 Dahl (1956). In his view, collective decision-making in modern political communities comes about through the interplay of interest groups, of which the leaders exert a certain influence in the political arena.

49 Van Ham (2001) 157-160.

input-legitimacy to Communitarian decision-making. A first incentive to such pragmatism may be found in the work of Bovens, which offers the simple but revealing insight that public accountability can serve more than only popular sovereignty purposes.[50] It can also serve 'cybernetic' purposes, which means that public accountability can stimulate the executive to learn from past experiences, for example, when a parliamentary inquiry – especially when broadcasted on TV – forces administrators to justify and adjust their policies. Public accountability can also serve 'constitutional' purposes, which means that it aims to prevent the abuse of executive power, for example, when a constitutional court controls whether governmental regulation respects regional autonomy in certain matters.

The crux is that these functions do not ask for a (difficult to organise) continuous influx of parliamentary viewpoints in the decision-making process. Rather, they ask for the creation of incidents: specific moments on which specific issues are politicised or legally disputed. In this perspective, we may, for a start, be more positive about the subsidiarity check, that may not lead to a significant national parliamentary influence on the content of EU-decisions, but that could well lead to 'moments of shock' that are beneficial to the EU's development. Furthermore, we may start to envision new forms of accountability of European institutions, notably the Commission, to national parliaments. It is also conceivable that national parliaments become more active in bringing cases before the ECJ, thus turning the EU's political accountability into a legal one.[51] In short: letting go of the *idée-fix* of input-legitimacy opens a window of opportunities.

3.5 A Plea for More Debate in National Parliaments

However, the most crucial role awaiting national parliaments is to establish a better communication about EU affairs within their own countries. Rather than sitting and waiting for the proper tools to be handed to them, national parliaments should become aware of the fact that in principle they *are* the tools.

To illustrate this final point, one may first recall that the contributions to this volume reveal a low level of involvement in European affairs among members of national parliaments. With the exception of the Finnish Eduskunta, MPs tend to treat the EU as an issue requiring special expertise and leave it up to the specialists to deal with it.[52] This may be caused by the committee system, a lack of insight in European affairs, a sense of not being able to exert influence on EU decision-making anyway, a reluctance to produce disagreement between political (coalition) parties, or by the fact that members of national parliaments are primarily interested in controversial domestic issues over which they can score politically. Anyhow, it has a negative effect on the democratic process. The fact

---

50 Bovens (2006).

51 In France and Germany there is a legal basis for these actions. See: Besselink (2006) 127.

52 Raunio describes how all Finnish MP's, regardless of their political preferences and status, are more or less forced to handle EU affairs due to delegation of authority to specialised committees.

that EU affairs are discussed less frequently and widely in national parliaments implies that the will of citizens is more weakly and less congruently voiced in these matters. In other words, it implies that national parliaments do not represent the people well.

As far as these matters *are* discussed, it can furthermore be noted that the style of debate leaves room for improvement. Laso Peréz, for example, states that the debates in the Spanish Joint Committee for European Affairs are 'excessively predictable' and follow a very strict party line. In other contributions, the parliamentary treatment of EU matters is described with terms such as 'technical', 'flat', 'silently positive' and 'with lack of constructive debate.'[53] This implies an impoverishment of the political process in the sense that national parliaments are apparently not contributing optimally to the so-called 'public deliberation' on EU matters.[54] They tend to refrain from substantive, politically engaged debate about EU affairs, and thereby miss a chance to involve the people in what Curtin describes as 'a European political public sphere'.[55] A poignant illustration can be found in the treatment of the European constitutional treaty in the Dutch parliament. Throughout the constitution-building process, the main parties have to a large extent shared the same concerns and preferences, and, in the end, they have almost unanimously supported the constitutional treaty. In other words, there has not been much political conflict. The negative outcome of the referendum on the constitutional treaty indicates that the Dutch people have not been well represented in this respect.[56]

This absence of fundamental political debate may be connected to the aforementioned culture of parliamentary democracy, in particular, in the consensual variant. As signalled in a number of contributions to this volume, this culture affects the way parliaments control their governments. Rather than a polarisation between parliament and the executive, thus realising the idea of *checks and balances*, we witness a certain degree of unification of governments on the one hand and parliamentary majorities on the other. This type of co-operation is often cherished for its stability and ability to produce practical results, but it also has downsides, especially where it comes to parliamentary control of EU decision-making. Firstly, the ties between cabinets and coalition-parties tend to turn the latter into 'supportive' rather than critical scrutinisers.[57] On that basis, it has been argued that the most thorough and critical scrutiny of EU decision-making must come from opposition parties.[58]

---

[53] Laso Pérez (2006). This study was presented at the conference *Political control in a European and constitutional perspective*, held February 9-10 in Maastricht.

[54] For a deliberative perspective on European democracy, see: Eriksen & Fossum (2000).

[55] Curtin (1997) 56.

[56] Of the 63% that made it to the ballot box 61,5% said no, whereas over 85% of the MPs – judging from the statements of their spokesmen – said yes. See: Tans (2006).

[57] In this way, Thym characterises the Bundestag's control over EU decision-making as 'supportive scrutiny'.

[58] On the role of parliamentary opposition in European scrutiny, see: Holzhacker (2005)/(2002).

Secondly and more generally, consensus oriented parliamentary practice entails that political differences of opinion tend to be handled informally and behind closed doors, which has a negative effect on the intensity and openness of parliamentary debate. Again, this can be interpreted to be a nice and peaceful result of the aforementioned experience in coping with diversity, but it can also be argued to represent an erosion of the deliberative function of parliamentary debate. By engaging in debate and conflict, a parliament can feed and reflect public awareness about political issues. Deliberation, one may say, lies at the heart of what a parliament is supposed to do, namely, represent the voters in the expression of political will. As it stands, however, national parliaments do a poor job in producing a discourse that makes sense to the public, a discourse in which European affairs are fundamentally and critically discussed, a discourse in which something is at stake, in which choices are made on the basis of recognisable arguments.

4 Conclusion

In this chapter, the role of national parliaments in the European Union has been discussed in the following way. Answering the research question that is formulated in the introductory chapter of this book, an attempt was made to formulate a common ground in the organisation of national parliamentary control of EU decision-making. In a nutshell, this common ground was found to consist of (adherence to) the principle of democracy, (adherence to) the principle of ministerial responsibility, a parliamentary practice in which European affairs committees have a leading role in both the information- and influence-aspect of European scrutiny, and a political culture in which the executive-legislative relation is characterised by a considerable degree of mutual dependence.

In light of the EU's future (constitutional) development, this chapter has furthermore presented a critical assessment of this common ground. The main argument is that present day European scrutiny is primarily directed at redressing the EU's democratic deficit by organising national parliamentary input in the Communitarian decision-making process, even though this attempt to establish more input-legitimacy runs up to a number of practical complications. Therefore, it has been suggested that it may be wiser to seek other national parliamentary contributions to European democracy. For example, these institutions could become more active in directly calling European institutions to account, or in bringing cases before the ECJ. Most of all, however, it has been argued that national parliaments should take the lead in firing up domestic discourses on European affairs, that remain flat and technical, whereas vivid, fundamental public debate is needed to inspire European citizens to start identifying with the EU.

References

S. Andersen & K.A. Eliassen, "Introduction: Dilemmas, Contradictions, and the Future of European Democracy", in: *The European Union: How Democratic is it?* (London: Sage, 1995) 1-11.

M.J. Baun, "The Federal Republic of Germany", in: D.P. Franklin & M.J. Baun, *Political Culture and Constitutionalism. A Comparative Approach* (London/New York: M.E. Sharpe, 1995) 79-97.

T. Bergman & E. Damgaard (eds.), *Delegation and Accountability in European Integration. The Nordic Parliamentary Democracies and the European Union* (Abington/New York: Frank Cass, 2000).

L.F.M. Besselink, "National Parliaments in the EU's Composite Constitution. A Plea for a Shift in Paradigm", in: Ph. Kiiver (ed.), *National and Regional Parliaments in the European Constitutional Order* (Groningen: Europa Law Publishing, 2006) 117-132.

L.F.M. Besselink, "Aard en grondslag der ministeriële verantwoordelijkheid", in: *De ministeriële verantwoordelijkheid* (Antwerpen: Interuniversitair centrum voor staatsrecht, 1991).

S. van Bijsterveld, *The Empty Throne. Democracy and the Rule of Law in Transition* (Utrecht: Lemma, 2002).

M. Bovens, "Analysing and Assessing Public Accountability. A Conceptual Framework", *European Governance Papers* (EUROGOV: 2006), no. C-06-01: <http://www.connex-network.org/eurogov/pdf/egp-connex-c-06-01.pdf>

M. Bovens, *The Quest for Responsibilty* (Cambridge: Cambridge UP, 1998)

D.M. Curtin, *Postnational democracy, The European Union in search of a political philosophy* (The Hague: Kluwer, 1997)

A.J. Cygan, *National Parliaments in an Integrated Europe, an Anglo-German perspective* (The Hague/London/New York: Kluwer Law International, 2001).

R.A. Dahl, *A Preface to Democratic Theory* (Chicago: Chicago UP, 1956).

E. Damgaard, "Conclusion: The Impact of European Integration on Nordic Parliamentary Democracies", in: T. Bergman & E. Damgaard (eds.), *Delegation and Accountability in European Integration* (Abingdon/New York: Frank Cass, 2000) 151-174.

E.O. Eriksen & J.E. Fossum (eds.), *Democracy in the European Union. Integration through deliberation?* (London/New York: Routledge, 2000).

H. Eulau, "The Congruence Model Revisited", *Legislative Studies Quarterly* 12 (1987) 171-214.

J.D. Fearon, "Electorial accountability and the control of politicians: Selecting good types versus sanctioning poor performance", in: A. Przeworski, S.C. Stokes & B. Manin (eds.), *Democracy, accountability, and representation* (Cambridge: Cambridge UP, 1999) 55-97.

W. van Gerven, *The European Union. A Polity of States and Peoples* (Oxford and Portland (Oregon: Hart Publishing, 2005).

P. van Ham, *European Integration and the Postmodern Condition. Governance, Democracy, Identity* (London/New York: Routledge, 2001).

C. Harlow, *Accountability in the European Union* (Oxford: Oxford UP, 2002).

R. Holzhacker, "The Power of Opposition Parliamentary Groups in European Scrutiny", *The Journal of Legislative Studies* 11 (2005) 428-445.

R. Holzhacker, "National Parliamentary Scrutiny over EU Issues", *European Union Politics* 3:4 (2002) 459-479.

Ph. Kiiver, *The National Parliaments in the European Union. A Critical View on EU Constitution-Building* (The Hague/London/New York: Kluwer Law International, 2006).

A. Lijphart, *Patterns of Democracy. Government Forms and Performance in Thirty-Six Countries* (New Haven/London: Yale UP, 1999).

A. Maurer & W. Wessels (eds.), *National Parliaments on their Ways to Europe: Losers or Latecomers?* (Baden-Baden: Nomos, 2001).

Ph. Norton, "National parliaments in Western Europe", in: Smith, E. (ed.), *National parliaments as cornerstones of European integration* (The Hague: Kluwer, 1996) 179-186

D.M. Olson & Ph. Norton (eds.), *The New Parliaments of Central and Eastern Europe* (London/ Portland: Frank Cass, 1996).

J.A. Peters, "National Parliaments and Subsidiarity: Think Twice", *European Constitutional Law Review* 1:1 (2005) 68-72.

T. Raunio, "Holding governments accountable in European affairs: Explaining cross-national variation", *Journal of Legislative Studies* 11:3-4 (2005) 319-342.

T. Raunio & M. Wiberg, "Does Support Lead to Ignorance? National Parliaments and the Legitimacy of EU
Governance", *Acta Politica* 35 (2000) 146-168.

T. Raunio, *Two Steps Forward, One Step Behind? National Legislatures in the EU Constitution* (paper, The Federal Trust for Education and Research, London: 2004)

M. van Schendelen, "The Council Decides: Does the Council Decide?", *Journal of Common Market Studies* 34 (1996).

K. Strøm, "Delegation and accountability in parliamentary democracies", *European Journal of Political Research* 37 (2000) 261-289.

K. Szalay, *Scrutiny of EU Affairs in the National Parliaments of the New Member States – comparative analysis* – (Budapest: Hungarian National Assembly, 2005).

O.J. Tans, "The Dutch Parliament and the European Constitution: How Yes Led to No", in: P. Kiiver (ed.), *National and Regional Parliaments in the European Constitutional Order* (Groningen: Europa Law Publishing, 2006) 79-95.

O.J. Tans, "The Constitutional Theatre", *Res Publica. Journal of Legal and Social Philosophy* 8:3 (2002) 231-248.

D. Travers, H. Coppolecchia, A. Tomlins (preparation), *European Affairs Committees. The Influence of National Parliaments on European Policies* (Brussels: European Centre for Parliamentary Research and Documentation, 2003)

A. Verhoeven, *The European Union in Search of a Democratic and Constitutional Theory* (The Hague: Kluwer, 2002).

H. Vos, "The performance of national parliaments in the European Union-democratic legitimacy and European decision-making", paper in the series *Democracy and Accountability in the Enlarged European Union*, published by the SWP: < http://www.swp-berlin.org/common/get_document.php?asset_id=695>

J.H.H. Weiler, *The Constitution of Europe* (Cambridge/New York: Cambridge UP, 1999) 336-343.

W. Wessels, "The EC Council: The Community's Decision-making Center", in: S. Hoffmann & O. Keohane (eds.), *The New European Community. Decision-making and Institutional Chance* (Boulder, Colo.: Westview, 1991).

Contributors

The Editors

Olaf Tans is a legal philosopher and political scientist. He defended his PhD-thesis in 2003, which analyses the communicative function of constitutional claims on the basis of insights from legal/political philosophy and discourse theory. After working as a postdoc in the project 'Political Control in a European and Constitutional Perspective', he became assistant professor of legal philosophy at the Free University of Amsterdam in 2007. His current research interests are: (European) constitutionalism, discourse theory and evolution of law. He can be reached at: o.j.tans@rechten.vu.nl; olaf.tans@wanadoo.nl.

Carla Zoethout is associate professor of Constitutional and Administrative Law, Faculty of Law, University of Amsterdam. She has lectured for several years at the Free University of Amsterdam, Erasmus University Rotterdam and Leyden University. Her thesis is on Constitutionalism; A comparative study of limited government (1995). Main topics of scientific interest: (European) constitutional law and constitutional theory in comparative perspective, human rights and comparative politics (c.m.zoethout@uva.nl).

Jit Peters is professor of Constitutional and Administrative Law, Faculty of Law, University of Amsterdam. Earlier he worked as Deputy Director General at the Ministry of Interior, as Director at the Ministry of Environment and as Alderman and City Counsellor of the City of Leiden. At the University of Leiden, where he earlier was employed as associate professor, he wrote his thesis on the freedom of expression in The Netherlands and the USA (1981). His current research interests are the role of the judiciary in relation to the political process and the relationship between national constitutions and the international constitutional order (j.a.peters@uva.nl).

The Authors

Barbara Blümel is working at the Austrian Parliamentary Administration, Department of Communication (barabara.bluemel@parlament.gv.at).

Martina Coxová is currently on leave and may be reached at: (coxovi@yahoo.com).

Adam Cygan: Senior Lecturer in law, Faculty of Law, University of Leicester (ajc33@leicester.ac.uk).

Carl Devos: Professor in Belgian Politics at the Ghent University (carl.devos@Ugent.be).

Angéla Juhász-Tóth: Legal Advisor at the Hungarian National Assembly, Committee on European Affairs (angela.juhasz-toth@parlament.hu).

Christine Neuhold: Vice Dean of International Affairs and Director of Studies of the European Public Affairs (Master at the Faculty of Arts and Social Sciences at the University of Maastricht) (c.neuhold@politics.unimaas.nl).

Jan Orbie: Assistant Professor in European Politics at the Ghent University (jan.orbie@Ugent.be).

Lenka Pítrová: Head of the Unit for European Union, Parliamentary Institute, Chamber of Deputies, Parliament of the Czech Republic and Assistant

Professor in Administrative Law and Administrative Science at the Law Faculty, Charles University, Prague (pitrova@psp.cz).

Tapio Raunio: Professor of political science, University of Tampere (tapio.raunio@uta.fi).

Peter Riis: Head of Section, International Secretariat of the Danish Parliament (Folketinget)(Peter.Riis@ft.dk).

An Schrijvers: Researcher European Politics at the Ghent University (an.schrijvers@Ugent.be).

Sofie Staelraeve: Assistant in Belgian Politics at the Ghent University (sofie.staelraeve@Ugent.be).

Klára Szalay: Senior Legal Advisor at the Hungarian National Assembly, Committee on European Affairs (klara.szalay@parlament.hu).

Olaf Tans: Assistant Professor in Legal Philosophy at the Free University of Amsterdam (o.j.tans@rechten.vu.nl).

Daniel Thym: Senior Research Associate at the Walter Hallstein-Institute for European Constitutional Law at Humboldt-University, Berlin (daniel@thym.de).

Hilde Van Liefferinge: Assistant in Belgian Politics at the Ghent University (hilde.vanliefferinge@Ugent.be).

Hendrik Vos: Professor in European Politics at the Ghent University (hendrik.vos@Ugent.be).